Nichts als Farbe | *Nothing but Paint*

EDUARD TAUSS

Inhalt | *Contents*

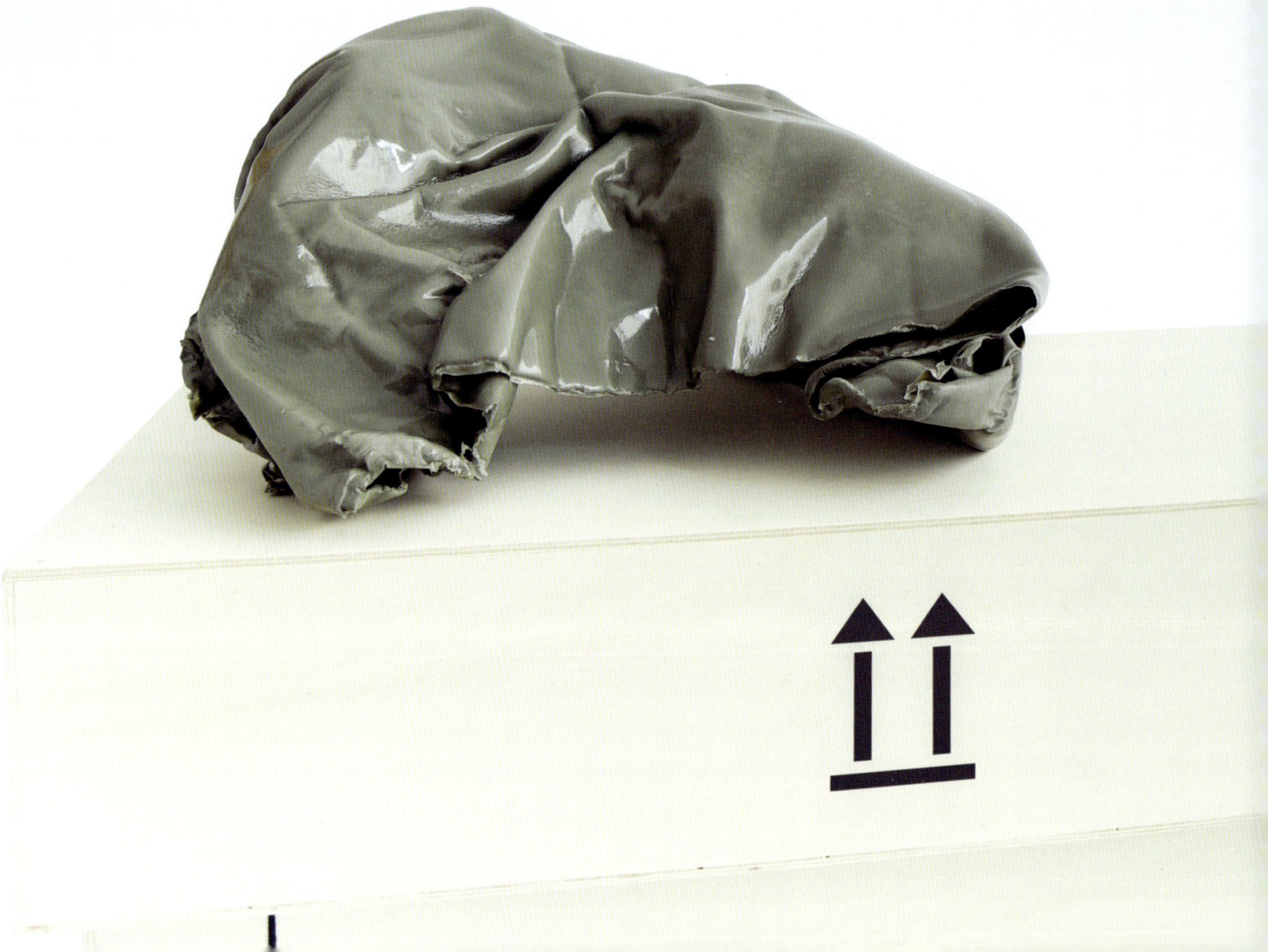

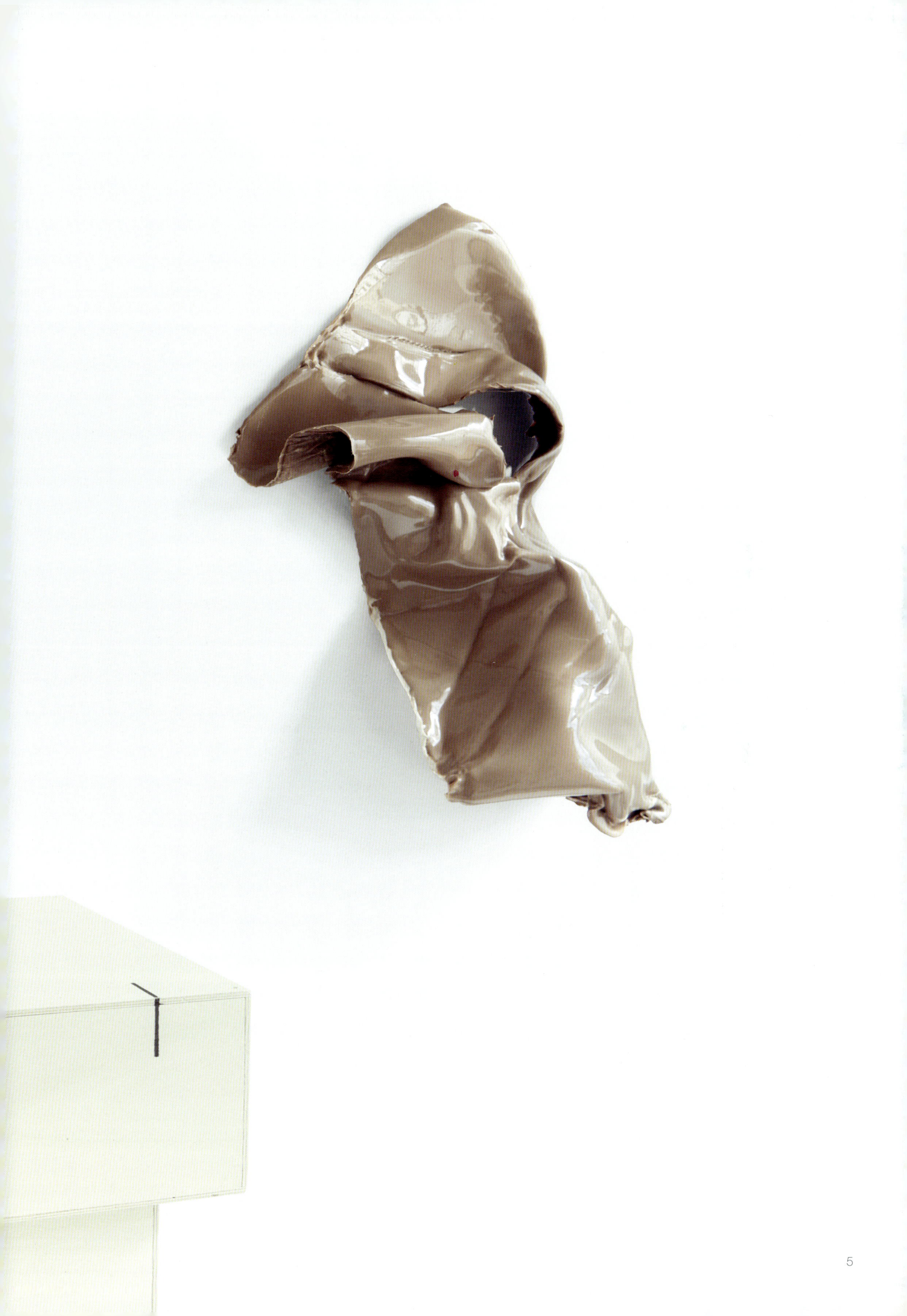

Angela Stief

Direktorin | *Director* Albertina Modern

Matter Matters, oder: Nichts als Farbe

Matter Matters, or: Nothing but Paint

Farbe. Nichts als Farbe. In unterschiedlichen Nuancen und Kombinationen. Meistens sind es gedeckte Töne in grünlichen, gelblichen, rötlichen und bläulichen Schattierungen, die in ihrem subjektiven Ausdruckswert bewusst zurückgenommen wurden. Einmal ein ganz dunkler, fast schwarzer Ausreißer. Eine kontraststarke Betonung der Form, der Linienführung durch die Kontur, wenn sie sich von der Umgebung abhebt. Den Joker der Farbe, ihre ästhetische Eindringlichkeit und emotionale Überzeugungskraft, spielt Eduard Tauss nicht aus. Es ziehen den Betrachter weder schreiende Töne, wie man sie aus der Pop Art kennt, die sich der visuellen Sprache der Werbung anpasste, um die Masse zu gewinnen, noch die farbliche Sensationskraft, wie sie Künstler von Yves Klein über James Turrell bis Anish Kapoor erkundeten, in den Bann. Bei manchen Arbeiten denkt man an die monochromen Skulpturen von Angela de la Cruz und Hans Kupelwieser, die meistens mit industriell vorgefertigten Ausgangsmaterialien hantieren, die dann deformiert werden. Solche Vergleiche greifen jedoch zu kurz, da Tauss bei der Produktion seiner Objekte nie auf bereits bestehende materielle Versatzstücke zurückgreift.

Der Künstler, der sich in der Eleganz der Diskretion übt, ästhetische Superlative und auch eine apodiktische

Paint. Nothing but paint. In various nuances and combinations. Usually they are subdued hues, in greenish, yellowish, reddish and bluish shades that were consciously scaled back in their subjective expressive value. Occasionally a very dark, nearly black outlier. A contrast-rich emphasis on the form, of the line through the contour when it stands out against its surroundings. Eduard Tauss doesn't resort to playing the joker card of colour, with its aesthetic forcefulness and emotional persuasiveness. The viewer is captivated neither by screaming colours familiar to us from Pop Art – which adopted the visual language of advertising to win over the masses – nor by the sensational colouristic power explored by artists from Yves Klein and James Turrell to Anish Kapoor. Some works bring to mind the monochrome sculptures of Angela de la Cruz and Hans Kupelwieser, who generally make use of industrially prefabricated materials that are then deformed. But these kinds of comparisons fall short because in producing his objects, Tauss never resorts to the use of existing material components.

Eduard Tauss, who exercises the elegance of discretion and avoids both aesthetic superlatives and an apodictic terminology, blends liquid polyurethane with pigments of muted colouring, refines the shading and reduces the

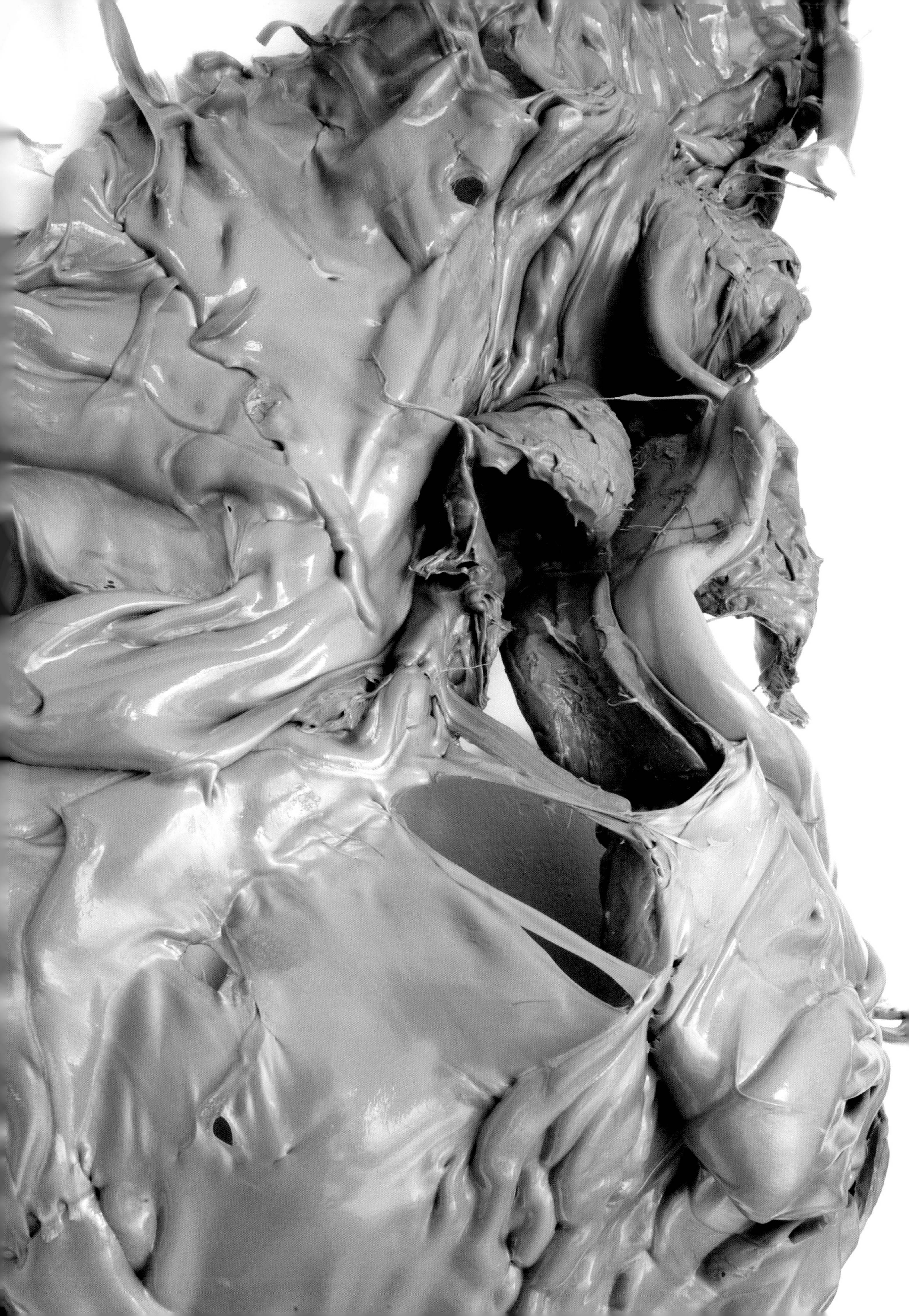

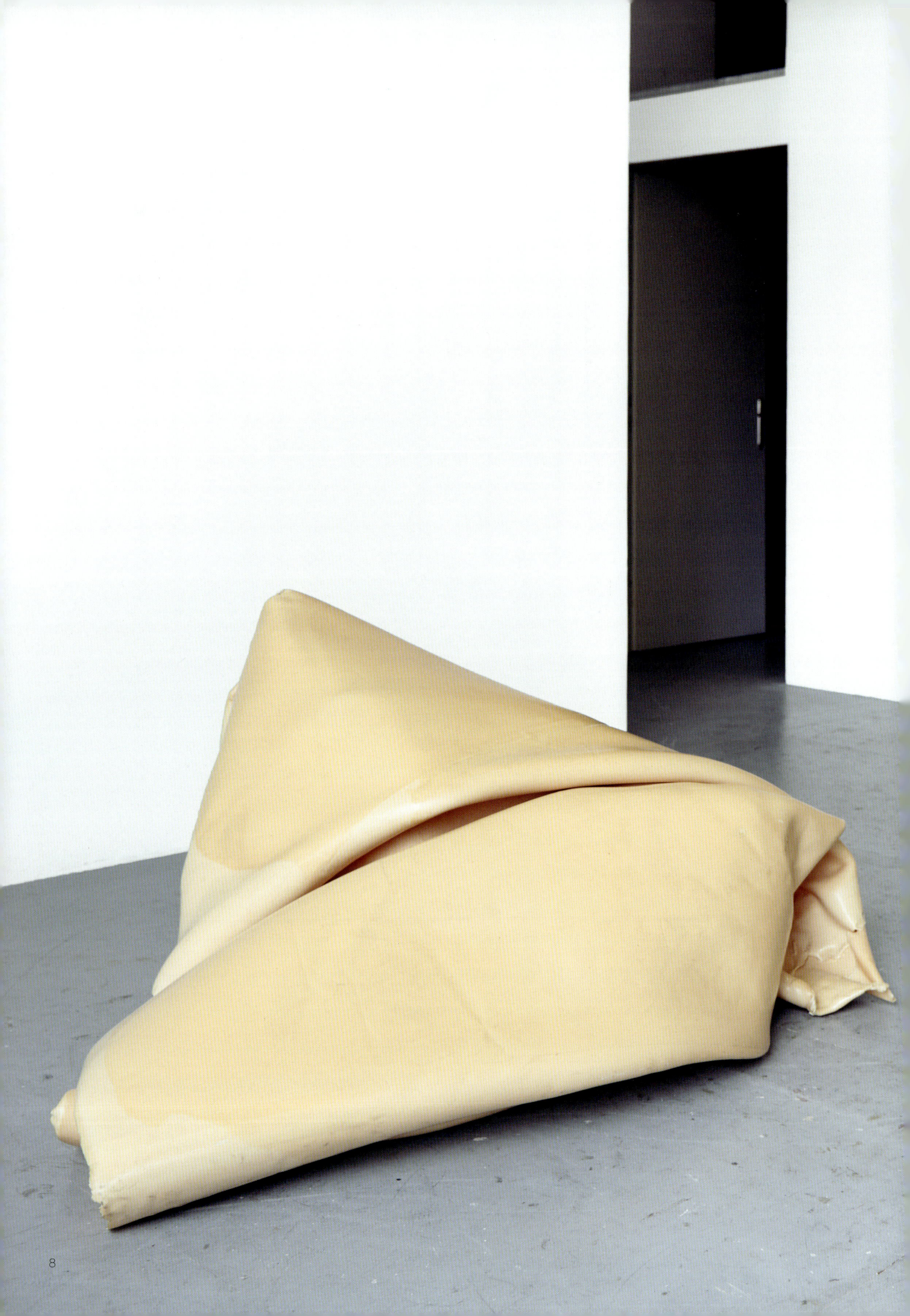

Begrifflichkeit meidet, vermischt flüssiges Polyurethan mit Pigmenten in gedämpftem Kolorit, kultiviert die Abtönung und nimmt den Effekt zurück, um die Aufmerksamkeit des Betrachters zu lenken. Trotz einer künstlerischen Haltung, die stets die Angemessenheit im Ausdruck sucht, schürt Tauss Zweifel: Einerseits konzentriert er sich auf die Ausschließlichkeit seines Mediums und andererseits verdeutlichen seine Arbeiten, dass es primär nicht um den Farbwert und um dessen langläufige Bedeutungshoheit geht: „Farbentscheidungen sind Differenzentscheidungen“[1], meint Tauss und negiert die Relevanz spezifischer Farbtöne, die ein Objekt „schlüssig machen“ und etwas anderes als eine Materialeigenschaft vermitteln. So kann beispielsweise die Farbskala von Haut von ganz hell über braun bis fast schwarz reichen und sagt dennoch kaum etwas über die ihr zugrundeliegende Materialität aus.

Die scheinbare Widersprüchlichkeit in der ästhetischen Aussage der Arbeit von Tauss – es geht um Farbe, aber doch nicht um Farbe (Farbe als Tonwert versus Farbe als Substanz) – schärft die Rezeption. Heinz Gappmayr schreibt: „Ihm geht es allerdings weniger um die höchst komplexe Realität der Farbe, sondern um den Prozess der Herstellung, um die Substanz des Materials, um die Beziehung zwischen Farbe und Stoff.“[2] Farbe findet in seinem Oeuvre eine extraordinäre Anwendung. Er verwendet sie diametral entgegengesetzt zum malerischen Gewohnheitseffekt als mehr oder weniger dick aufgetragenes Medium, das figurative oder abstrakte Zeichen auf einen Bildträger wie eine Leinwand appliziert. Er schafft Materialgesten, Farbobjekte, die von flächigen

1 Angela Stief im Gespräch mit Eduard Tauss im Atelier des Künstlers, Juni 2017, Wien.

2 Heinz Gappmayr: Eduard Tauss, Katalog, edition ps, Wien, 2003, S. 14.

effect in order to guide the viewer's attention. Despite an artistic attitude that constantly seeks appropriateness in expression, Tauss sows doubt: on the one hand he concentrates on the exclusivity of his medium, but on the other his works demonstrate that the primary concern is not the colour value and its long-time sovereignty of importance: "Decisions of colour are decisions of difference"[1], says Tauss, negating the relevance of specific hues that make an object "coherent" and convey something other than a material quality. The colour scale of skin, for example, can range from very light to brown to nearly black, but it still says little about its underlying materiality.

The apparent contradiction in the aesthetic message of Tauss's work – it's about colour but then again not about colour (colour as chromatic value as opposed to colour as substance) – sharpens the reception. As Heinz Gappmayr wrote: "He is less concerned with the highly complex reality of colour than he is with the process of production, with the substance of the material, with the relationship between colour and material."[2] Colour is utilized in an extraordinary manner in Tauss's oeuvre. He uses it in a way that is diametrically opposed to the habitual painterly manner of a more or less thickly applied medium that affixes figurative or abstract characters to an image carrier such as a canvas. He creates material gestures, colour objects that range from flat – only a few millimetres thick – to completely sculptural figures. In doing so he resorts neither to an additive (modelling) nor to a subtractive (carving) process. The artist usually gives the works self-referential names such as

1 Angela Stief in conversation with Eduard Tauss in the artist's studio, June 2017, Vienna.

2 Heinz Gappmayr: Eduard Tauss, exh. cat., edition ps, Vienna, 2003, p. 14.

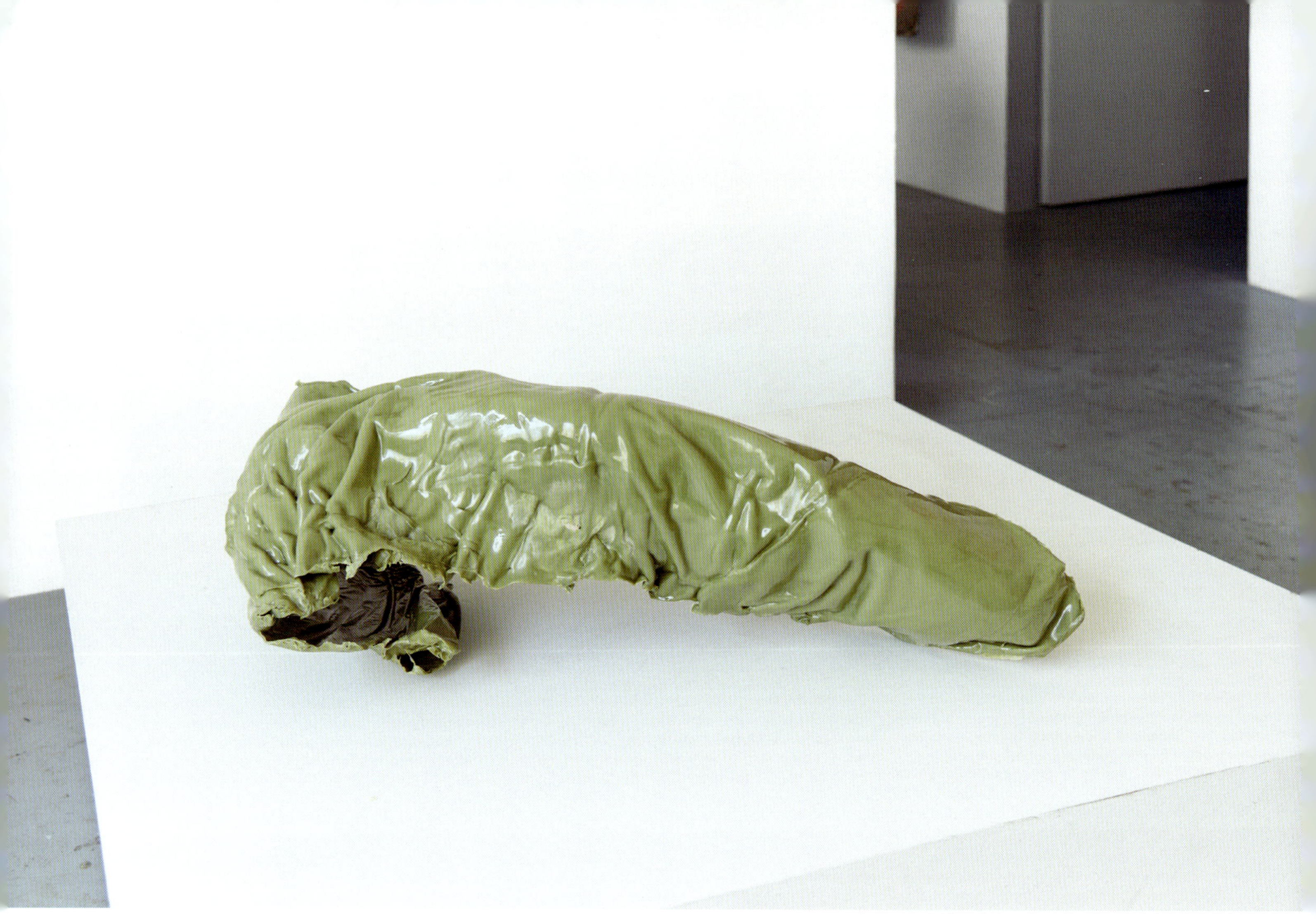

– wenige Millimeter dicken – bis zu gänzlich plastischen Gebilden reichen. Dabei bedient er sich weder eines additiven (Plastik) noch eines subtraktiven (Skulptur) Verfahrens. Der Künstler bezeichnet die Werke meist selbstreferentiell als „Farbkörper", „Farbfläche", „Offene Form", usw., je nach Beschaffenheit und Machart. Farbe und Form begreift er als enge Verbündete, die sich als Einheit im Objekt zusammenfinden und sich räumlich entfalten: „Die Autonomie der Farbe, ein Begriff, der im Kontext der gegenstandsfreien Malerei entstanden ist, erfährt hier seinen Fortgang: Die Farbe hat sich sogar von ihrem Bildträger befreit und macht sich mittels ihrer eigenen plastischen Substanz zum Ausdruck ihrer selbst und zum Gegenstand ihrer Betrachtung im Raum."[3] Die Farbe gewinnt dadurch

3 Michael Post, Heiner Thiel: „Zu den Farbkörpern von Eduard Tauss", im Ausst. kat.: Embodying Colour, Kunsthalle Wiesbaden, Edition PT, Wiesbaden, 2013, S. 67.

"Colour Body", "Colour Plane", "Open Shape", etc., depending on their qualities and style. He regards colour and form as close allies that unify in the object and develop spatially: "The autonomy of colour, a concept that emerged in the context of non-figurative painting, is carried on here: colour has even liberated itself from its image carrier and through its own plastic substance becomes an expression of itself and an object of examination in space."[3] Colour thereby gains maximal autonomy, and the memorability of these objects has the power of a signature. In describing them, one is tempted to use a vocabulary that sounds as if it were borrowed from the field of textiles and metals: one then speaks of invaginations, folds, indentations, smudges, bulges, burrs, fold falls, draperies and wrinkled

3 Michael Post, Heiner Thiel: "On the Colour Bodies by Eduard Tauss," exh. cat.: Embodying Colour, Kunsthalle Wiesbaden, Edition PT, Wiesbaden, 2013, p. 72.

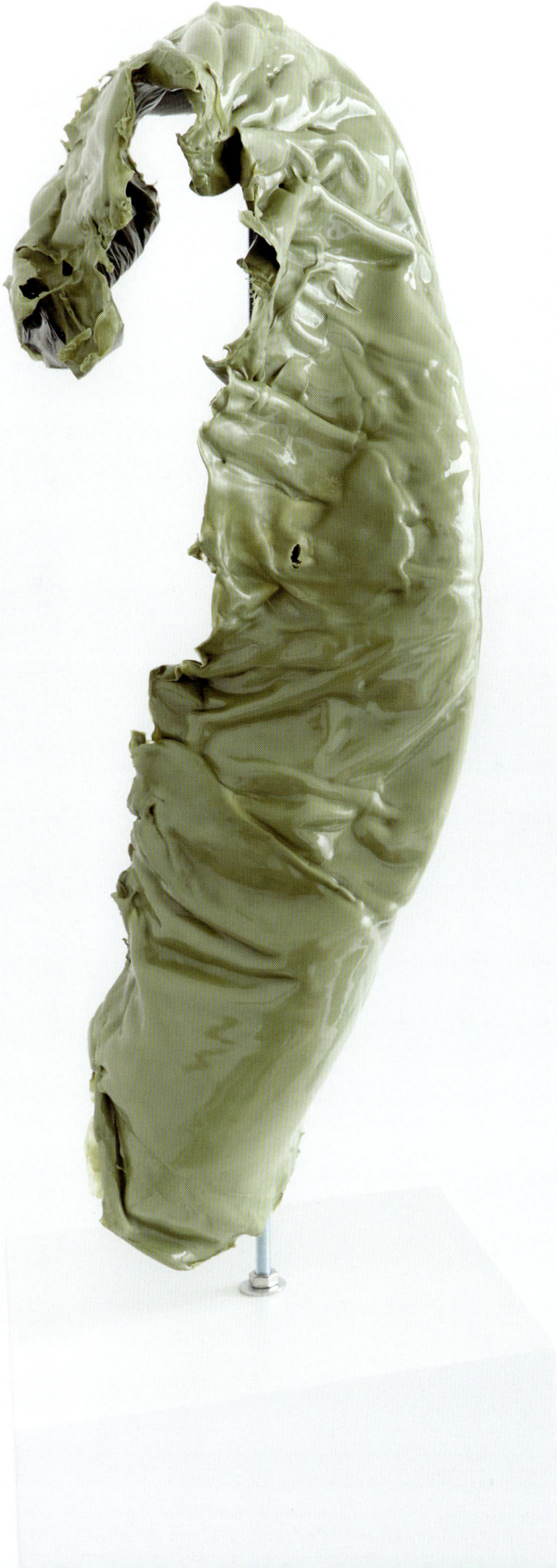

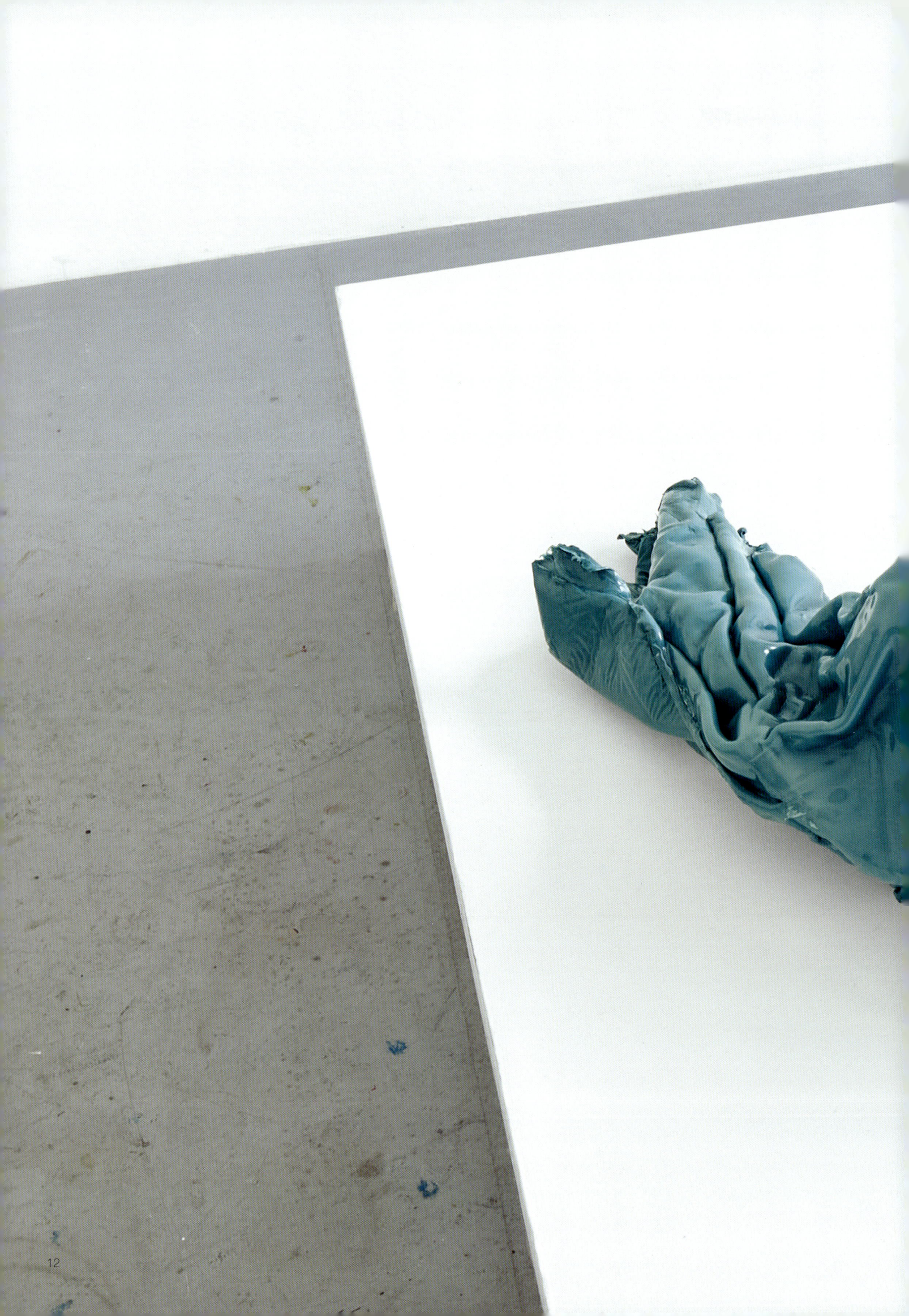

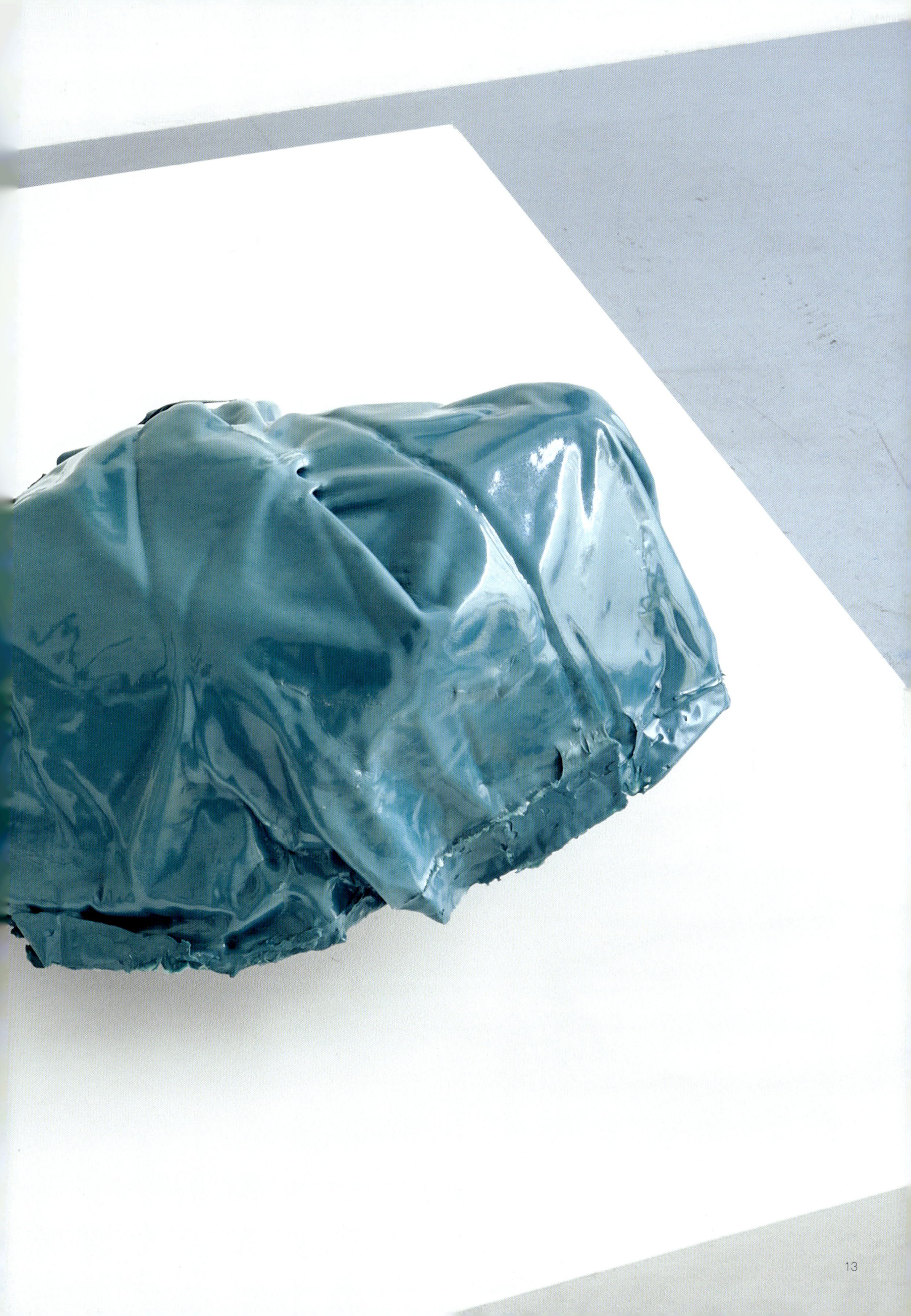

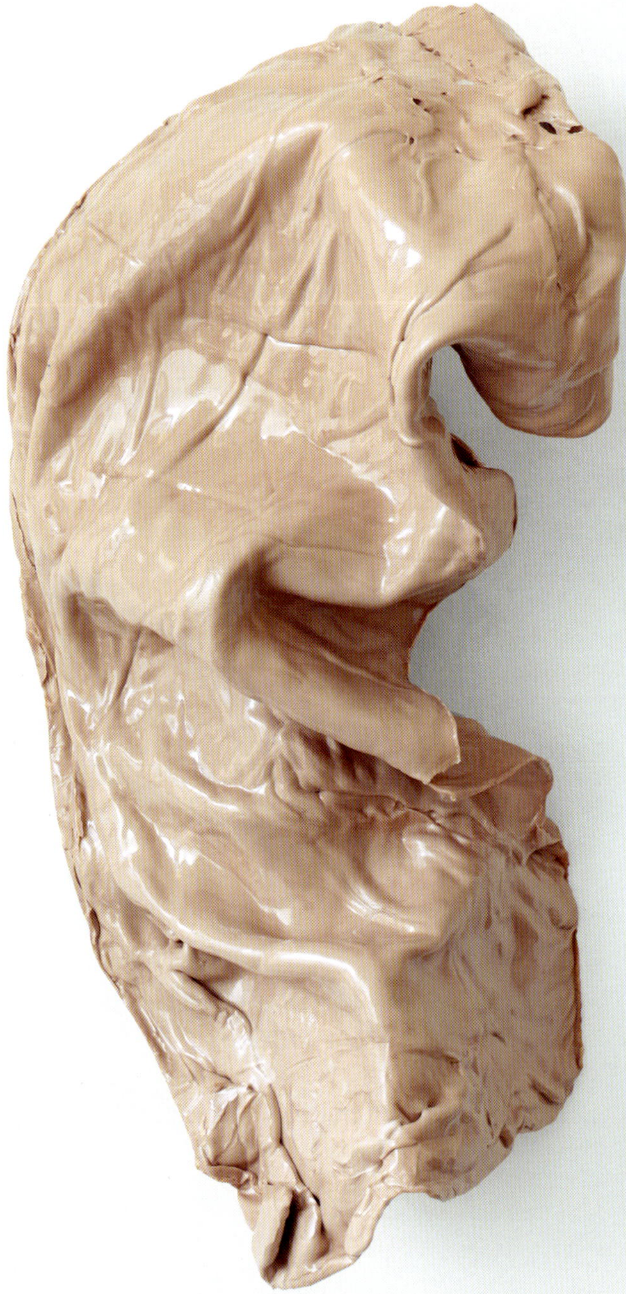

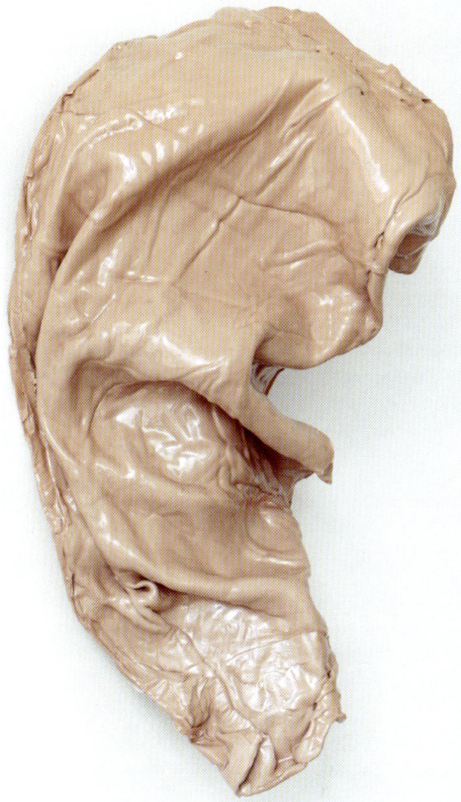

maximale Autonomie und der Wiedererkennungswert dieser Objekte hat signatorische Kraft. Wenn man sie beschreibt, möchte man sich eines Vokabulars bedienen, das klingt, als wäre es der Textil- und Metallbranche entlehnt: Die Rede ist dann von Einstülpungen, Faltungen, Dellen, Schlieren, Ausbeulungen, Ausfransungen, Faltenwürfen, Drapierungen und zerknitterten Flächen in monochromer oder manchmal auch zweifarbiger Ausführung. Meistens sind es Abweichungen von geometrischen Axiomen und intakten Formen, die beim Betrachten Irritationen auslösen: „Formation und Deformation sind Gestaltungsmittel, die sich gegenseitig bedingen"[4], sagt der Künstler. In seinem Werk erkennt man selten scharfe Kanten noch spitze Ecken, sondern unre-

4 Angela Stief im Gespräch mit Eduard Tauss im Atelier des Künstlers, Juni 2017, Wien.

surfaces in monochrome and sometimes even bichrome executions. Generally it is the departures from geometric axioms and intact forms that cause confusion on the part of viewers: "Formation and deformation are artistic means that are mutually dependent"[4], says the artist. In his works one seldom perceives sharp edges or pointed corners but rather irregular reliefs, soft transitions and organic curves. Modulated surfaces produce volume in a playful manner.

4 Angela Stief in conversation with Eduard Tauss in the artist's studio, June 2017, Vienna.

gelmäßige Reliefs, weiche Übergänge und organische Rundungen. Modulierte Flächen erzeugen spielerisch Volumen.

Es liegt auf der Hand, bei manchen dieser Objekte an die Skulpturen aus gepresstem Autoschrott von John Chamberlain oder die bemalten Kühlerhauben von Richard Prince zu denken. Doch ist diese erste Ähnlichkeit ein optischer Trugschluss. Bei Tauss geht es weder um die Wiederverwertung von ausrangierten Gütern noch um die Auseinandersetzung mit Alltagsobjekten und Klischees beziehungsweise Statussymbolen, sondern um die innovative Nutzung eines Materials, eine von ihrer Historie und ihrem applikativen Charakter befreite und nicht mehr an

It is not surprising that some of these objects bring to mind John Chamberlain's sculptures made of crushed automobile parts or Richard Prince's painted car hoods. But this initial resemblance is a visual deception. Tauss is concerned neither with recycling scrapped goods nor with the study of everyday objects, clichés or status symbols. What interests him is the innovative utilization of a material, a material visibility that has been liberated from its history and its applicative character and is no longer bound to its exclusive flatness. Despite or because of their abstraction, these sculptures repeatedly trigger associations and in the case of certain work series bring to mind the materiality of blankets and pillows.

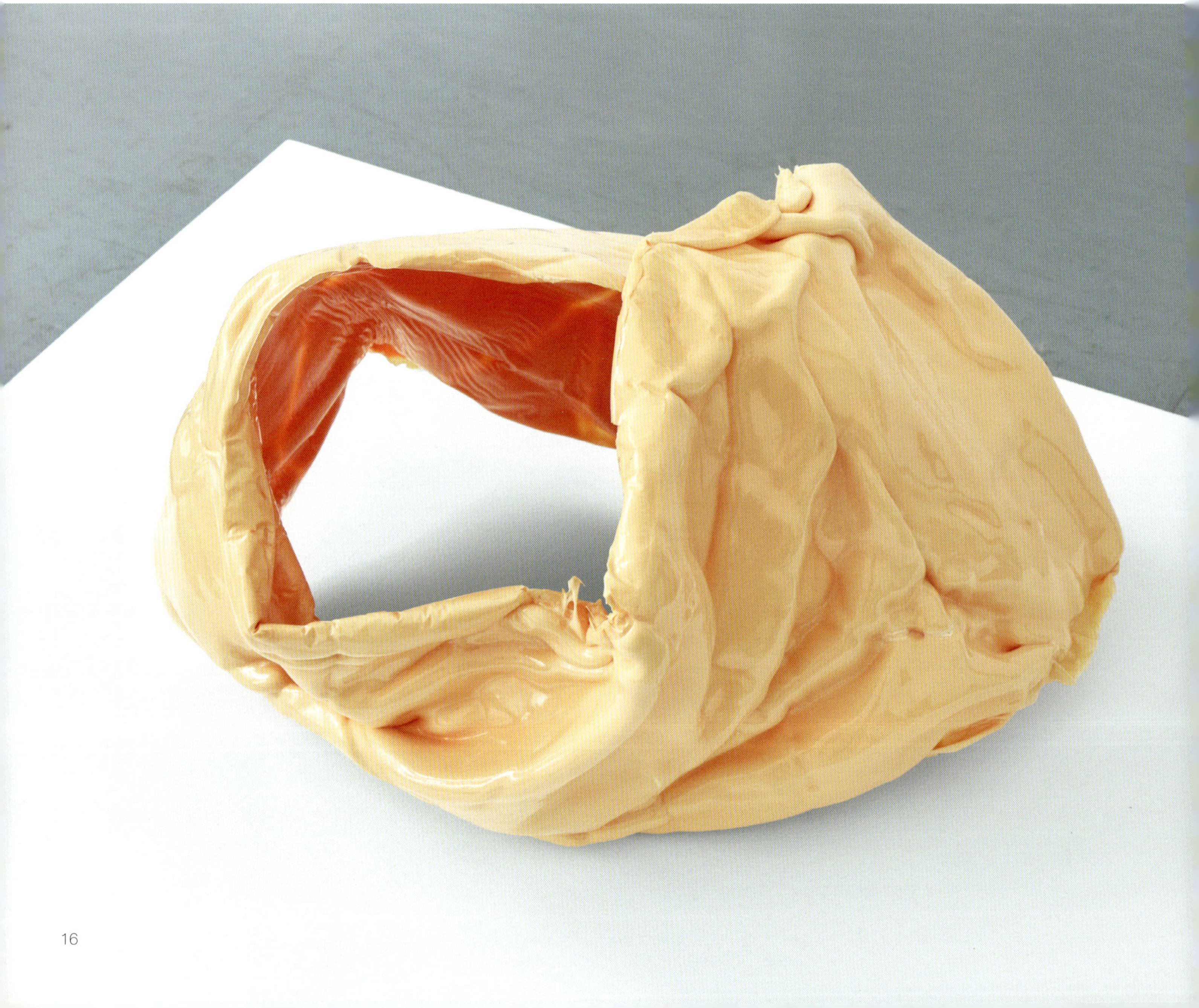

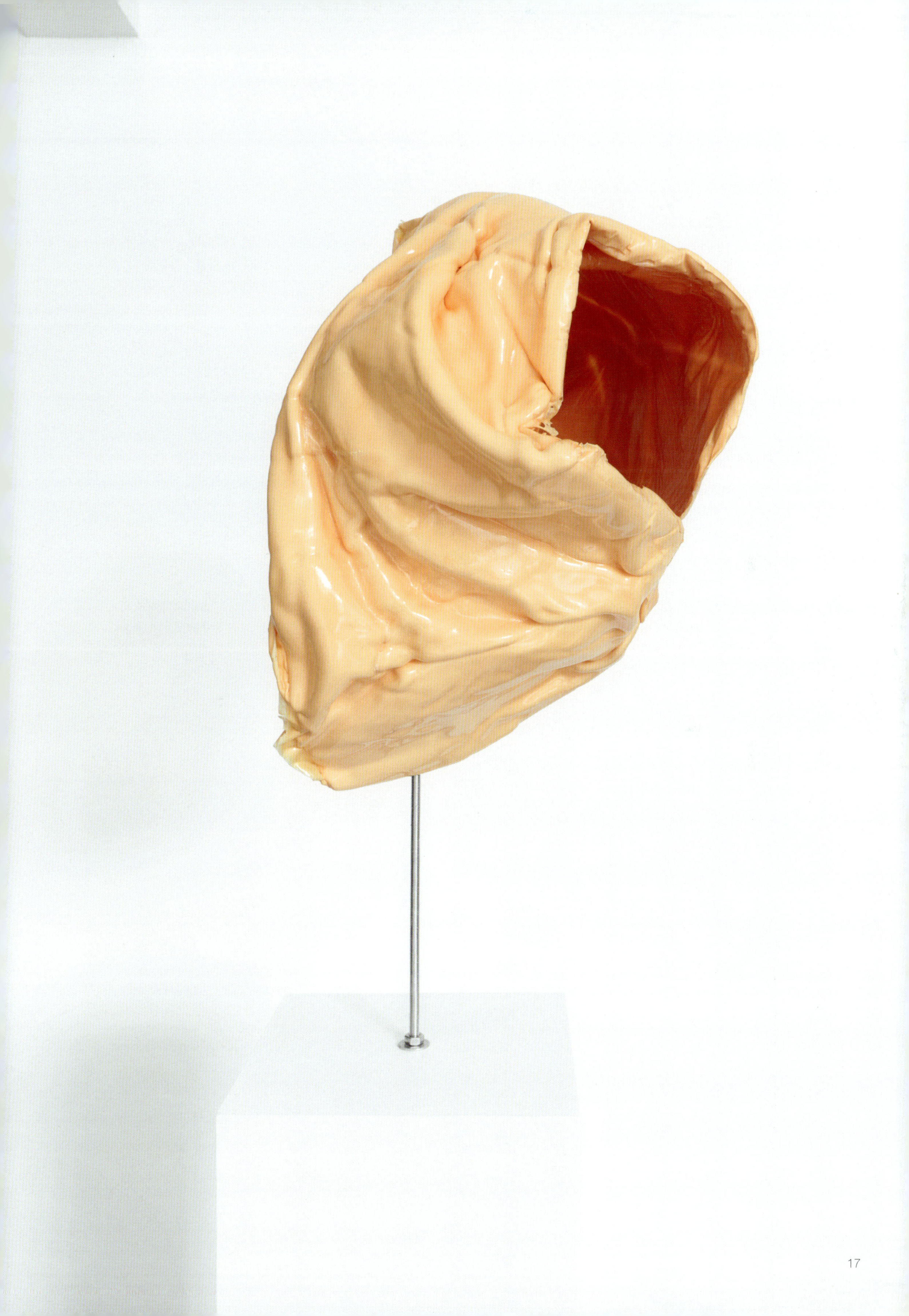

ihre exklusive Flächigkeit gebundene Materialansichtigkeit. Trotz oder gerade wegen ihrer Abstraktion setzen diese Skulpturen immer wieder Assoziationen frei und lassen bei bestimmten Werkserien an die Stofflichkeit von Decken und Kissen denken. Obwohl der Künstler sagt, dass ihn der Realismus nicht interessiere, und versucht, „bewusst keine gegenständlichen Zusammenhänge und Ähnlichkeiten mit Design und Natur herzustellen“[5], sind verschiedene Assoziationen und Realbezüge nicht von der Hand zu weisen. Manche Arbeiten haben etwas Organisches, erinnern an Adern, Haut, Fleisch und den Mythos des gehäuteten Marsyas.

All diese Interpretationen widersprechen jedoch dem künstlerischen Anspruch auf Neutralität. Man sollte sie besser unterlassen, sie schwächen die Autonomie der Objekte, ihren Werkstatus – die Materialimmanenz. Manchmal ist es die Grundvoraussetzung für eine gelingende Rezeption, sich zu disziplinieren, in der Zurückweisung von voreiligen Analogien und, wenn man so will, sich in einem Willen zur Abstraktion zu üben und damit ein allzu verspieltes und funktionales Denken abzulehnen.

Man könnte Mutmaßungen über das Selbstverständnis von Eduard Tauss anstellen und sich fragen, ob er ein Maler ist, der sich bildhauerisch betätigt oder eher ein Bildhauer, der malt. Seit seinem Studium besteht die Faszination für den Werkstoff Plastik und seit seiner ersten Einzelausstellung beim *Steirischen Herbst* (1991) arbeitet er mit Kunstharz – zunächst Polyester, dann Polyurethan – und beschäftigt sich mit der Materialität des Mediums. Daraus hat sich ein stringentes Konzept entwickelt, das man als die Kunst der Farbform, als ein Erkunden der

5 Angela Stief im Gespräch mit Eduard Tauss im Atelier des Künstlers, Juni 2017, Wien.

Although the artist insists he is not interested in realism and consciously avoids "producing figurative relationships and similarities to design and nature"[5], various associations and references to reality cannot be denied. Some works have an organic nature and are reminiscent of veins, skin, flesh and the myth of the flayed Marsyas.

All of these interpretations, however, contradict the artistic demand for neutrality. One would do better to abstain from them, as they weaken the autonomy of the objects, their work status – their material immanence. Sometimes the basic prerequisite for the successful reception of a work is to discipline oneself, to repudiate premature analogies and to strive, as it were, to accept abstraction and thus reject an overly playful and functional thought process.

One could speculate about Eduard Tauss's self-conception and wonder if he is a painter who sculpts or rather a sculptor who paints. Even as a student he was fascinated by plastic materials, and since his first solo exhibition at the Steirischer Herbst *(1991) he has worked with synthetic resin – first with polyester, then with polyurethane – and studied the materiality of this medium. From this a stringent concept developed that one could describe as the art of the colour form, as an exploration of the aggregate states between liquid and solid. Put in Neoplatonic terms, it is about the idea of colour that has lost its accidental status and constantly gains in substance in the display – pure paint that is not subjected to any hybridization with other materials and thus stands for the purity requirement of an Apollonian conception of art.*

5 Angela Stief in conversation with Eduard Tauss in the artist's studio, June 2017, Vienna.

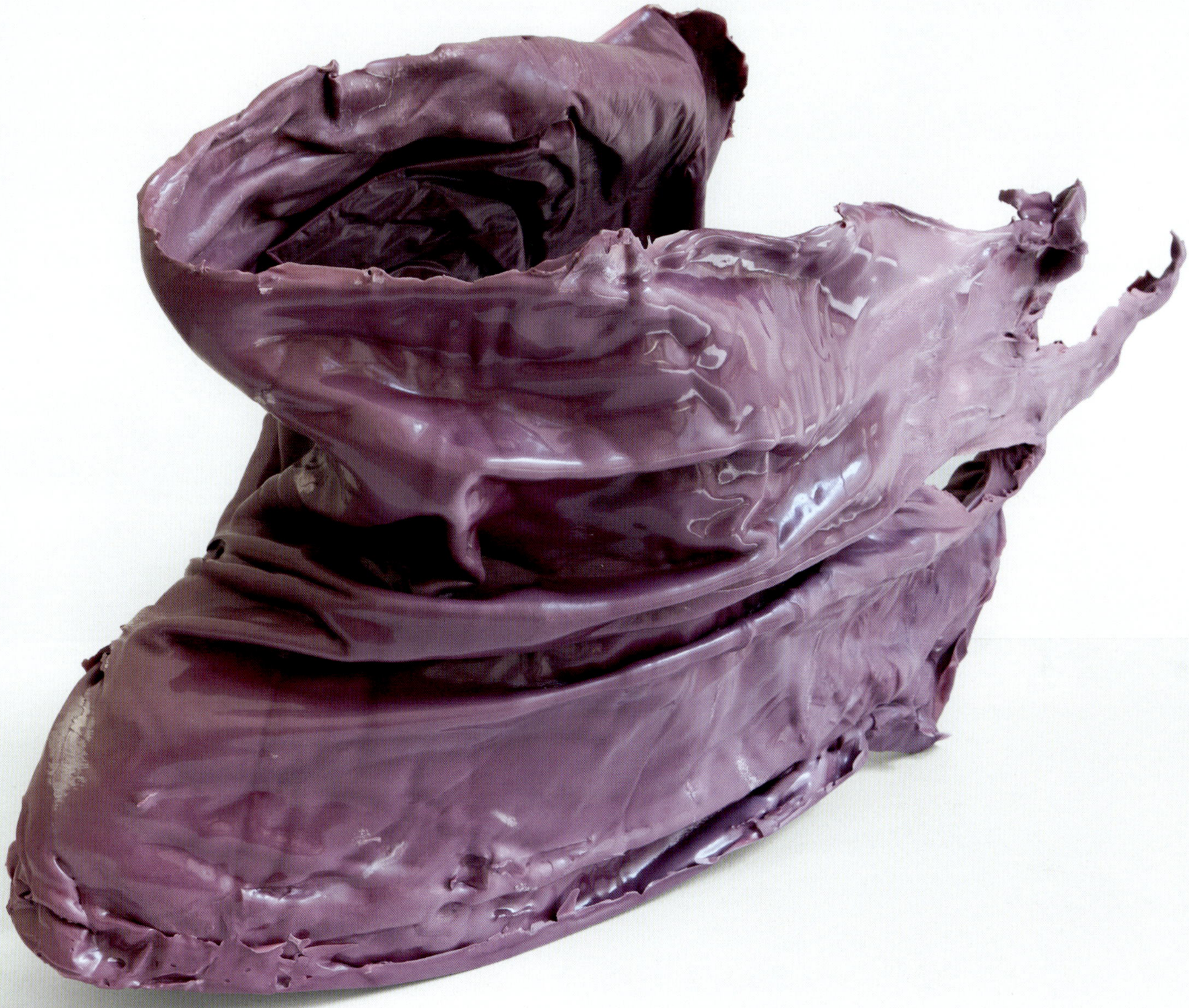

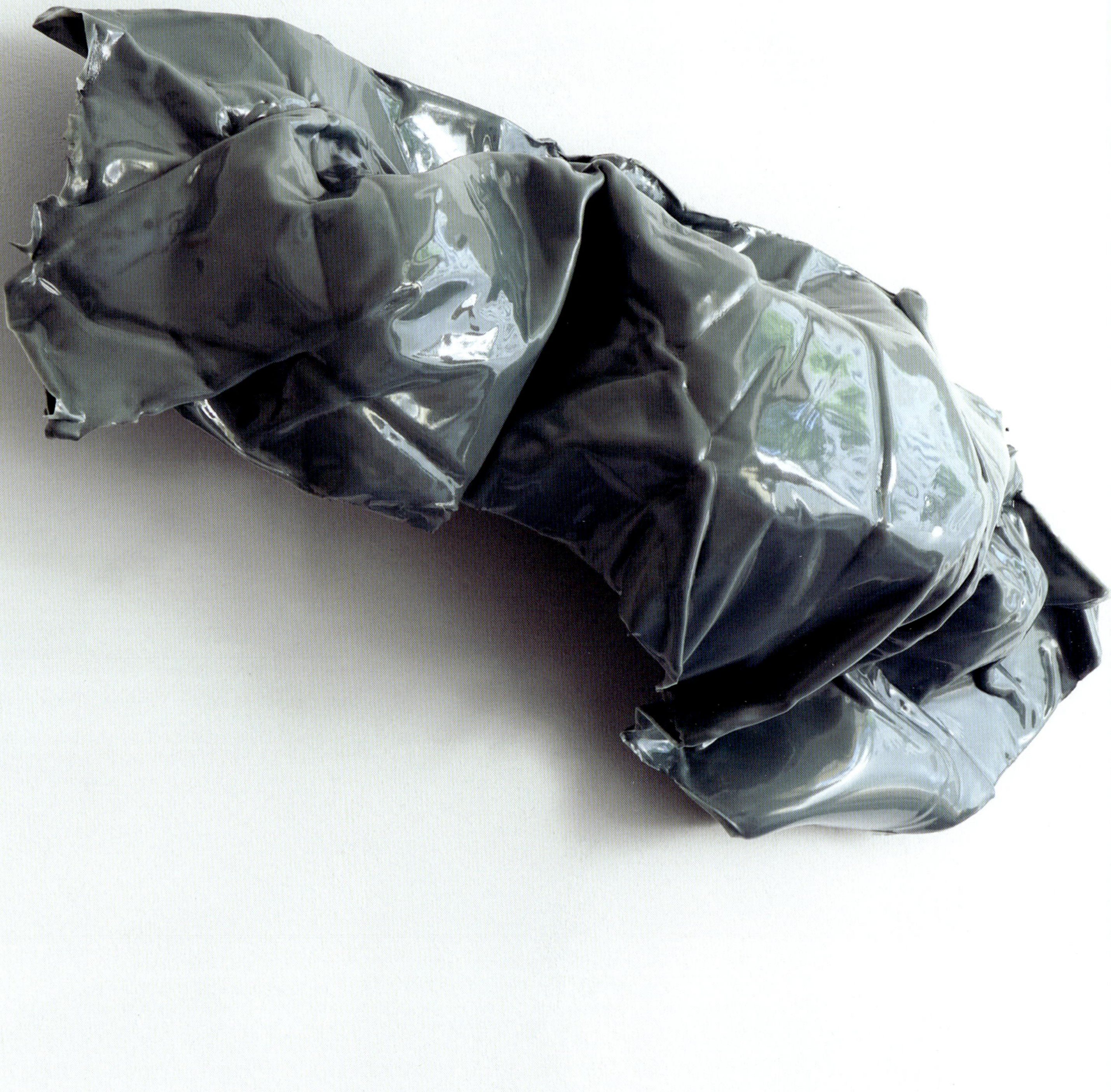

Aggregatzustände zwischen flüssig und fest beschreiben könnte. Neoplatonisch formuliert geht es um die Idee von Farbe, die ihren akzidentiellen Status verloren hat und in der Darstellung permanent an Substanz gewinnt. Pure Farbe, die keine Hybridisierungen mit anderen Materialien eingeht und deshalb auch für das Reinheitsgebot eines apollinischen Kunstverständnisses steht.

Das Oeuvre von Eduard Tauss folgt der Zielgeraden der L'art pour l'art. Es kommt ausschließlich um seiner selbst willen zur Geltung. Den Diensten an der gesellschaftlichen Integration oder Exklusion, der politischen Verbesserung, der Meinungsbildung, dem Anspruch zu informieren oder irgendeiner wie auch immer gearteten stilistischen oder ideologischen Verpflichtung ist die Kunst hier enthoben. Tauss negiert die sowieso viel zu langen kunsthistorischen Narrative des Abbildens, Aneignens, Assemblierens, Bricolierens, Recycelns und Zitierens. Seine künstlerische Lösung entfaltet sich in der materialästhetischen Reduktion und gerät trotzdem nie in den Verdacht des Fetischismus. Den ergebnisoffenen Arbeitsprozess versteht Tauss als Allianz mit dem Material. Ein ständiges Lernen vom Medium und mit ihm, ein Durchformulieren von Materialmöglichkeiten. In der Wiederholung von räumlich ausladenden Skulpturen, planen Werken, die an das Bildgeviert erinnern, und Arbeiten, die auf einem im Atelier gespannten Draht aushärten, schafft er Ordnungskategorien in unterschiedlich raumgreifenden Varianten. Diese Serialität ohne zwangsläufige Chronologie strukturiert das Oeuvre. Die glatten Oberflächen reflektieren das von Außen einfallende Licht, so als wollten sie auf ihre spezifische Eigenart verweisen, Denkprozesse in Gang setzen, sich im

Eduard Tauss's oeuvre follows the finishing straight of l'art pour l'art: his works are visually effective purely for their own sake. Here, art is absolved of its service to social integration or exclusion, to political betterment, to opinion-forming; it is absolved of its requirement to inform and of any other kind of stylistic or ideological obligation. Tauss negates what is in any case a much too long-lived art-historical narrative of depiction, acquisition, assemblage, bricolage, recycling and citation. His artistic solution develops the material-aesthetic reduction, but without ever coming under suspicion of fetishism. Tauss views the open-ended work process as an alliance with the material, as a perpetual process of learning with and from the medium, as a systematic formulation of material related possibilities. In the repetition of spatially expansive sculptures, of flat works reminiscent of the square picture, of objects hardening on a wire hanging in the studio, he creates ordering categories of differently sized variants. This serialism without a compulsory chronology is what gives the oeuvre structure. The smooth surfaces reflect the light falling from outside as if they wanted to point out their own specific uniqueness, set thought processes in motion, assert themselves as the exceptional solution in the field of innumerable contemporary artistic approaches and individual actions. The sheen inherent in them is usually broken: "I do not strive to create perfect surfaces; rather, I allow chance to surprise me."[6] The actually quite simple but nonetheless never practised concept of visualising colour during the form-finding process, of investigating the stress behaviour and fragility of form, demands the restriction of authorial control during the production. The artist's abstractly expressive gesture, the pouring on of

6 Angela Stief in conversation with Eduard Tauss in the artist's studio, June 2017, Vienna.

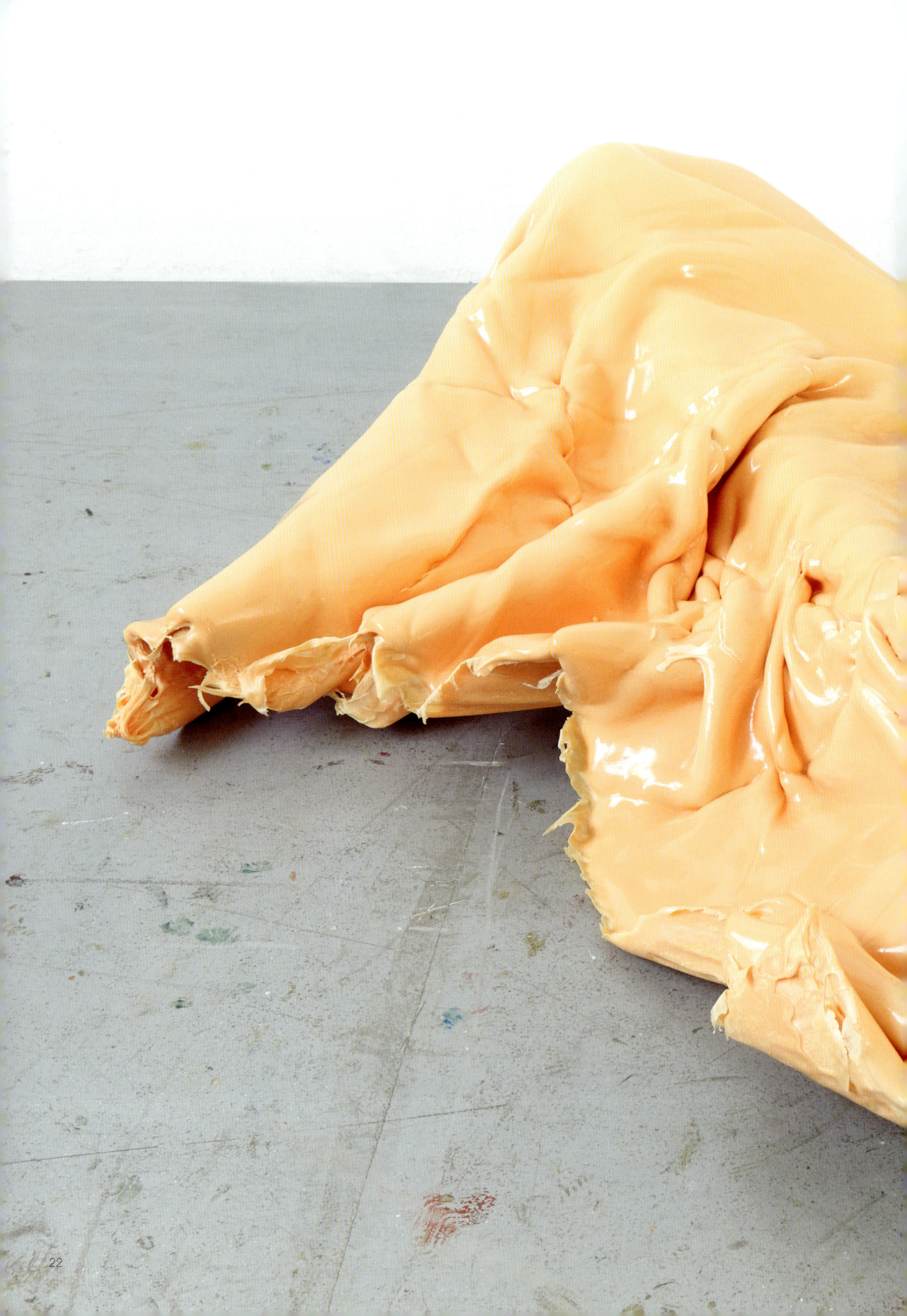

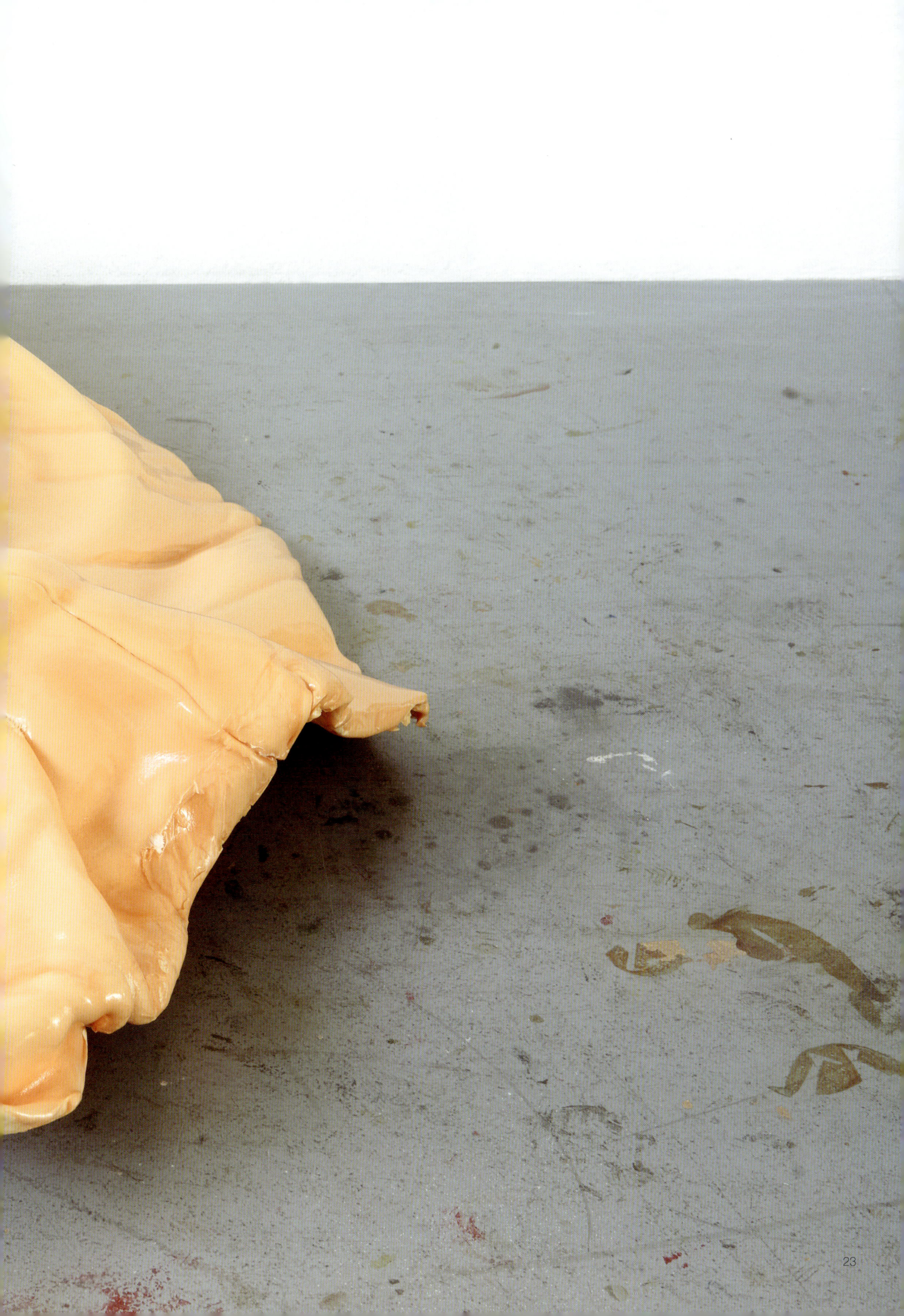

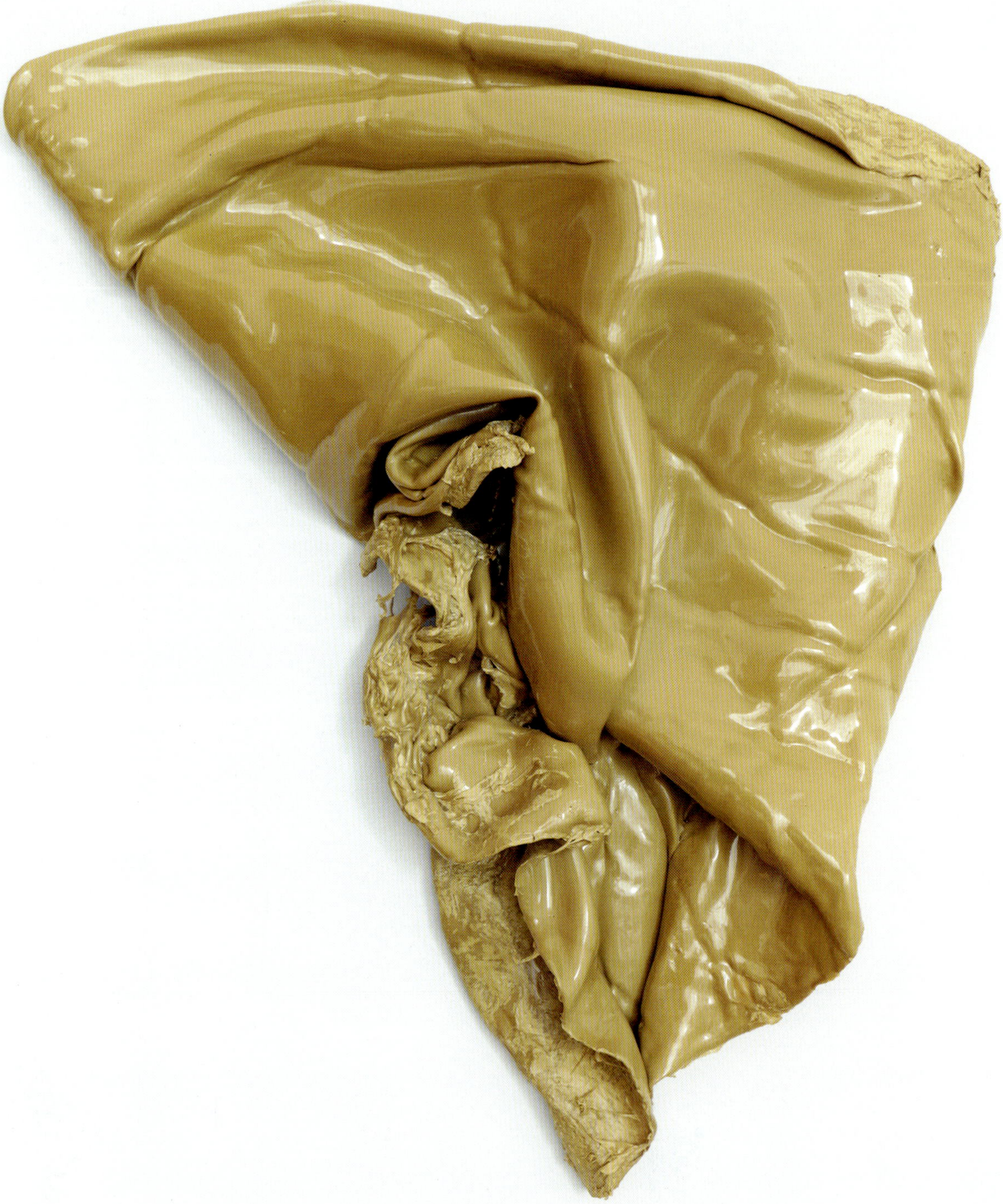

Spannungsfeld von x-beliebigen zeitgenössischen künstlerischen Ansätzen und individuellem Tun als herausragende Lösung behaupten. Der Glanz, der ihnen anhaftet, ist meist gebrochen: „Ich strebe keine perfekten Oberflächen an, sondern erlaube dem Zufall mich zu überraschen."[6] Das eigentlich ganz simple, aber dennoch nie praktizierte Konzept der Visualisierung von Farbe während des Formfindungsprozesses, die Untersuchung des Spannungsverhaltens und der Fragilität von Form sieht vor, die auktoriale Kontrolle während der Produktion einzuschränken. Die abstrakt-expressive Geste des Künstlers, das Schütten der Farbe, markiert die Akzentverschiebung vom statischen Werk zur Performanz der Herstellung und die Transformation eines klassischen Gussverfahrens.

Der Impuls, also die Menge an Bewegung, die auf das unfertige Objekt sowohl seitens des Künstlers als auch durch die Schwerkraft einwirkt, beschreibt die unmittelbare, in der Zeit verdichtete Interaktion von Künstler und Material: Tauss gießt das flüssige Kunstharz unter Berücksichtigung von Materialstärke und Ausdehnung flächig auf eine auf dem Boden liegende Plastikfolie. Wenn das Material „weitestgehend trocken, aber noch nicht ausgehärtet ist"[7], beginnt die Arbeit des Hängens, Biegens und Formens. Dabei beträgt die Reaktionszeit des Künstlers nur wenige Minuten. Danach gibt es keine Möglichkeit der Nachbearbeitung mehr. Die ganze Konzentration liegt in dieser Zeit darauf, „das Material zu seinem Eigenwert kommen zu lassen"[8] – ein Paradigma der künstlerischen Entwicklungen der 1960er-Jahre, in denen Materie, Material und Materialitäten gleichermaßen Ausgangspunkt und Inhalt

6 Angela Stief im Gespräch mit Eduard Tauss im Atelier des Künstlers, Juni 2017, Wien.

7 Ebenda.

8 Ebenda.

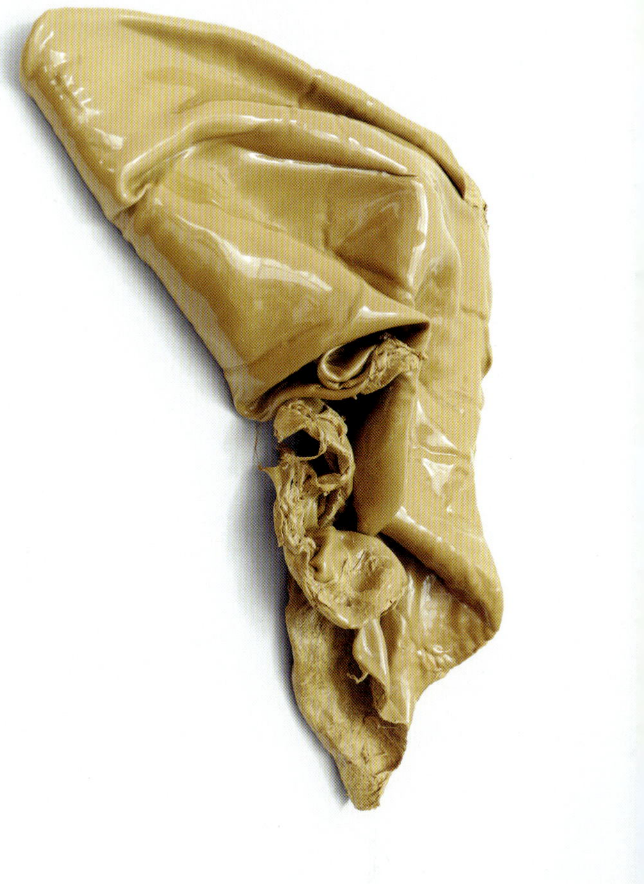

the paint, marks the shift of emphasis from a static work to a performance of the production and the transformation of a classic casting process.

The impulse – that is, the amount of movement by the artist as well as through gravity that impacts the unfinished object – describes the immediate interaction, condensed with regard to time, of artist and material: Tauss pours the liquid synthetic resin onto a plastic sheet on the floor, allowing for material thickness and expansion. When the material is "as dry as possible but has not yet hardened"[7], the work of hanging, bending and forming begins. Here, the artist is allowed only a few minutes of reaction time. Afterwards, post-processing is no longer possible. During this time the entire concentration is focussed on "allowing the material to realize its own intrinsic value"[8] – a

7 Angela Stief in conversation with Eduard Tauss in the artist's studio, June 2017, Vienna.

8 Ibid.

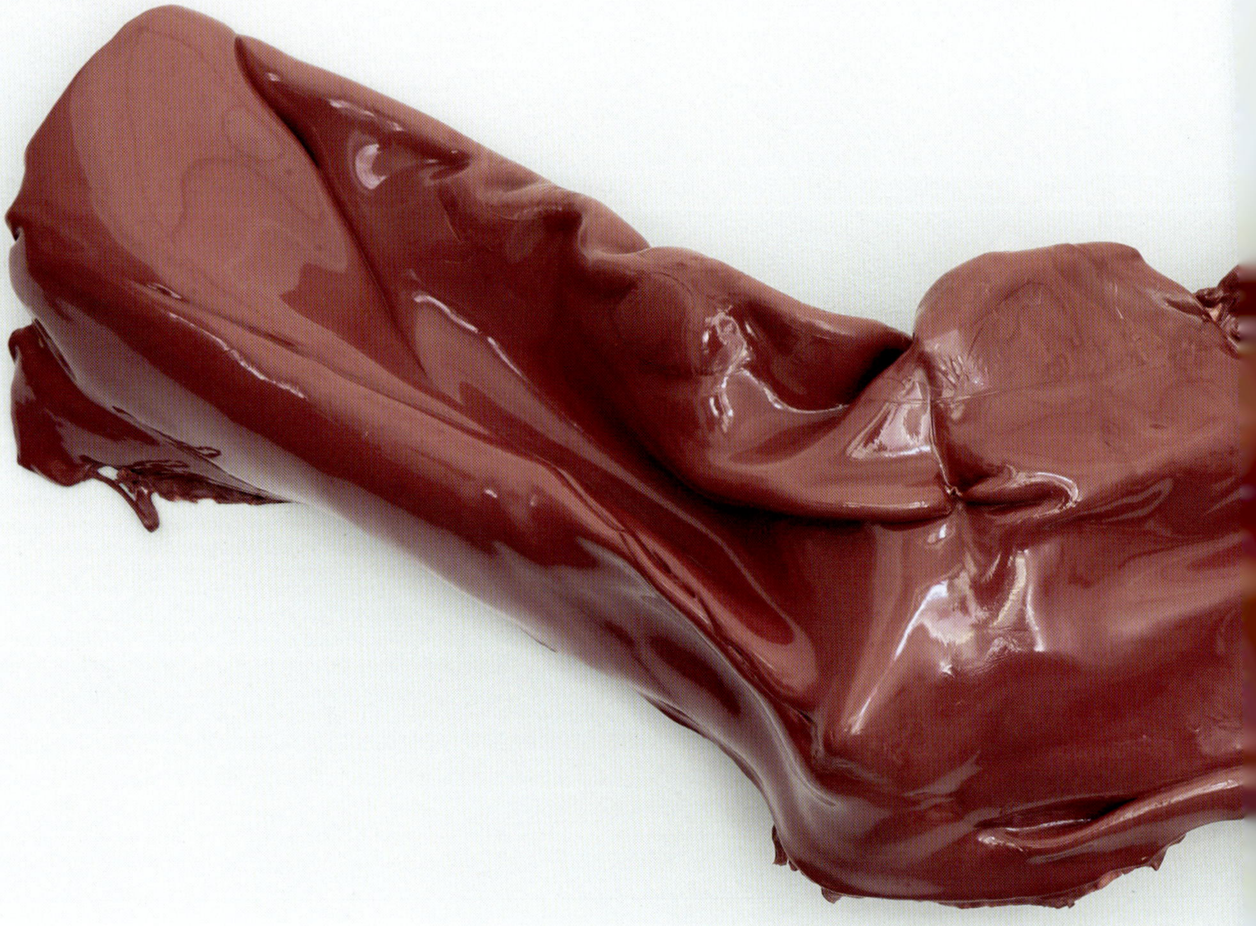

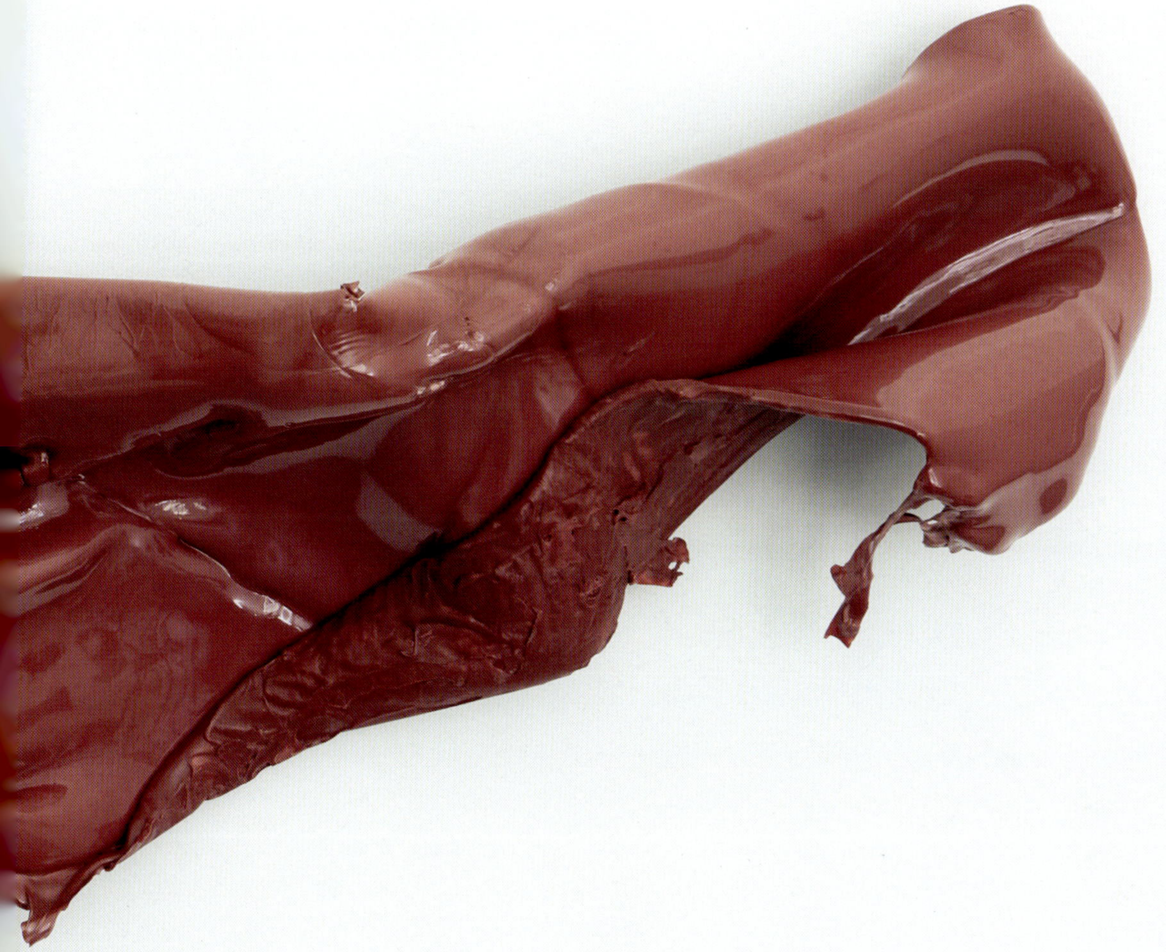

künstlerischer Produktion wurden. So standen etwa in der Minimal Art und bei Künstlern wie Robert Morris und Franz Erhard Walther die spezifischen Eigenschaften des jeweiligen Materials im Vordergrund. Auch Tauss will das Verhalten des Materials, wenn es trocken wird, Versehen, die während der Produktion entstehen, und die Endfarbigkeit der Objekte nur bedingt beeinflussen. Auch die Wahl von Vorder- und Rückseite passiert erst während des Arbeitsprozesses. Die Farbmasse wird während des Härtungsprozesses von der Schwerkraft moduliert: Sie wird ansichtig, wenn sie rinnt, verläuft, absackt und Falten wirft. Es sind dann Falten, manchmal auch Spalten und Knicke bis hin zu Brüchen, die die Werke bestimmen.

paradigm of the artistic development of the 1960s, when matter, material and materiality became both departure point and content of artistic production. In Minimal Art, for example, and with artists such as Robert Morris and Franz Erhard Walther, the specific qualities of the respective material were in the foreground. Tauss, as well, wants to have only limited influence on the behaviour of the material when it dries, on oversights that occur during production, and on the final colouring of the objects. The choice of front and back side is also made only in the course of the work process. The colour mass is modulated during the hardening process by gravity: It takes on a visual form when it drips, runs, sags and wrinkles. Then it is the folds, sometimes also

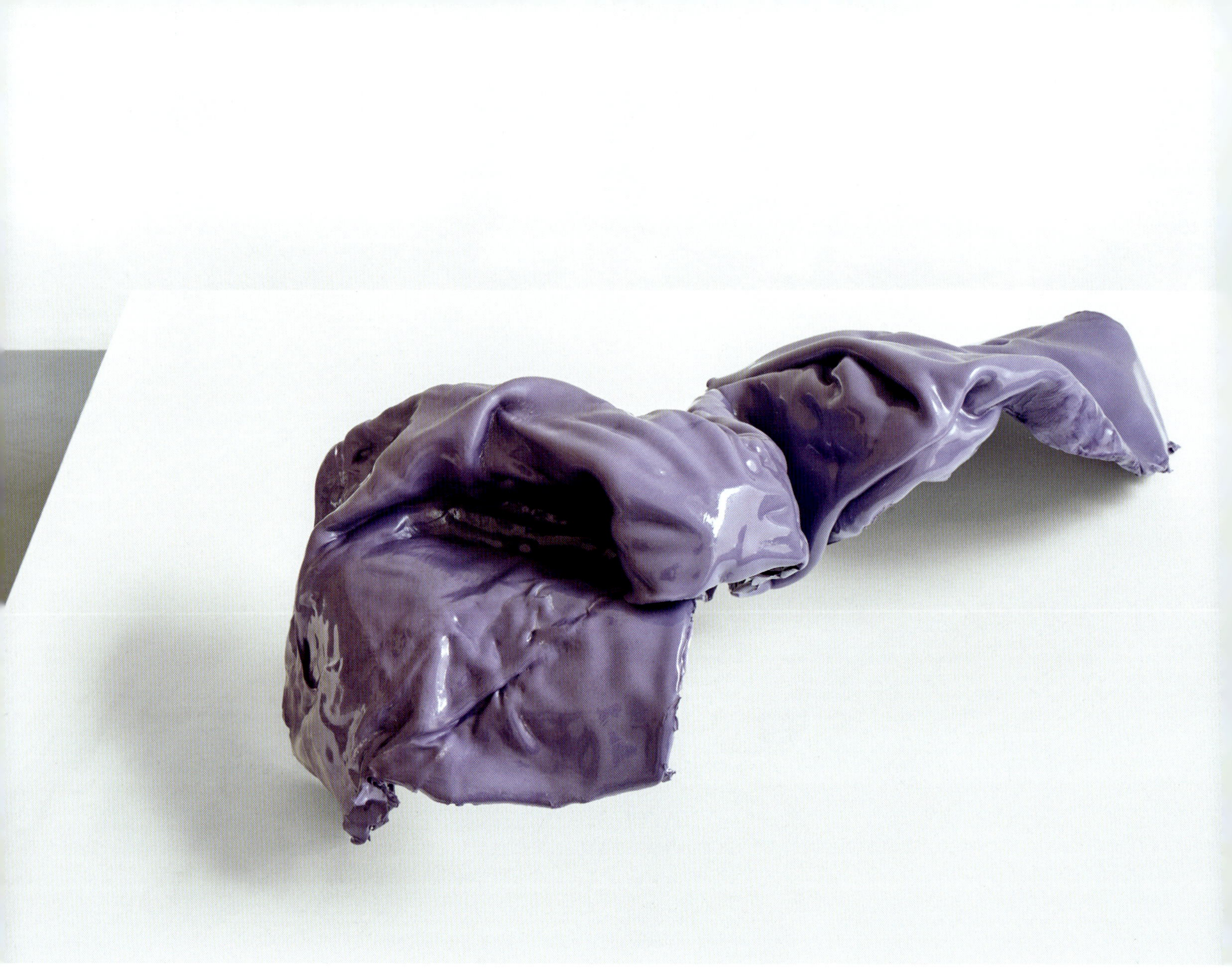

Letztendlich entfalten die Arbeiten des wohl klassischen White-Cube-Künstlers Eduard Tauss ihre Wirkungsmacht im Display. Die Modalitäten der Präsentation sind variabel und das breite Darstellungsspektrum reicht von Bodenobjekten bis zu Arbeiten, die lehnen, auf einem Podest liegen und an der Wand hängen. Es geht um vieles in dieser Kunst: um eine nicht-affirmative Ästhetisierung des Mediums, um das Einwirken physikalischer Kräfte während der Produktion, um Strukturaufweichung und um die Tautologie des Zähflüssigen. Aber vor allem geht es auch um eine sich im Raum entfaltende Malerei, die das Momentum der Interaktion zwischen Künstler und Material inszeniert.

crevices and kinks or even breaks, that determine the works.

Ultimately the works by Eduard Tauss, undoubtedly a classic White Cube artist, develop their full impact when displayed. The modalities of presentation are variable, the broad representational spectrum ranging from floor objects to works that lean, lie on a pedestal and hang on the wall. This art is concerned with many things: with a non-affirmative aestheticization of the medium, with an impacting of physical forces during production, with a softening of structure and with the tautology of the viscous. But above all it is concerned with painting that unfolds in the space, painting that stages the momentum of the interaction between artist and material.

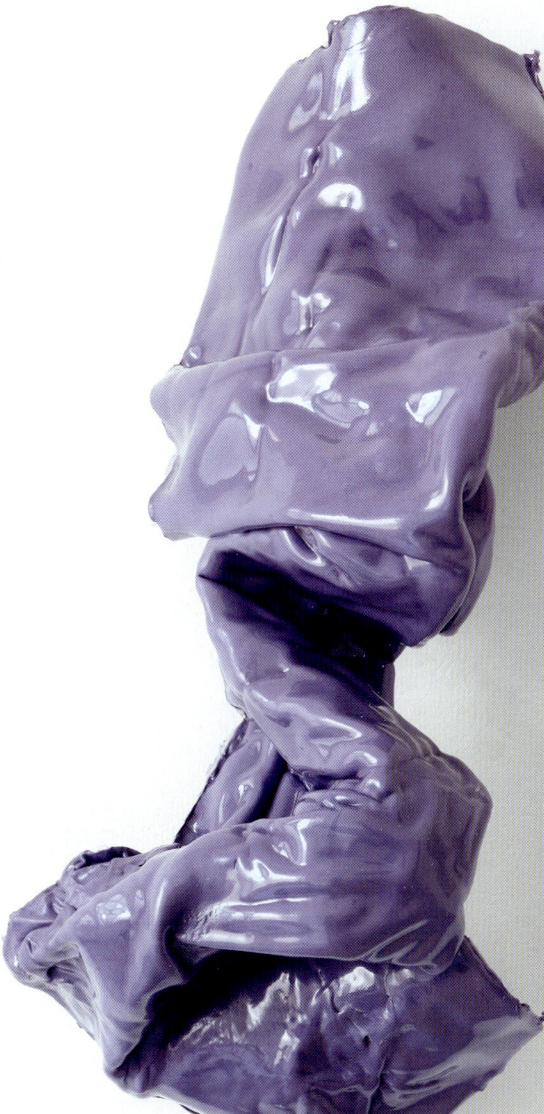

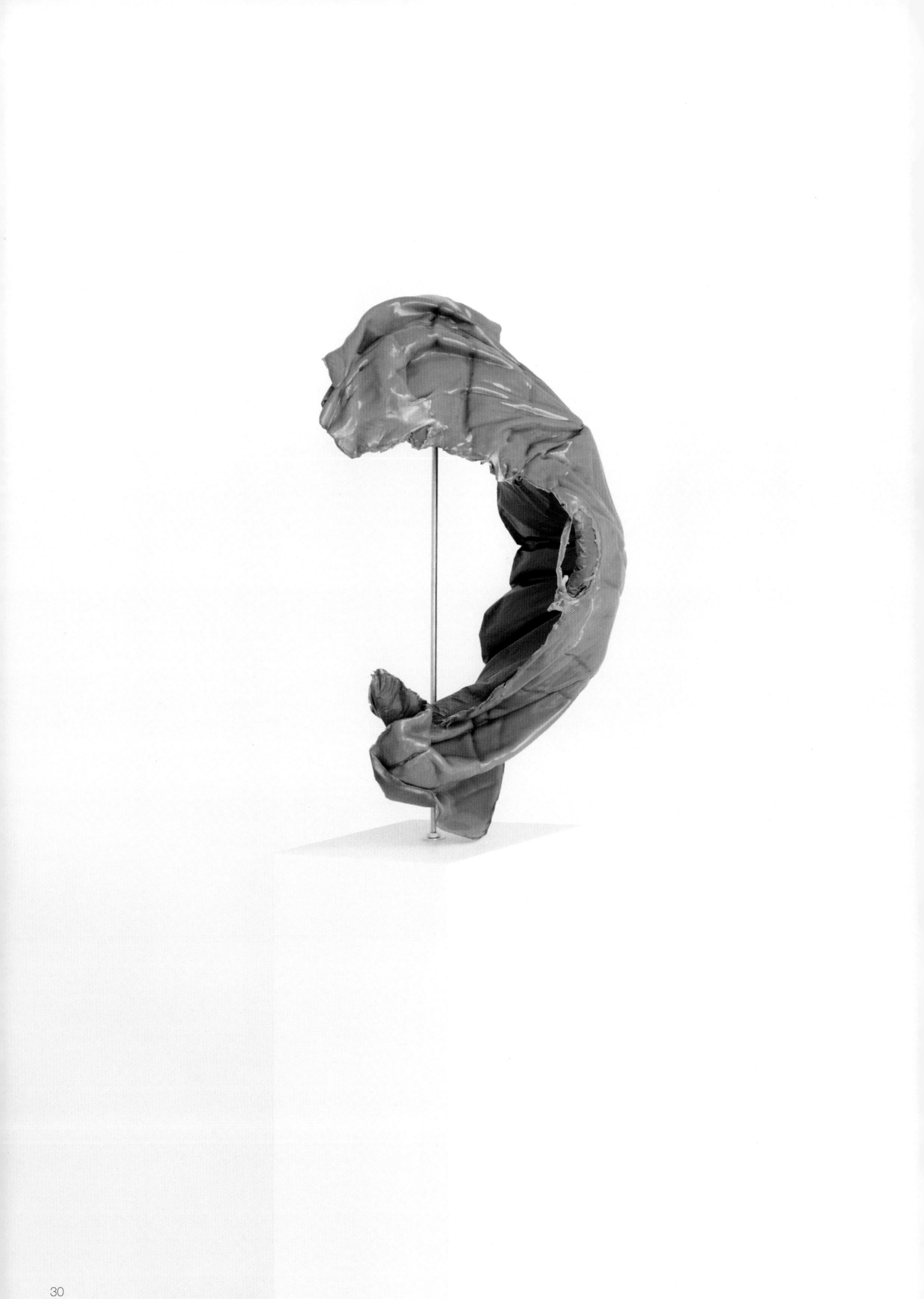

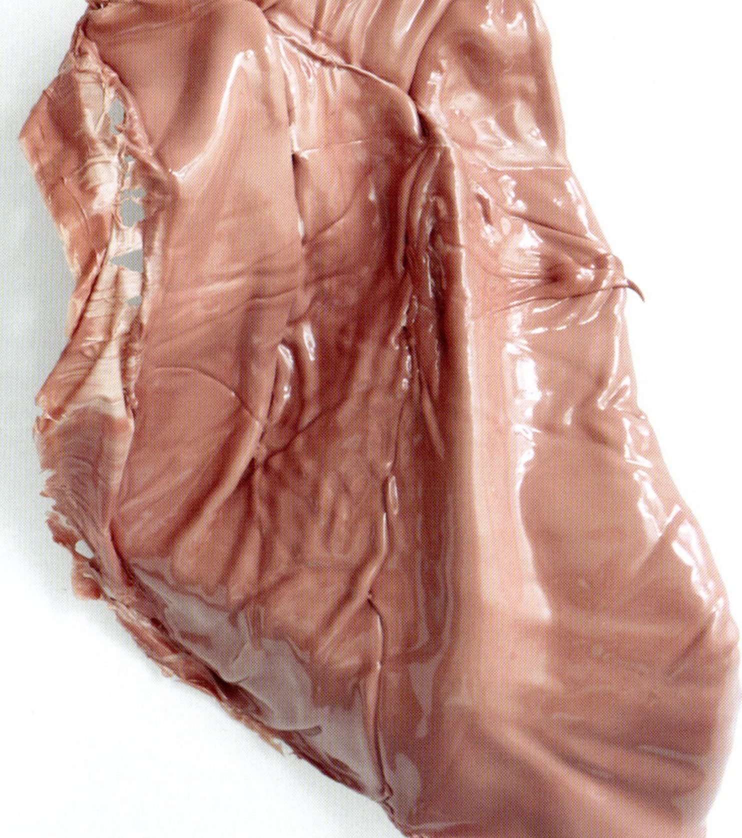

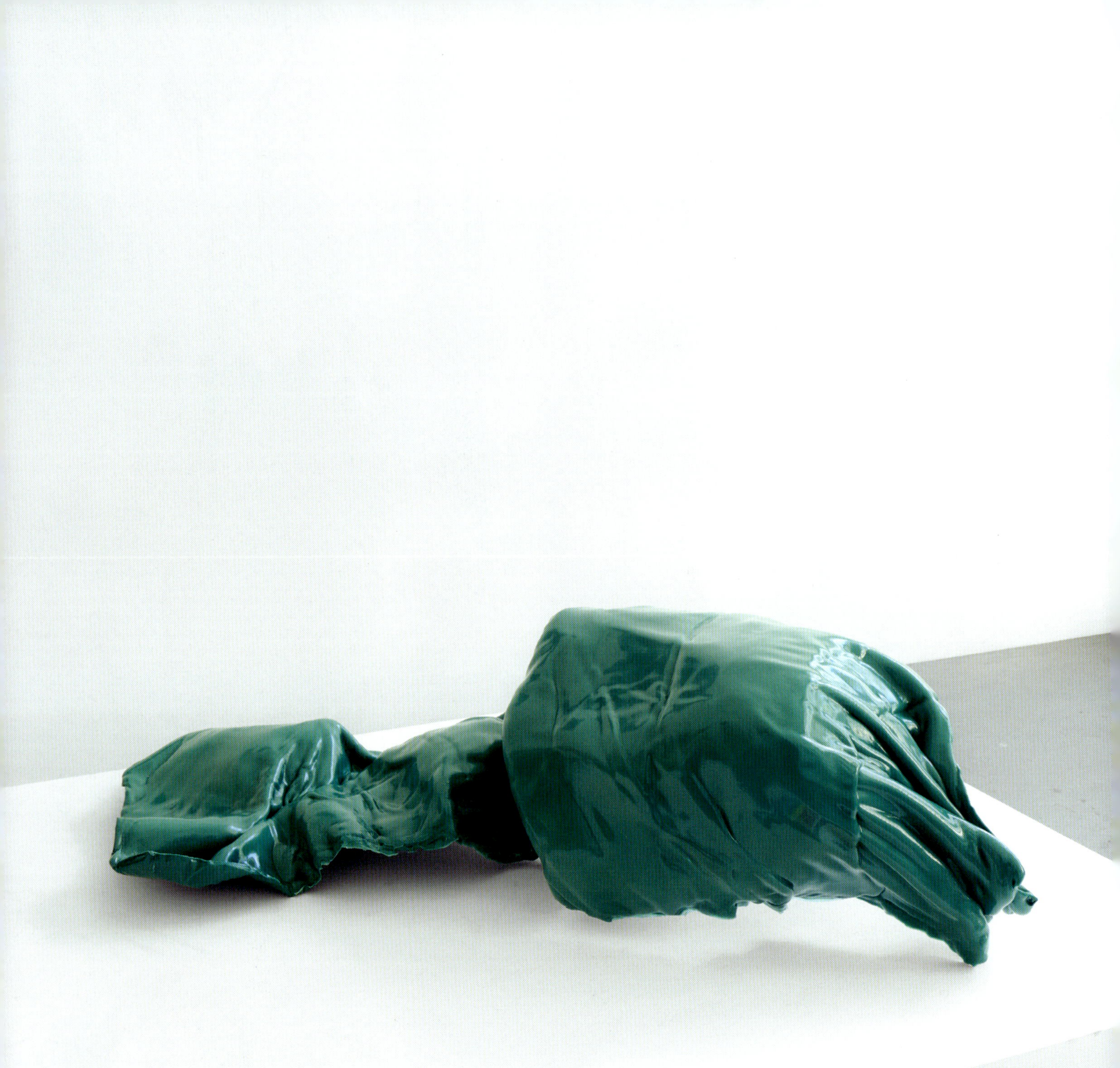

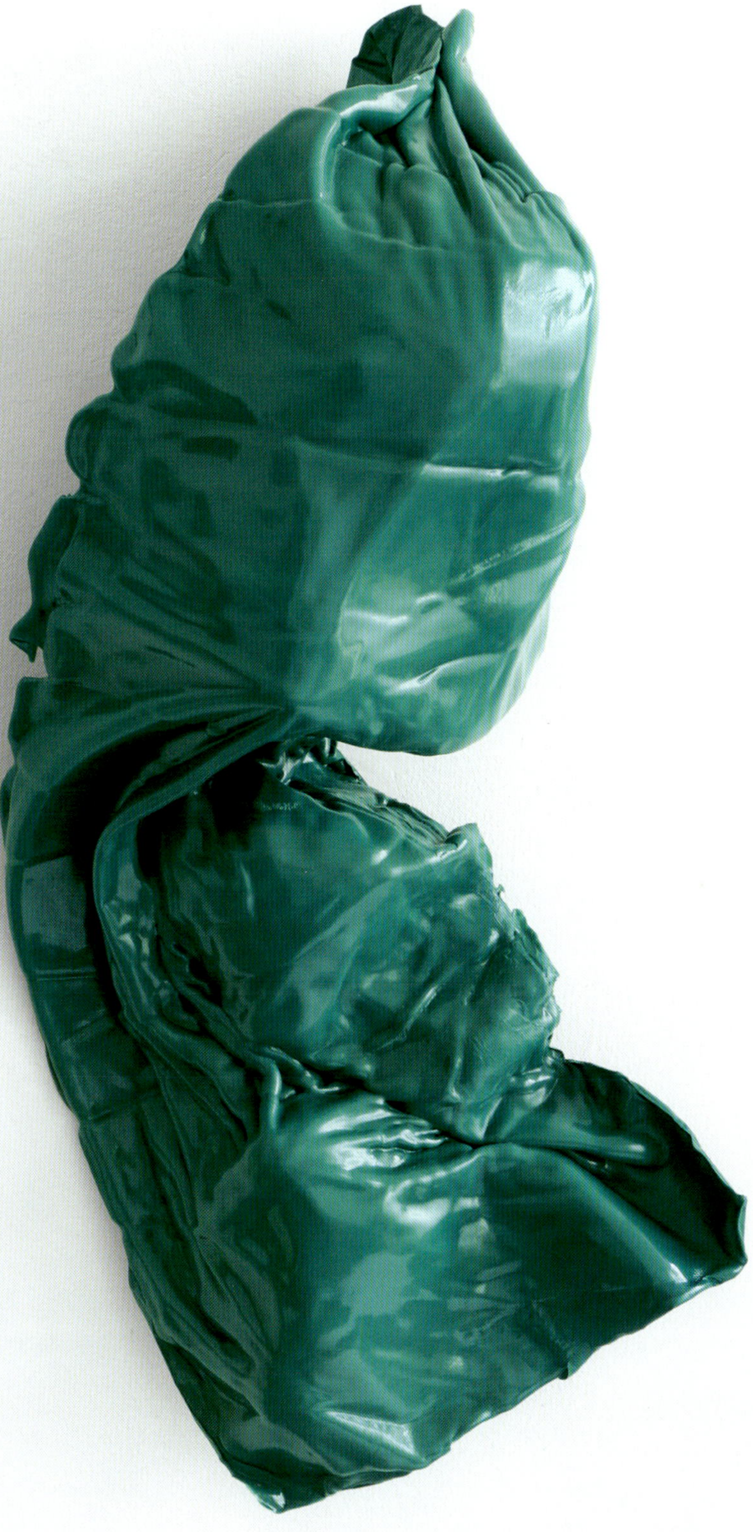

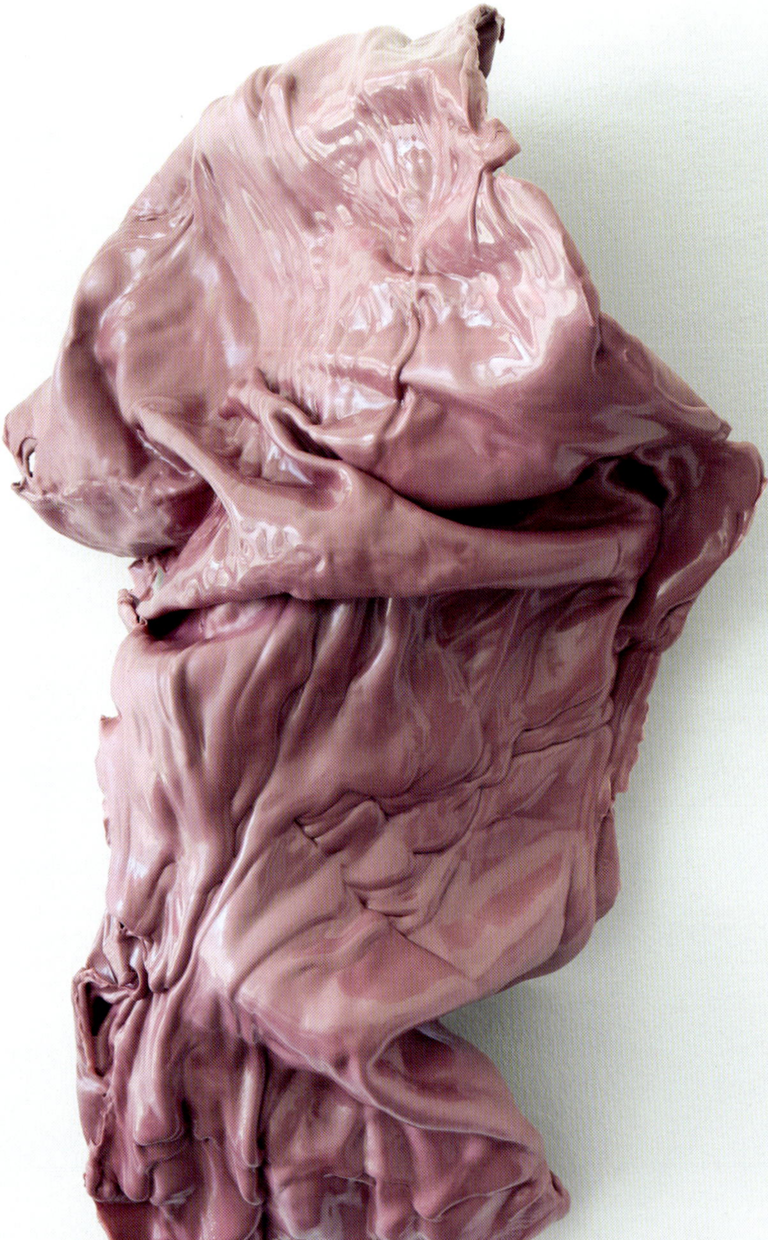

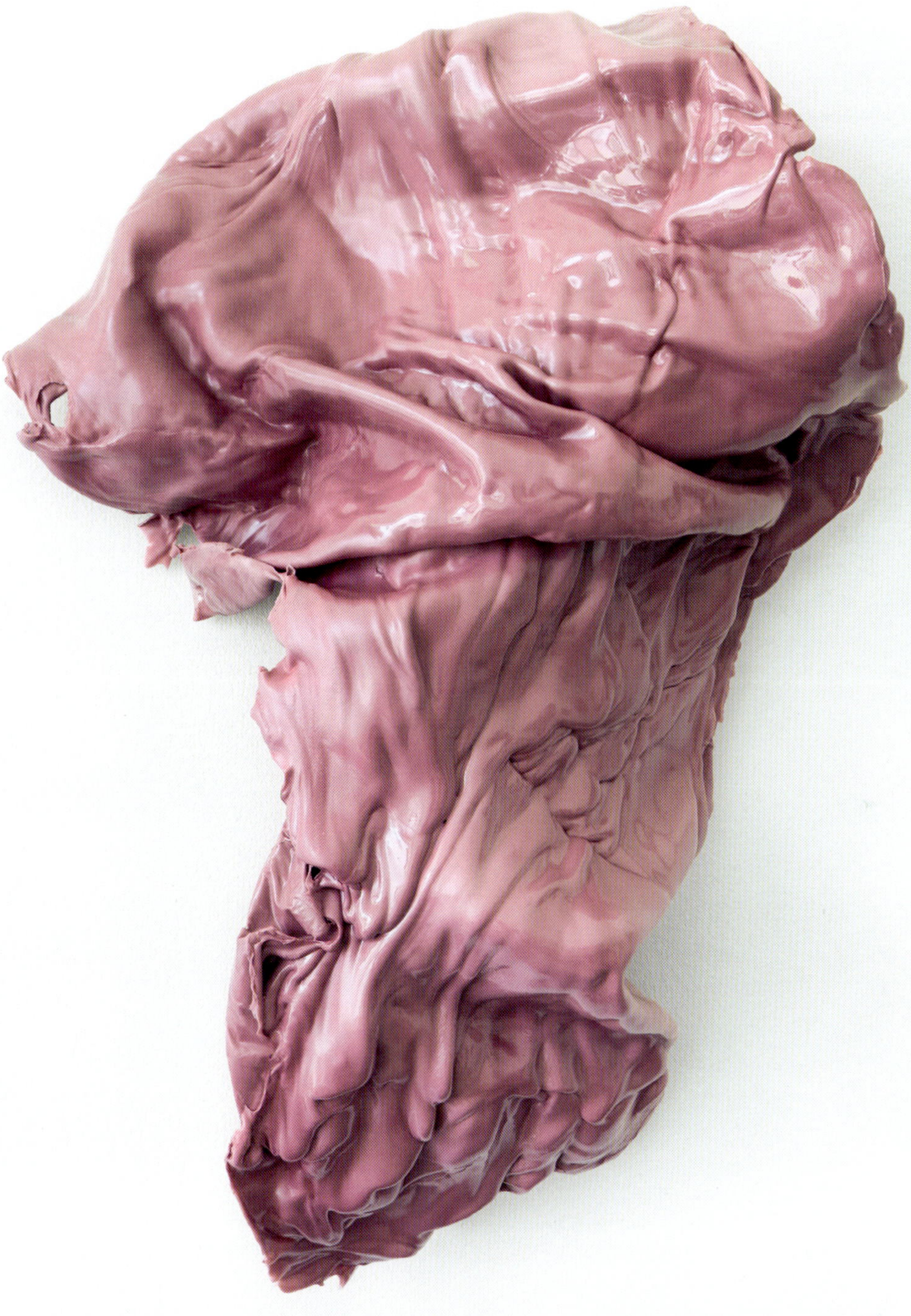

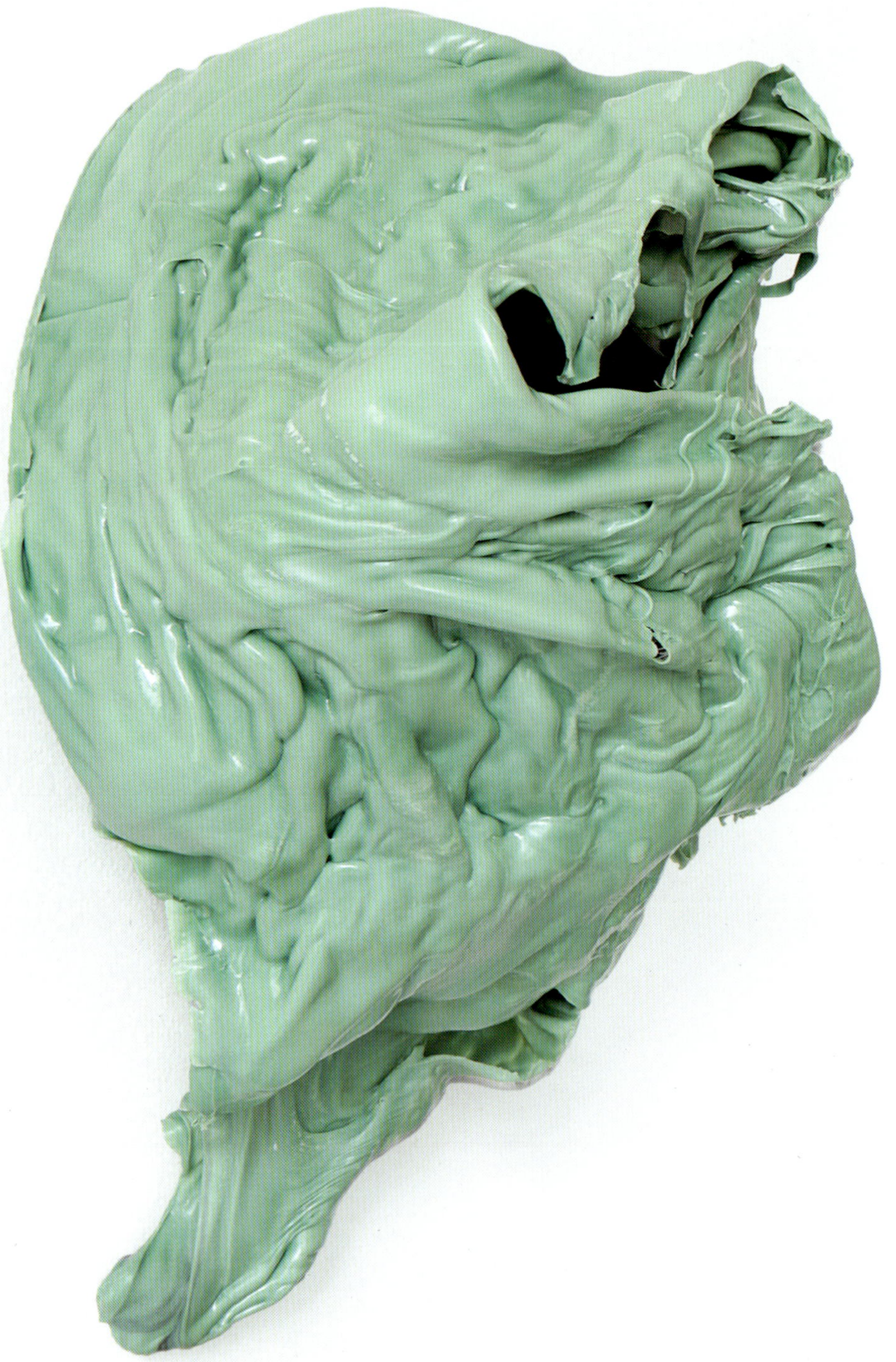

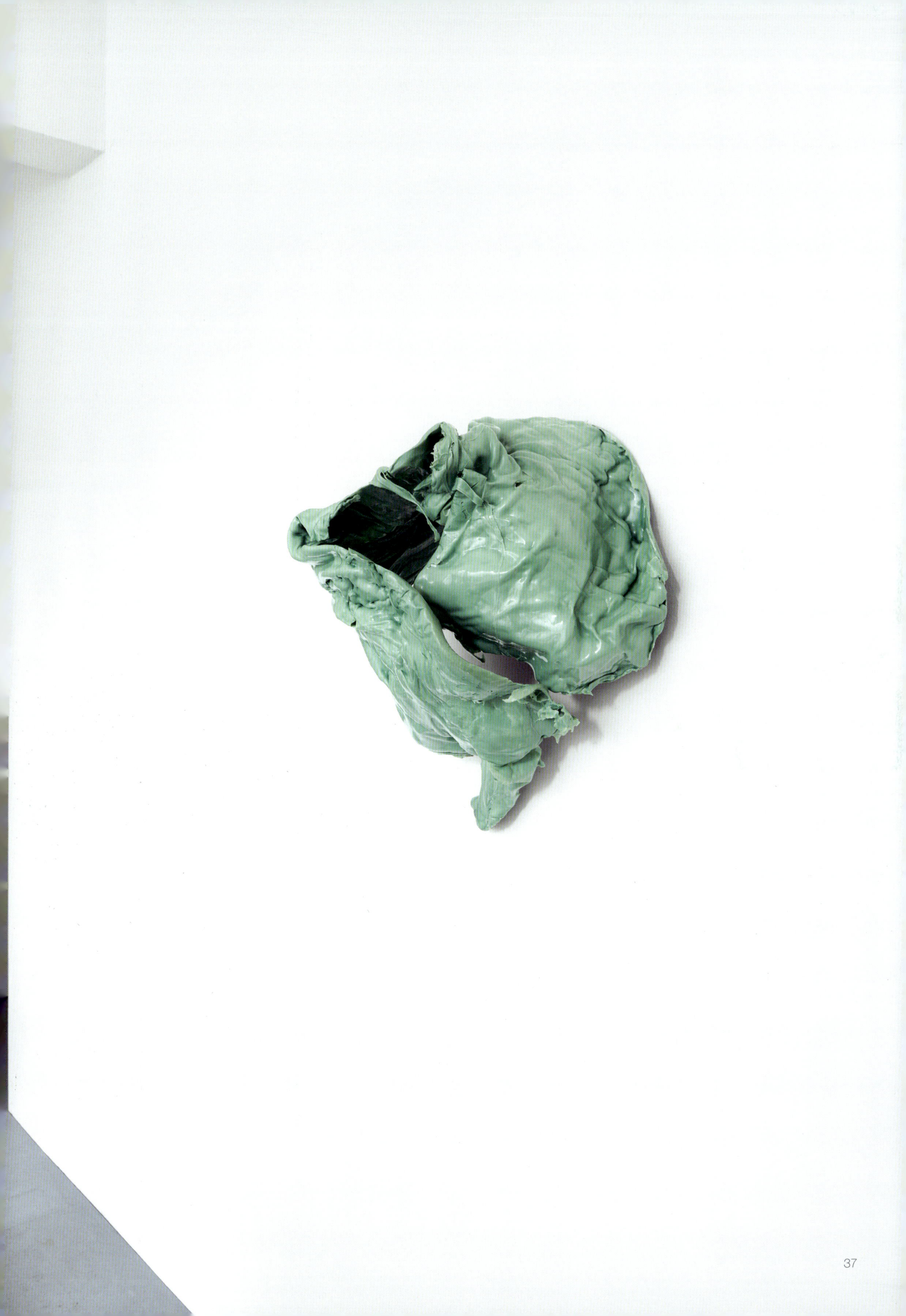

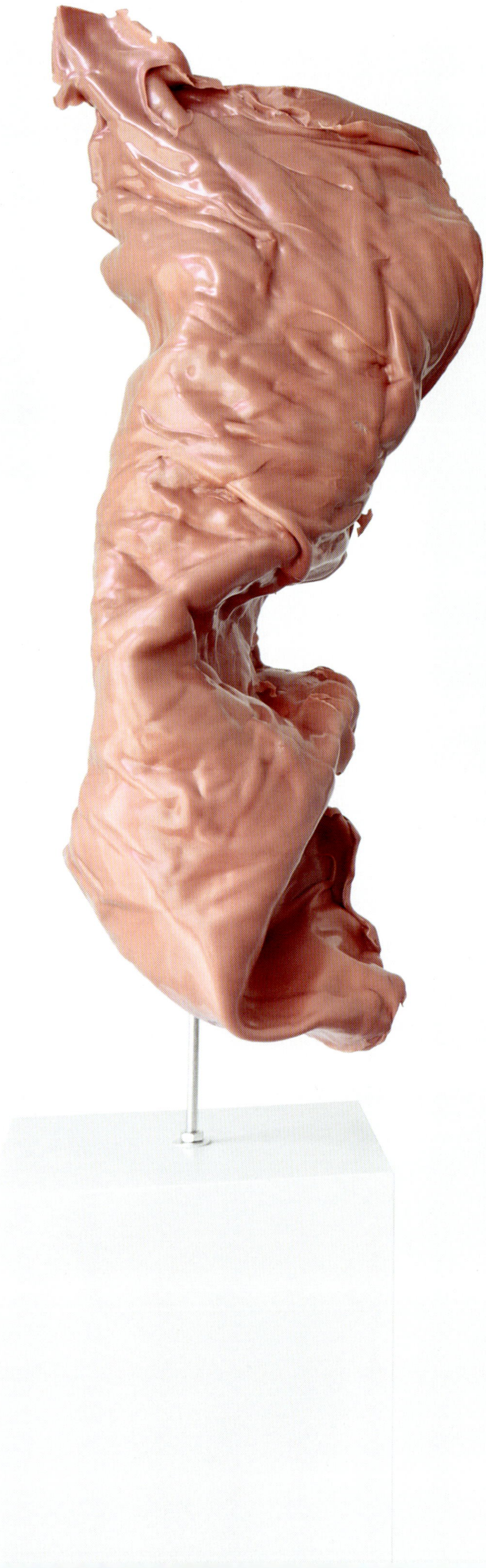

Florian Steininger

Direktor Kunsthalle Krems

Prozess – Farbe – Form

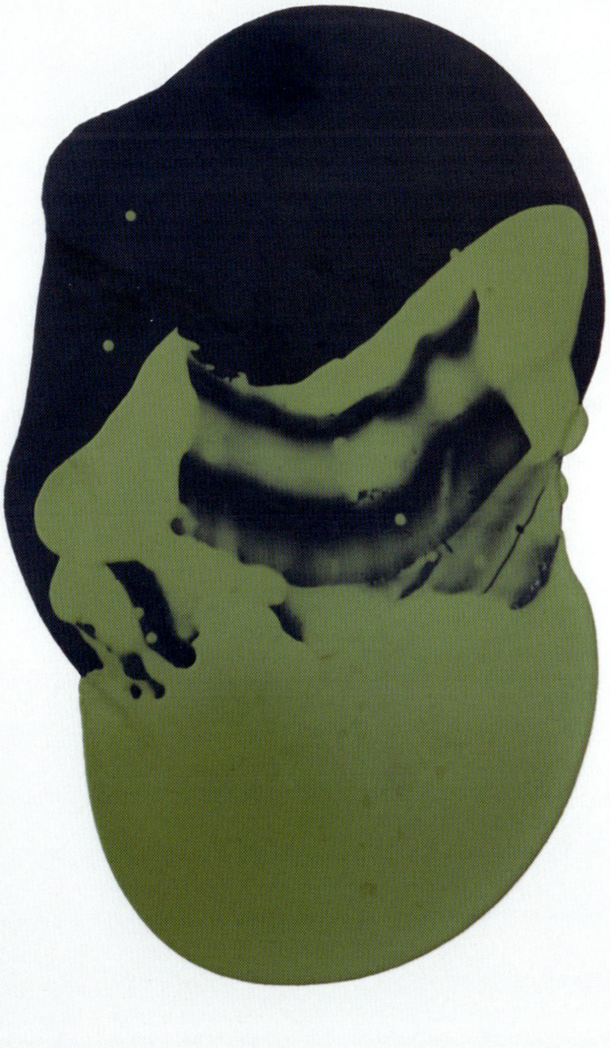

Farbe in ihrer materiellen Natur ist zentrales Thema in Eduard Tauss' künstlerischem Schaffen. Im Unterschied zur deutschen Sprache wird im Englischen zwischen „Colour" als optischem Wert und „Paint" als materieller Beschaffenheit differenziert. Eduard Tauss ist Painter/Maler im prozessual-formalen Sinne. Aktion und Substanz führen zu Form und Werk. Auf den mit Folie abgedeckten Atelierboden gießt der Künstler die flüssige, mit Farbpigment gemischte Polyurethanmasse. Leisten oder Latten dienen als flexible Gussform. Der Akt des Gießens ist jedoch keine auktorial-expressive Geste, sondern ein sachlich-prozessualer Vorgang.

Jackson Pollocks Ergüsse aus den Farbkannen oder Hermann Nitschs brachiale Schüttungen auf dem Bildträger resultieren aus einer psychischen Bewegtheit und einer körperlich-aktionistischen Kraft, ein aktives Markieren auf der Leinwand. Andy Warhol hat hierauf mit seinen Piss Paintings reagiert, indem Assistenten des Pop-Art-Künstlers auf den Bildträger urinierten und die kupferhaltige Farbe oxidierte. Tauss nimmt sich hingegen in seinem körperlich-gestischen Duktus auf ein Minimum zurück und lässt die Farbe ausfließen, sich innerhalb der Begrenzungen frei verteilen. Hierbei sei an Helen Frankenthalers Soak-Stain-Gemälde im Colour-Field-Painting-Stil verwiesen. Inspiriert wurde Frankenthaler von Jackson Pollocks Drip Paintings, vor allem den Black and White Paintings von 1950/51, deren ungrundierte Leinwand die geschüttete und getropfte schwarze Farbe vollends wie in einer Tuschezeichnung aufsog. Im Oktober 1952 malte Frankenthaler in ihrem New Yorker Atelier Mountains and Sea, indem sie die auf dem Boden ausgerollte, unbehandelte Leinwand mit verdünnter Ölfarbe beschüttete und die Farb-Lachen das Textil tränkten. Morris Louis und Kenneth Noland besuchten die junge US-amerikanische Malerin und waren überwältigt von ihren bahnbrechenden Soak-Stain-Bildern. Darauf entwickelten sie ihren spezifischen Colour-Field-Painting-Stil, indem die Farbe in großen Feldern die Leinwand benetzte. Sie ließen der Farbe ihren freien Lauf, lösten sich von der körperlichen Expressivität der Action Painter. Nun handelt es sich bei all den genannten Positionen um klassische Gemäldeformen. Das Fließen und Schütten verdichtet sich zu einer Malereifläche innerhalb des Bildgevierts, das auf den Keilrahmen gespannt wird. Oben, Unten, Links und Rechts werden festgelegt und schlussendlich wird das Bild an die Wand gehängt.

Eduard Tauss hingegen verlässt das klassische Bildfenster als rektanguläre Form, indem die geschüttete Farbe eine organische, plastische Form annimmt. Sie kann flache Lache sein oder körperlich-skulpturale Gestalt annehmen, indem der Künstler nach dem Schüttvorgang die Substanz, bevor sie aushärtet, formt und verformt. Assoziationen mit Körperteilen und Hautoberflächen treten auf, ohne dass der Künstler das Werk motivisch oder inhaltlich aufladen möchte. „Ich will keine Geschichte erzählen."[1] Die Werke sind autonome Existenzen – Artikulationen von Malerei. Die flachen Malerei-Lachen können wie ein Bild an die Wand gehängt oder, im Sinne ihrer Entstehung, auf dem Boden

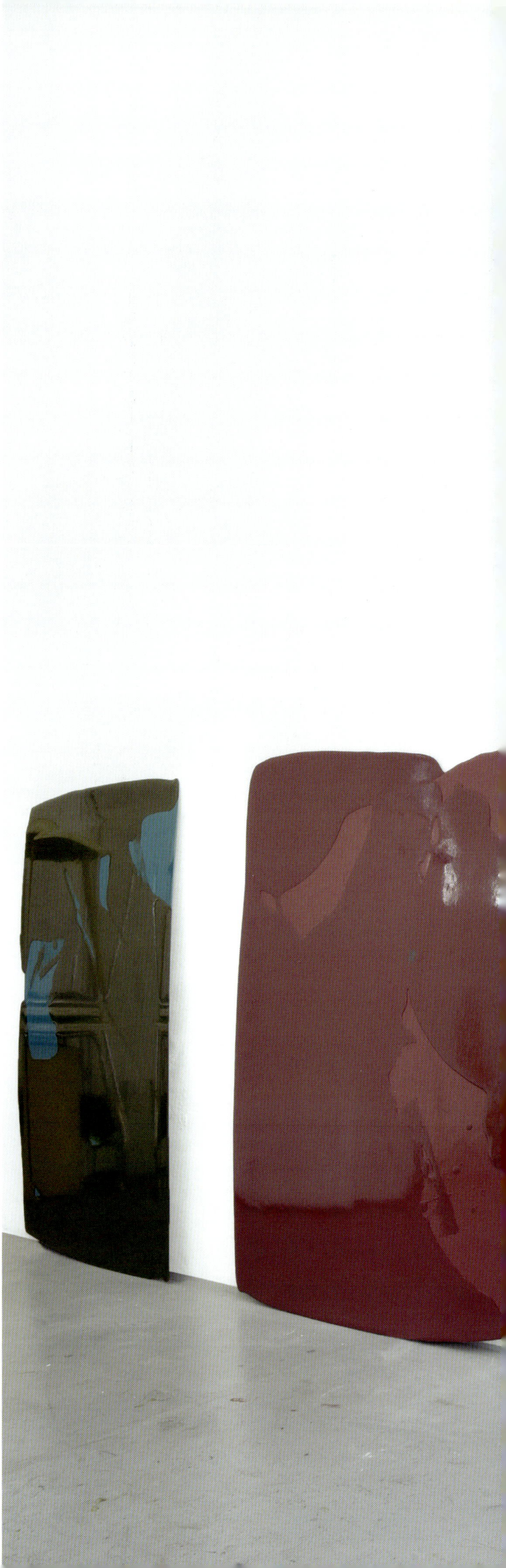

1 Florian Steininger im Gespräch mit Eduard Tauss im Atelier des Künstlers, März 2022, Wien.

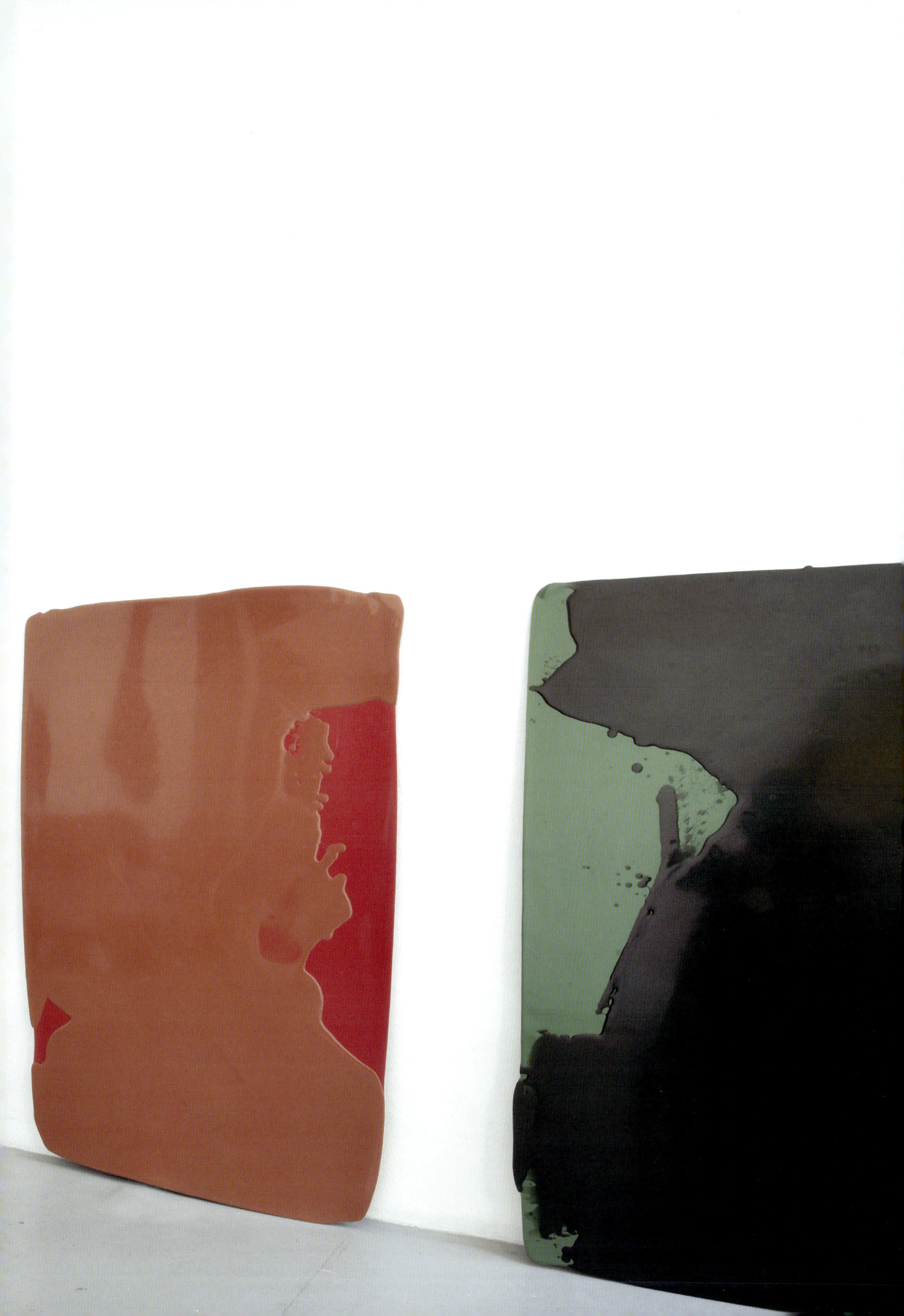

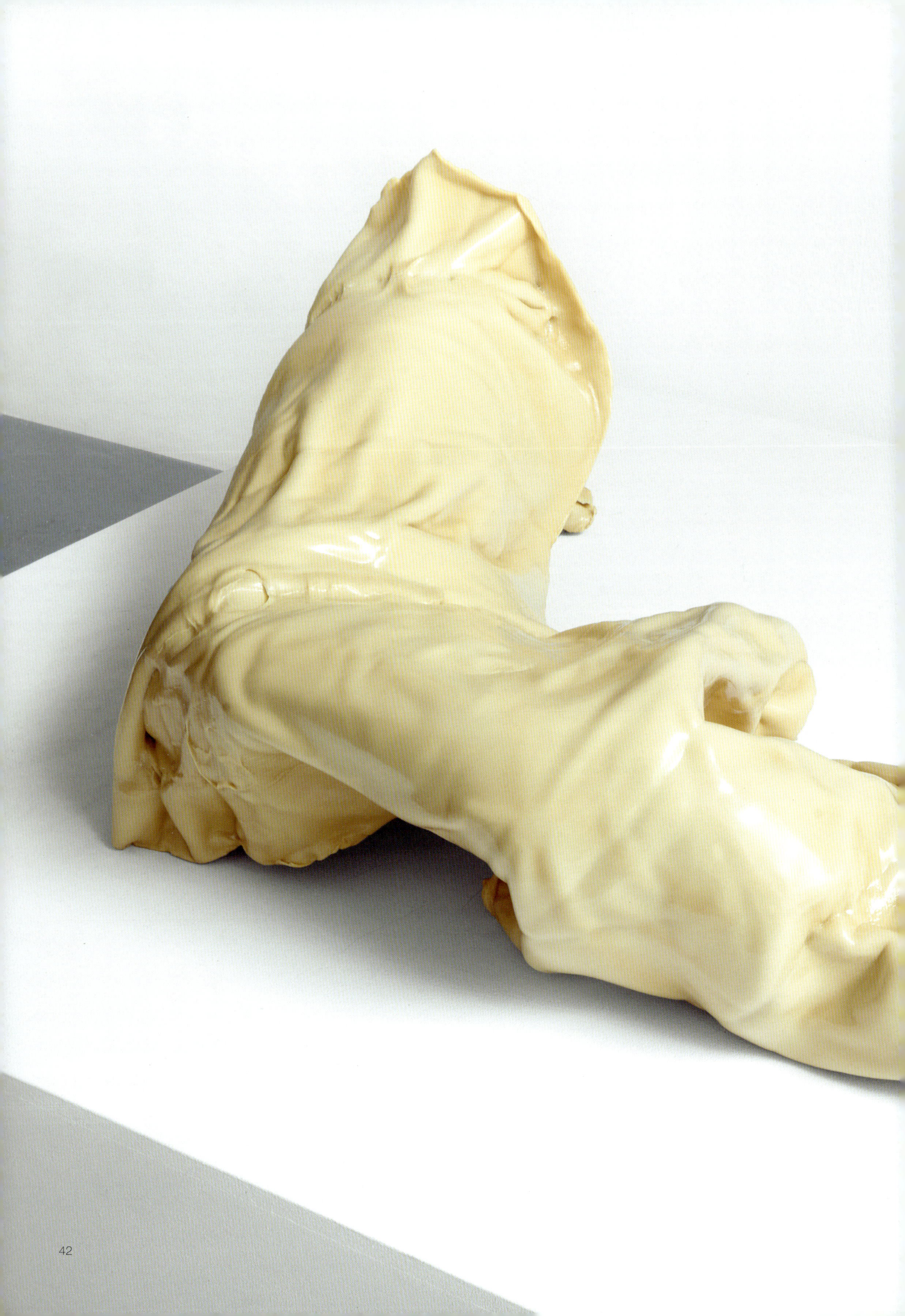

oder auf einem Sockel platziert werden. Im Unterschied zu den Colour-Field-Paintings von Frankenthaler und Louis sind Tauss' gemalte Oberflächen nicht transluzid, optisch illusionistisch, sondern opak, wie eine Haut. Der Künstler verwendet gedeckte Farben ohne poppigen Glanz, er verschließt das imaginäre Fenster der Malerei. Farbe ist Masse und Materialität. In der klassischen Malerei waren materielle Anhäufungen auf der Leinwand verpönt. Rembrandts und Courbets pastos-schmieriger Auftrag wurde von akademischer Warte aus als schmutziges und schlampiges Gekleckse kritisiert. Die Farbe sollte sich der illusionistischen Wiedergabe von Figur und Wirklichkeit als optisches Mittel unterordnen. In der Moderne wurde das Wesen der Malerei analysiert, wobei die Farbe als materielle Substanz an Bedeutung gewann – wie etwa van Goghs pastose Pinselstriche. So malte Alexander Rodtschenko 1921 drei Gemälde in den drei Grundfarben. Es ging um die Faktur, die malerische Oberflächenbeschaffenheit und Materialität und nicht um die Optikalität. Robert Ryman, Joseph Marioni oder Brice Marden folgten in der Nachkriegsmoderne diesem Primat der Materialität. Eduard Tauss' Malereien zeugen aufgrund ihrer materiellen Natur und prozessualen Geformtheit, die Parallelen zum Postminimalismus aufweisen, von einer gewissen skulpturalen Qualität. Richard Serra spritzte flüssiges Blei in die Raumecken, das sich zu skulpturalen Spuren verfestigte, Eva Hesse spann in Reaktion auf Pollocks kosmische Drip-Painting-Netze mit Schnüren ein Gewebe im Raum und Robert Morris schuf Antiforms, schlaff herabhängende Filzmatten an der Wand.

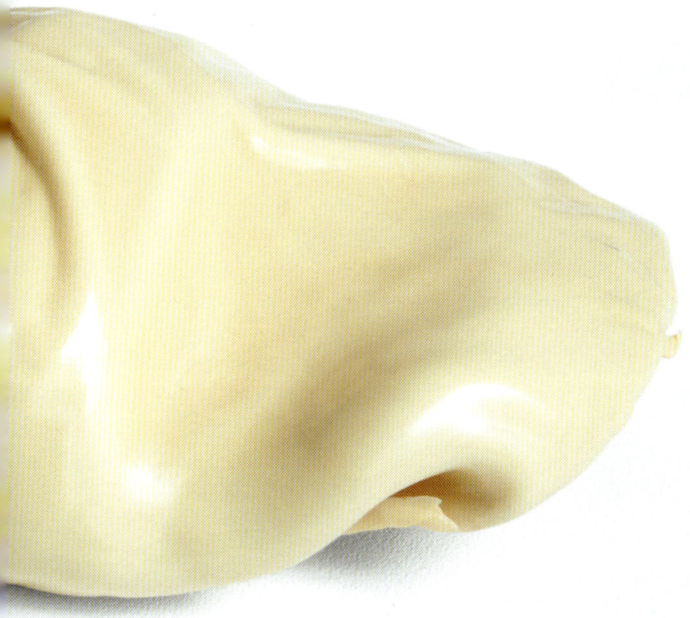

Im Wechselverhältnis zwischen Produktion und Analyse erschafft Eduard Tauss autonome Farb-Formen, die sich in ihrer malerischen Natur behaupten.

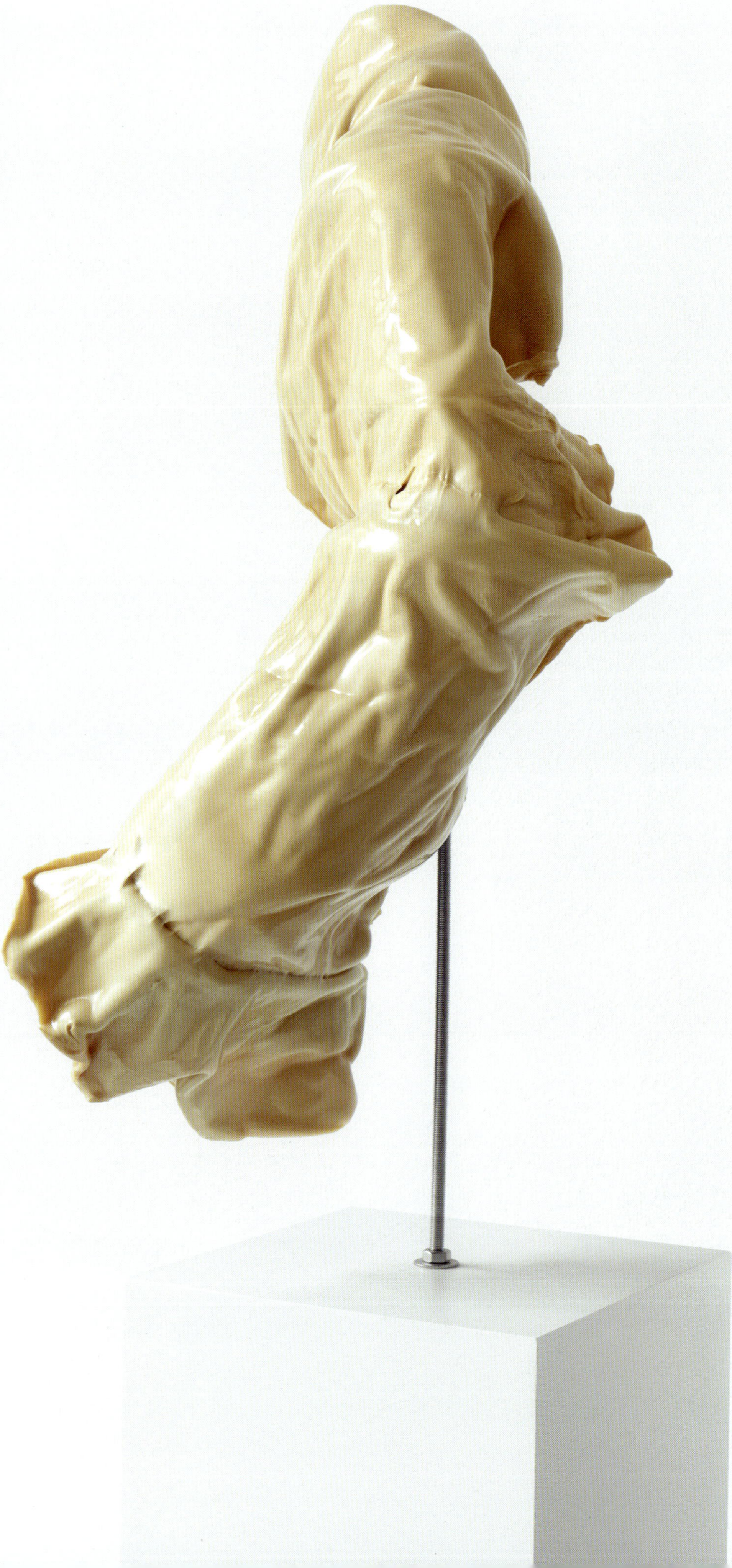

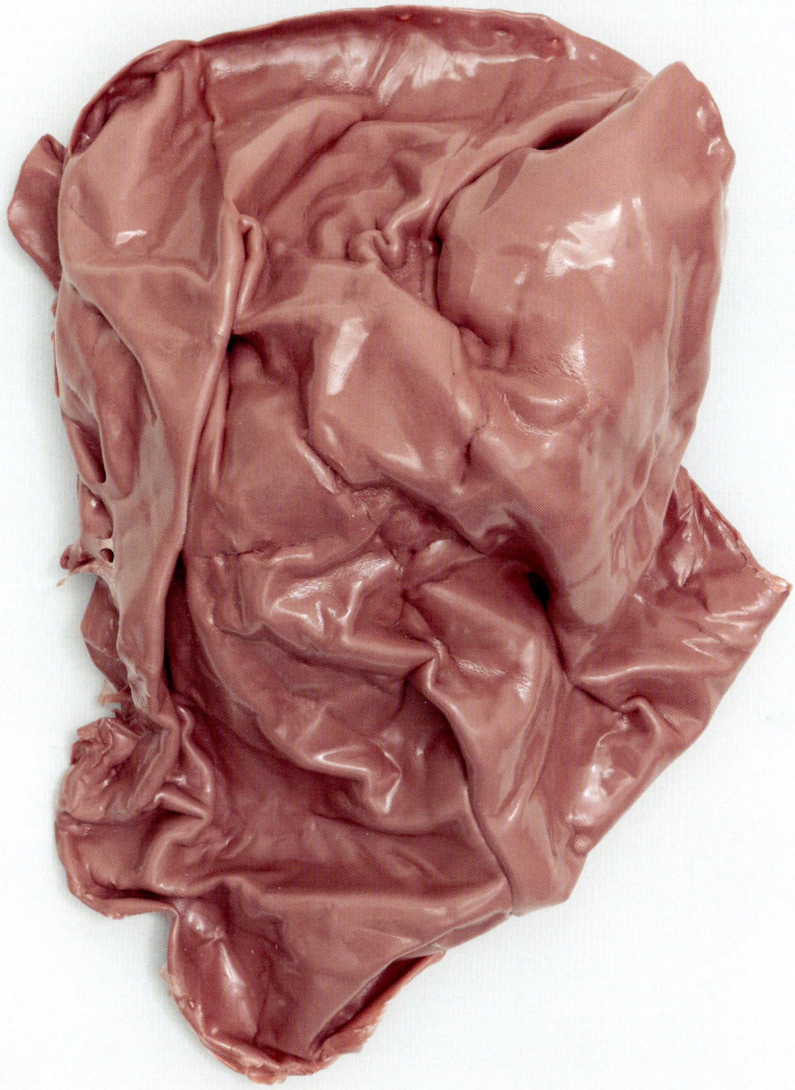

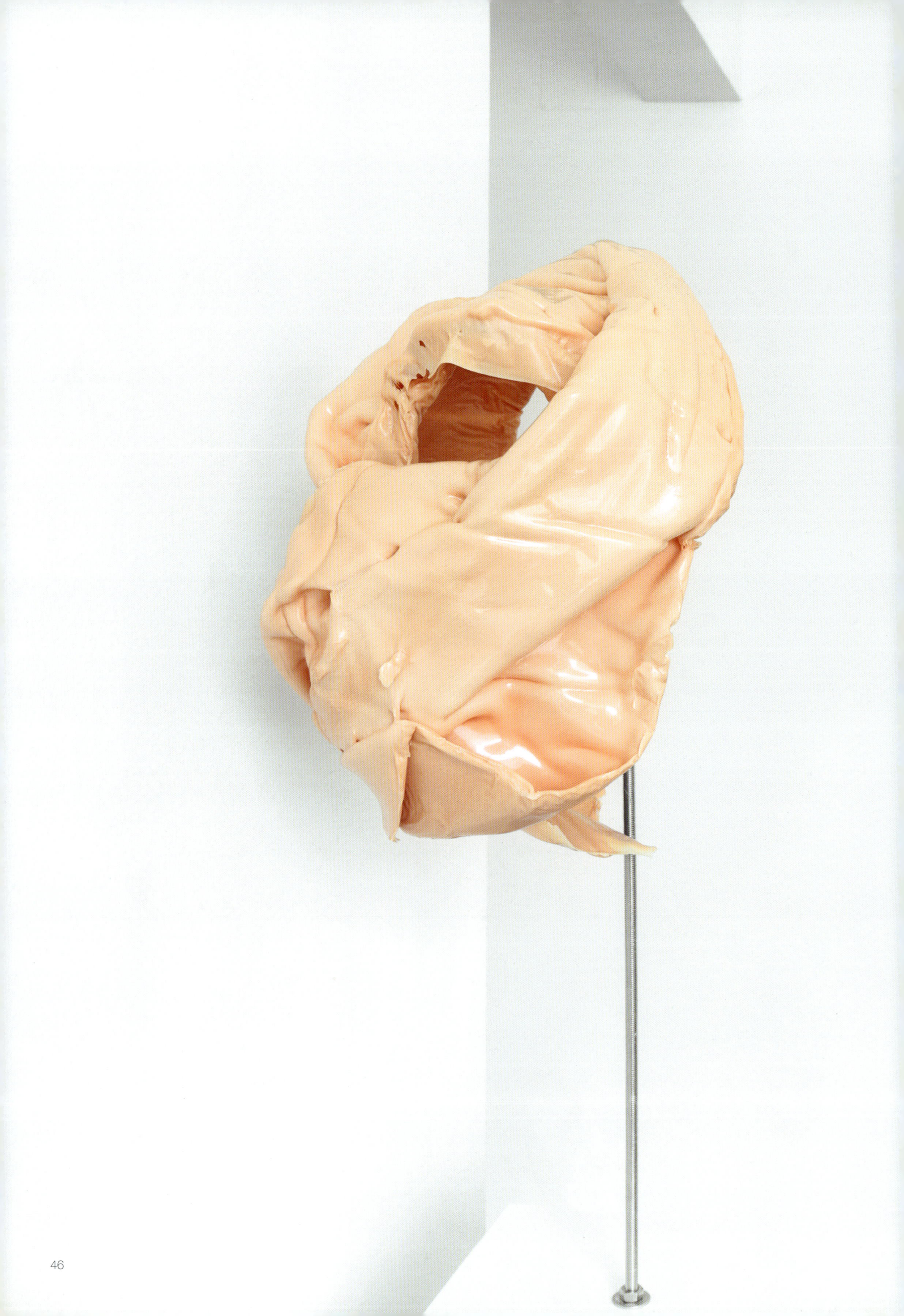

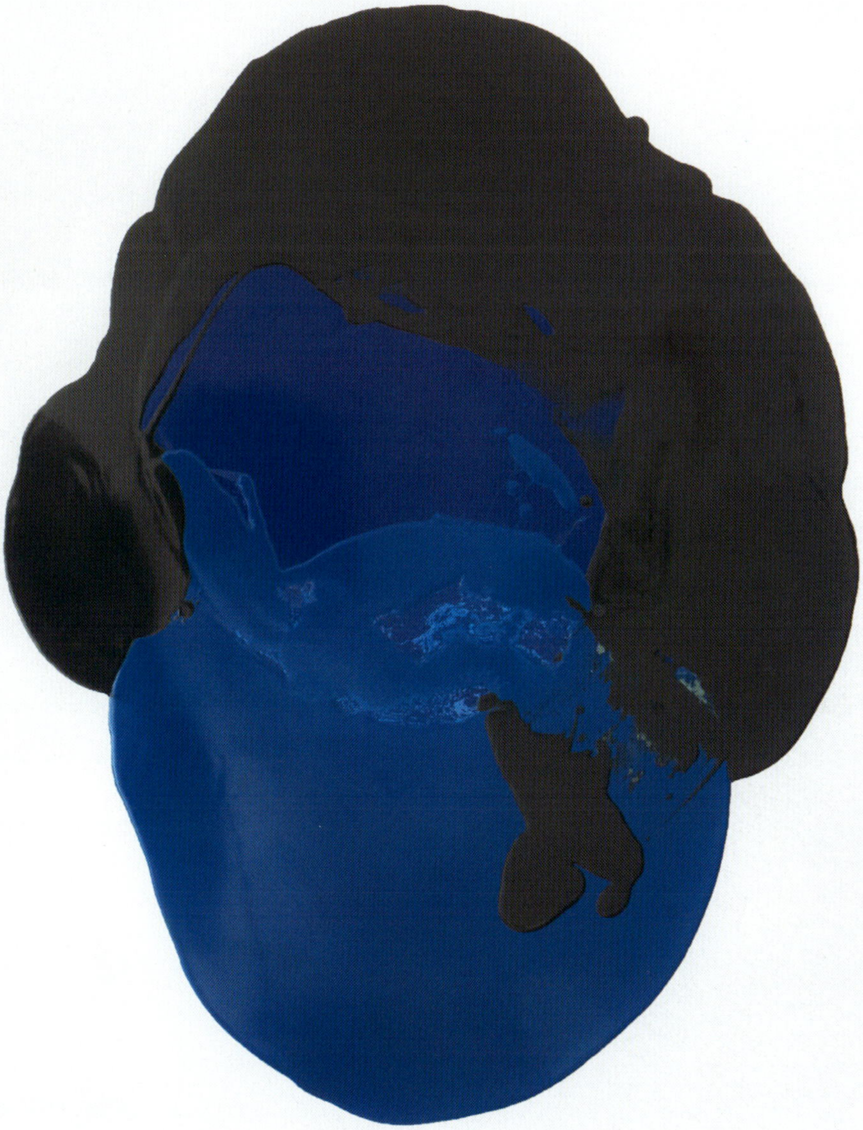

Florian Steininger

Director Kunsthalle Krems

Process – Paint – Form

Paint in its material nature is the central theme in the art of Eduard Tauss. In contrast to the German language, English differentiates between "colour" as optical value, and "paint" as material constitution. Eduard Tauss is a painter in terms of process and form. Action and substance lead to the form and the work. He pours the liquid compound of polyurethane mixed with pigment onto the foil-covered studio floor. Slats or bars act as flexible casting mould. The act of pouring however is not an authorial or expressionistic gesture, but an objective process.

Jackson Pollock's splashes from his cans of paint or Hermann Nitsch's violent splattering on the substrate are born of a mental turbulence, a physical and actionist energy, an active marking on the canvas. Andy Warhol reacted to this with his piss paintings; the assistants of the Pop artist urinated on the substrate, and the cupriferous paint oxidised, whereas Tauss holds himself back to a minimum in his characteristic physical and gestural style and lets the paint run out, lets it freely spread around within the limits. We are reminded here of Helen Frankenthaler's soak-stain paintings in the colour field painting style. Frankenthaler was inspired by Jackson Pollock's drip paintings and most of all by the black and white paintings of 1950/51, their untreated canvas thoroughly absorbing the splashed and dripped black paint in a kind of pen-and-ink drawing. In October 1952, Frankenthaler painted Mountains and

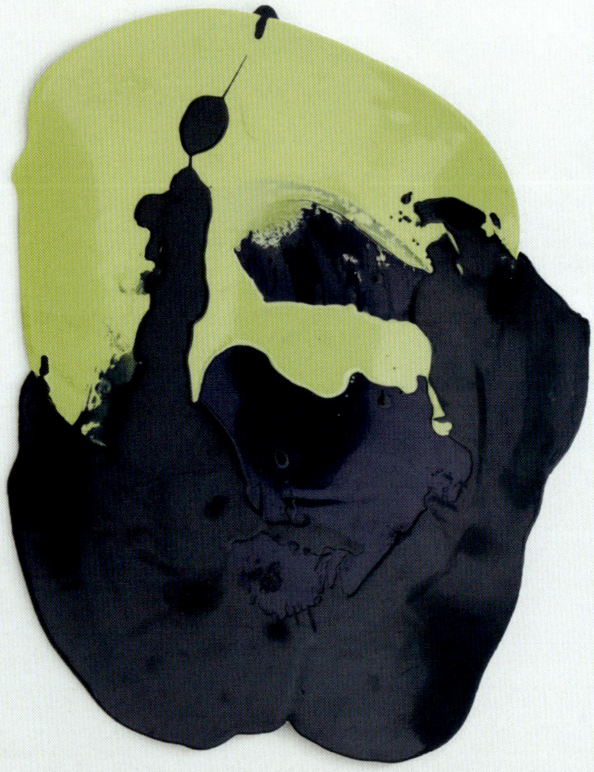

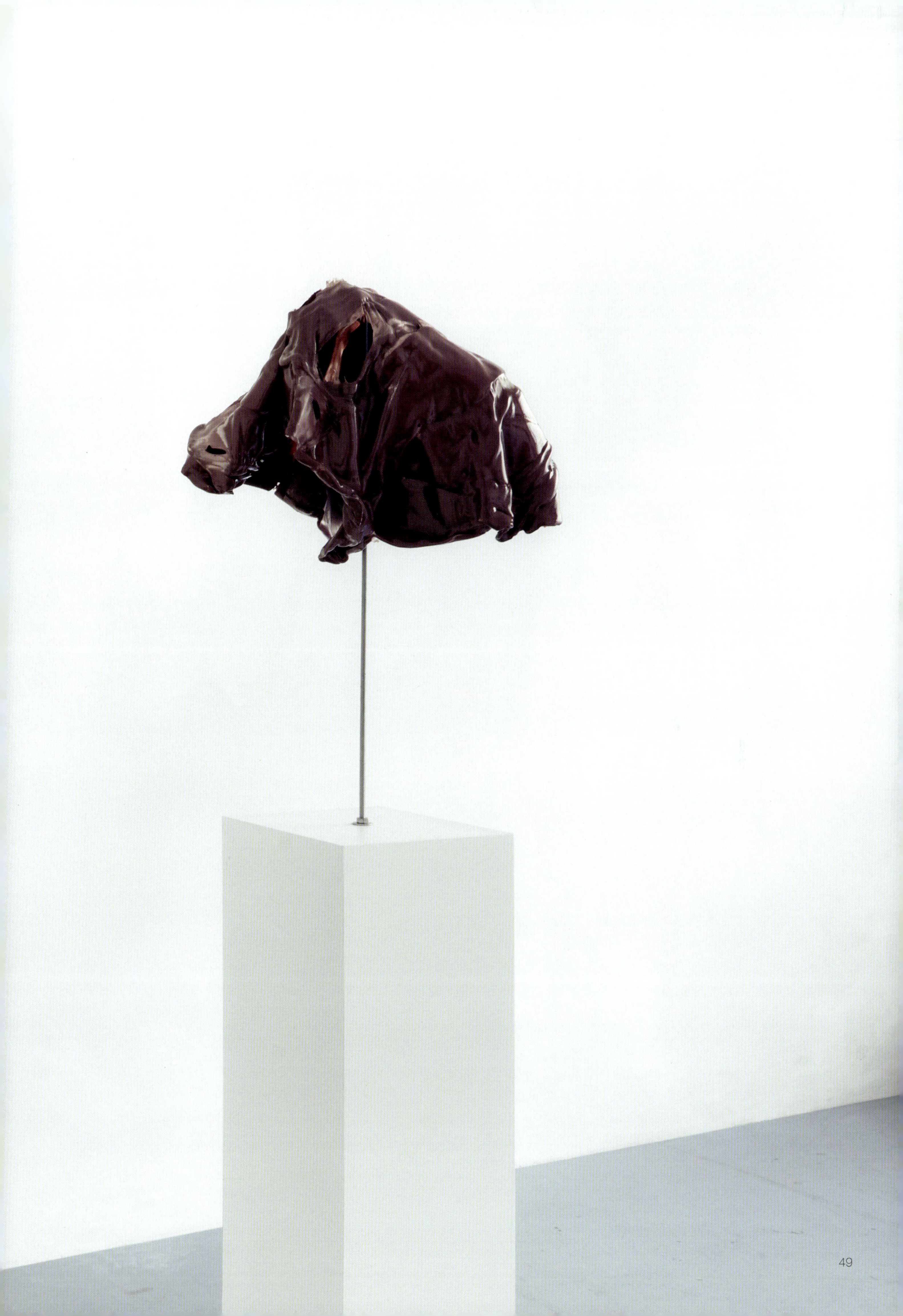

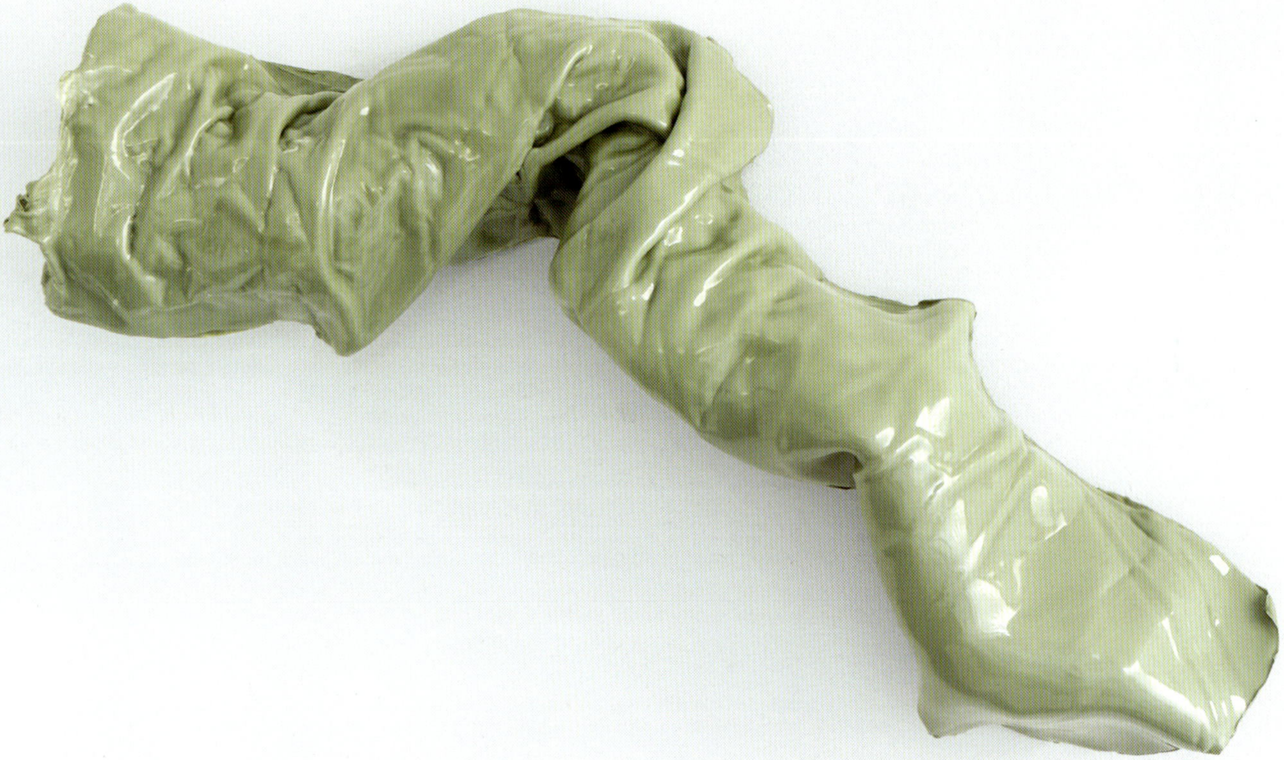

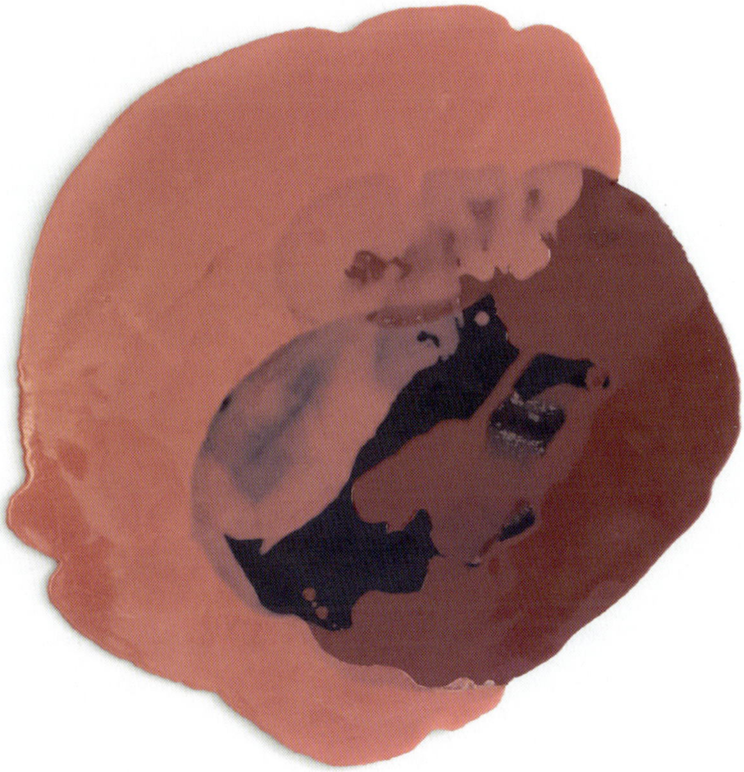

Sea in her New York studio; she rolled out the untreated canvas, splashed thinned oil paint onto it, and the textile absorbed the pigments. Morris Louis and Kenneth Noland visited the young American painter and were overwhelmed by her groundbreaking soak-stain pictures. Hence, they went on to develop their specific colour-field painting style; the paint wets the canvas in large sections. They let the paint run free, emancipated from the physical and expressionistic character of the action painter. But all the positions named here actually have to do with classical forms of painting. The flows and splashes densify into a painting surface within the picture quadrangle tensioned on the stretcher frame. Top, bottom, left and right are defined, and eventually the picture is hung on the wall.

In contrast, Eduard Tauss abandons the classical window picture as rectangular form by letting the poured paint take on an organic, sculptural form. It might be flat pigment, or take shape as something corporeal and sculptural; after the dripping and splashing process, Tauss forms and morphs the substance before it hardens. Associations with bodily parts and skin surfaces crop up without the artist wanting to charge the work with motif or content. "I don't want to tell stories."[1] The works are autonomous existences – articulations of painting. The flat pigment areas can be hung up on the wall like a picture, or, in the spirit of their creation, placed on the floor or on a pedestal. Unlike the colour field paintings of Frankenthaler and Louis, Tauss's painted surfaces are not translucid or optically illusionistic, but opaque, like skin. Tauss uses subdued colours, without pop gloss; he shuts the imaginary window of painting. Paint is mass and materiality. In classical painting, accumulated clods of material on the canvas were taboo. Rembrandt's and Courbet's pastose, smeared application was criticised by the echelons of academe as sordid and slovenly daubs. The paint should be subjected to the illusionistic rendering

---

1 Florian Steininger in conversation with Eduard Tauss in the artist's studio, March 2022, Vienna.

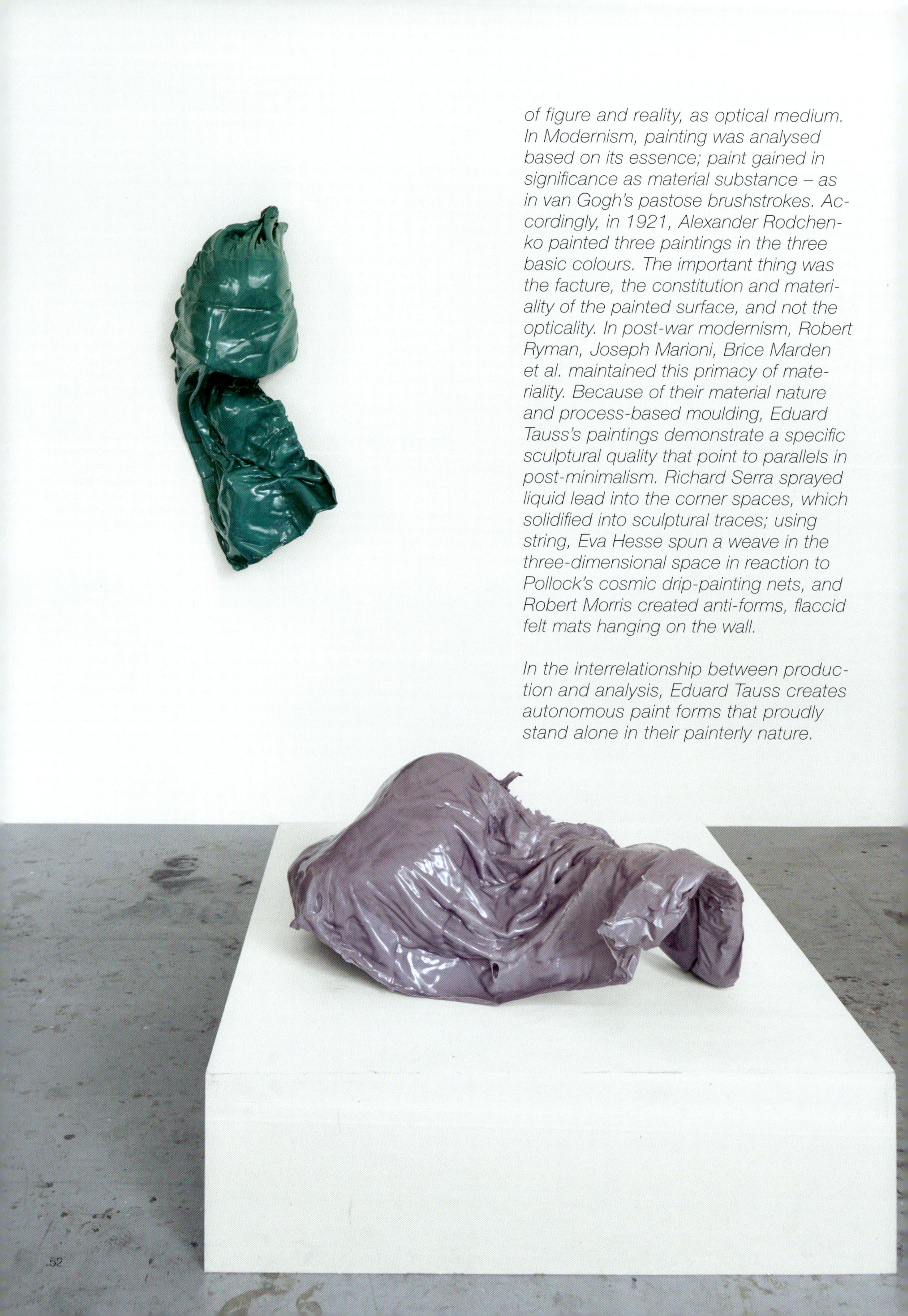

of figure and reality, as optical medium. In Modernism, painting was analysed based on its essence; paint gained in significance as material substance – as in van Gogh's pastose brushstrokes. Accordingly, in 1921, Alexander Rodchenko painted three paintings in the three basic colours. The important thing was the facture, the constitution and materiality of the painted surface, and not the opticality. In post-war modernism, Robert Ryman, Joseph Marioni, Brice Marden et al. maintained this primacy of materiality. Because of their material nature and process-based moulding, Eduard Tauss's paintings demonstrate a specific sculptural quality that point to parallels in post-minimalism. Richard Serra sprayed liquid lead into the corner spaces, which solidified into sculptural traces; using string, Eva Hesse spun a weave in the three-dimensional space in reaction to Pollock's cosmic drip-painting nets, and Robert Morris created anti-forms, flaccid felt mats hanging on the wall.

In the interrelationship between production and analysis, Eduard Tauss creates autonomous paint forms that proudly stand alone in their painterly nature.

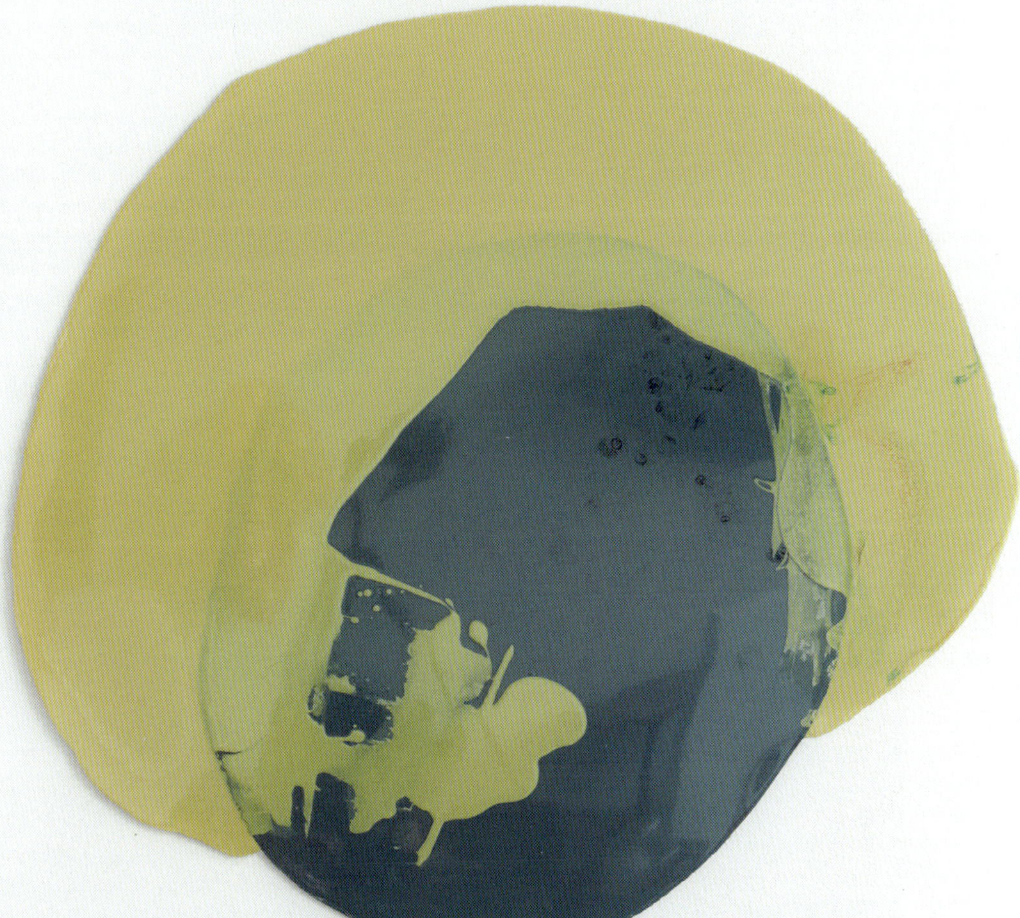

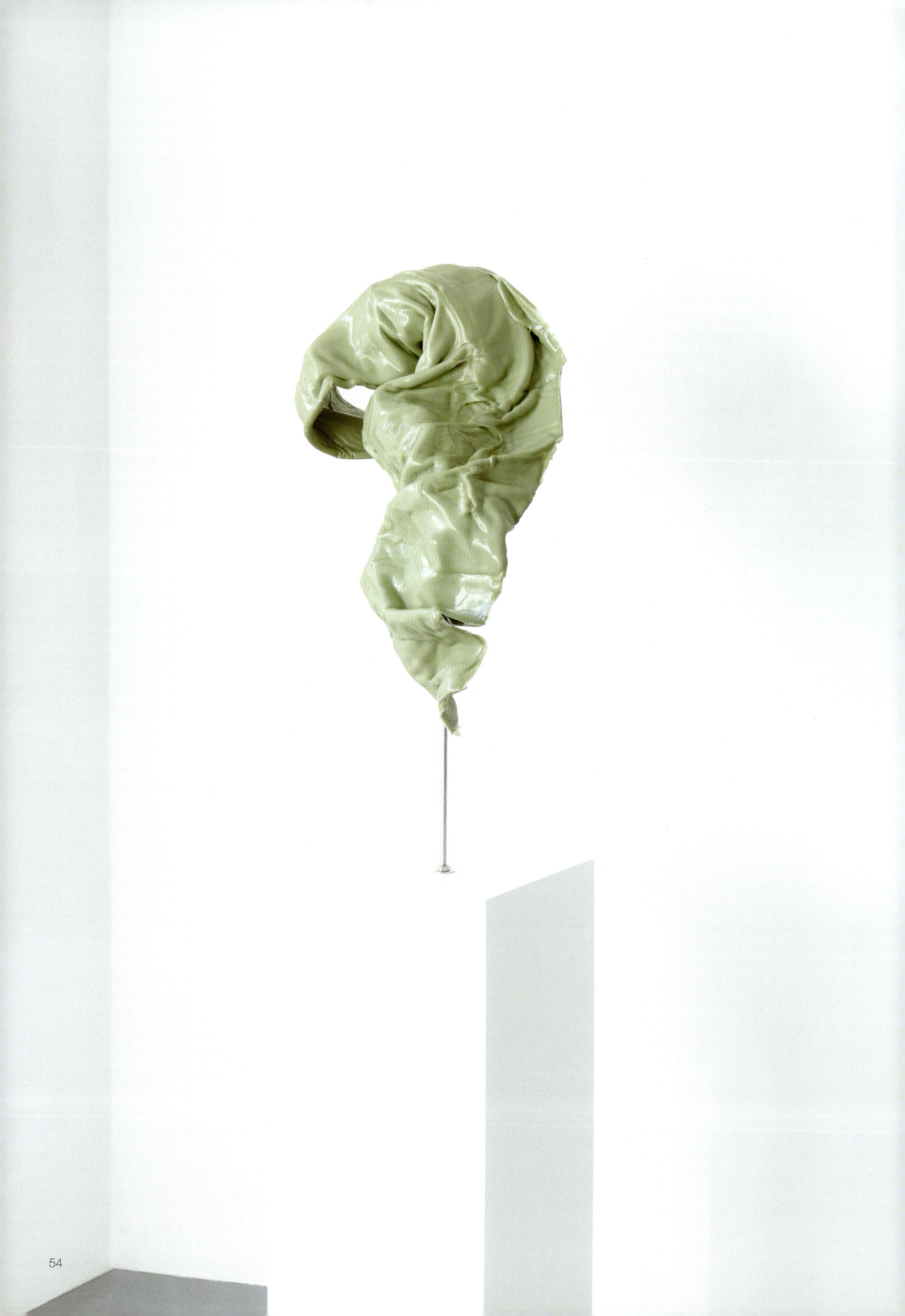

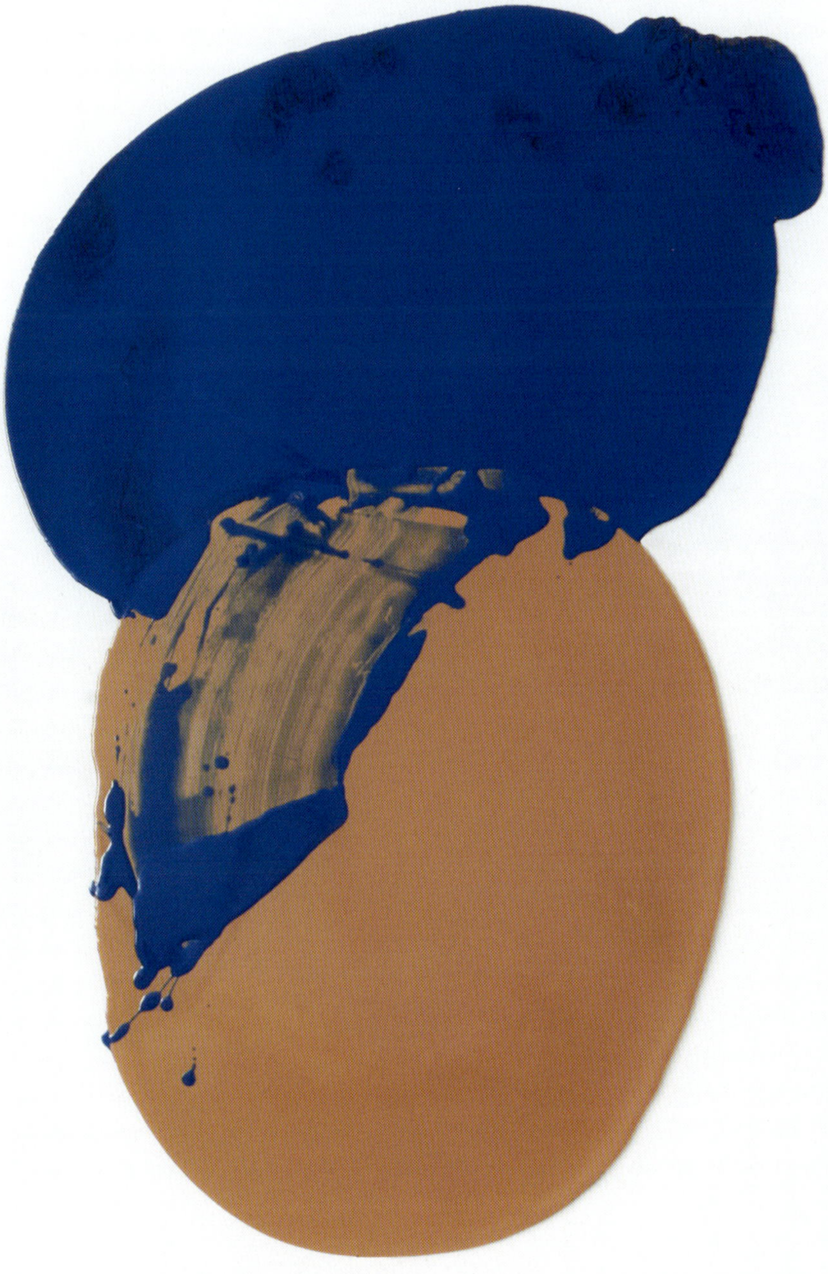

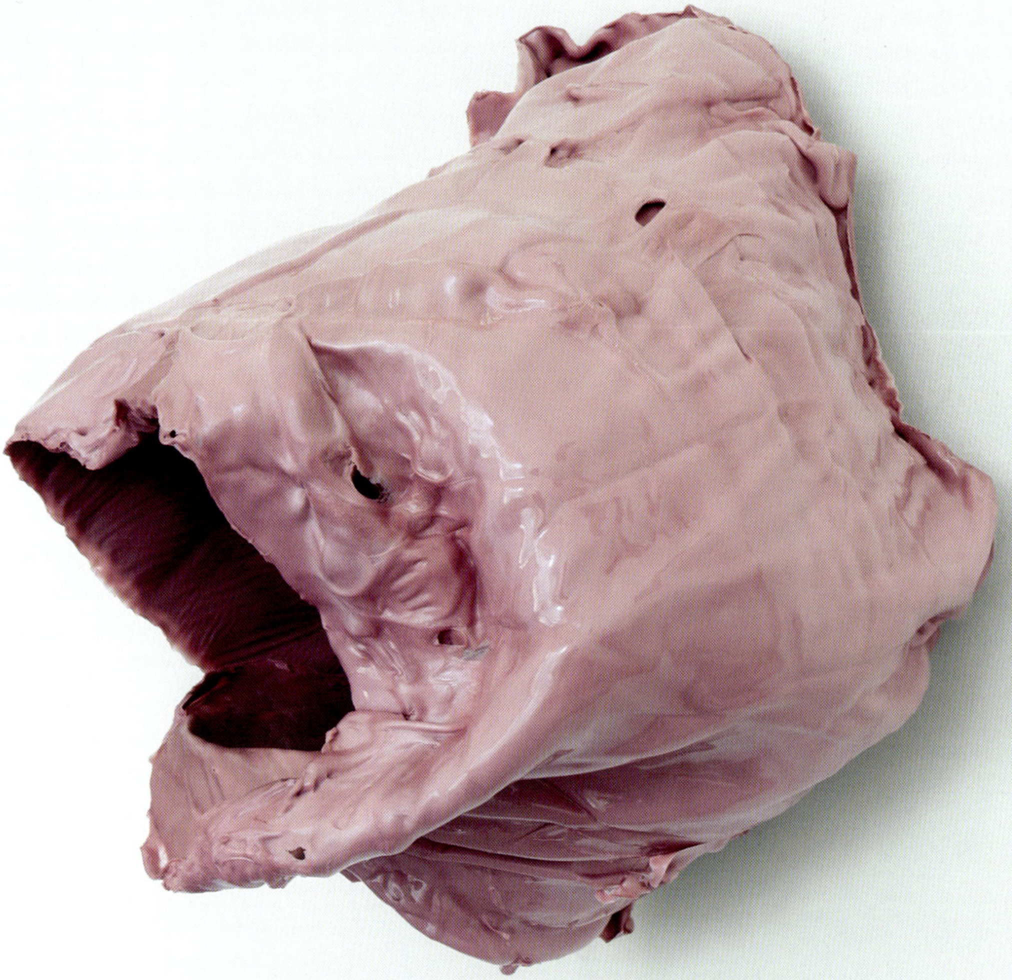

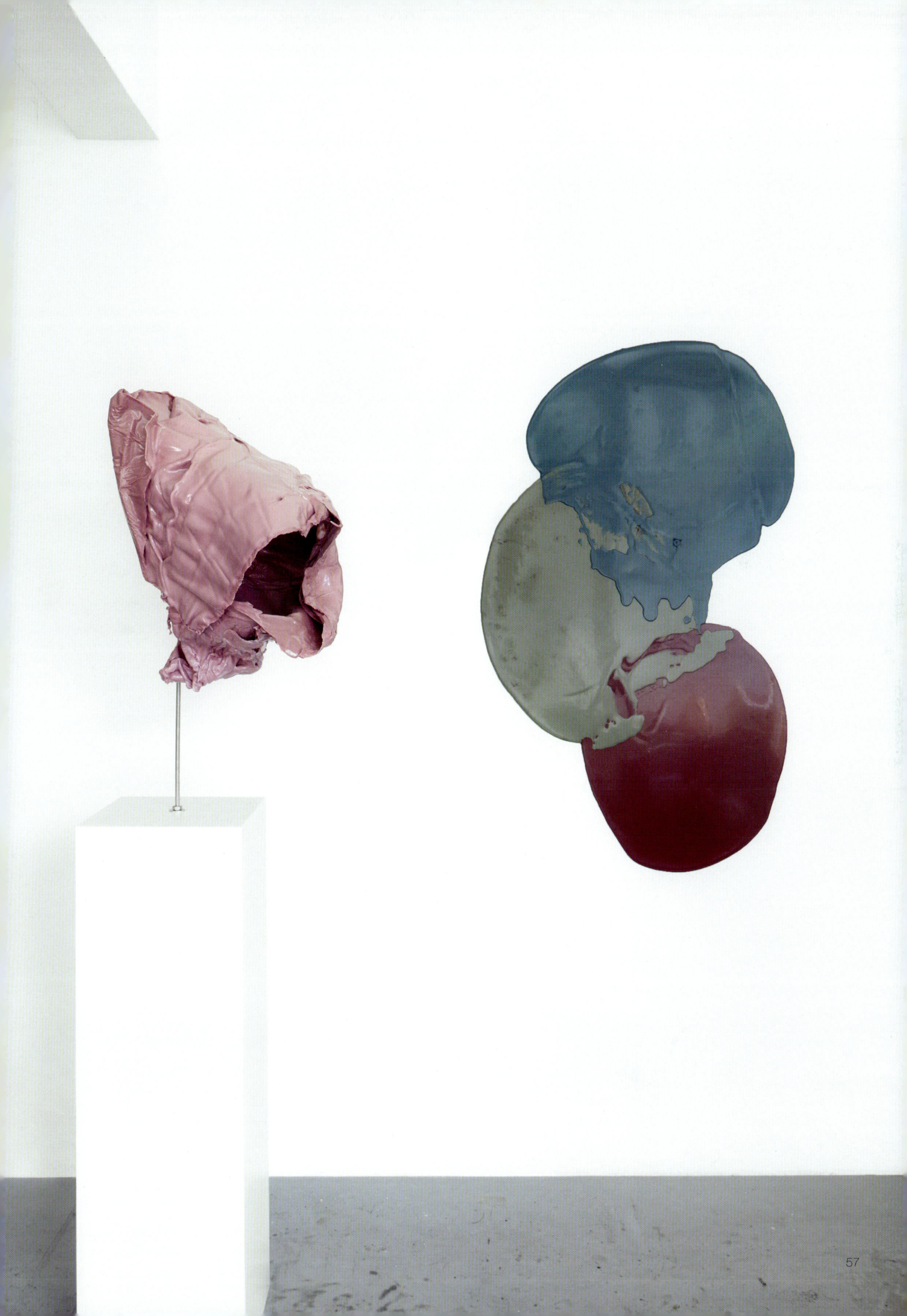

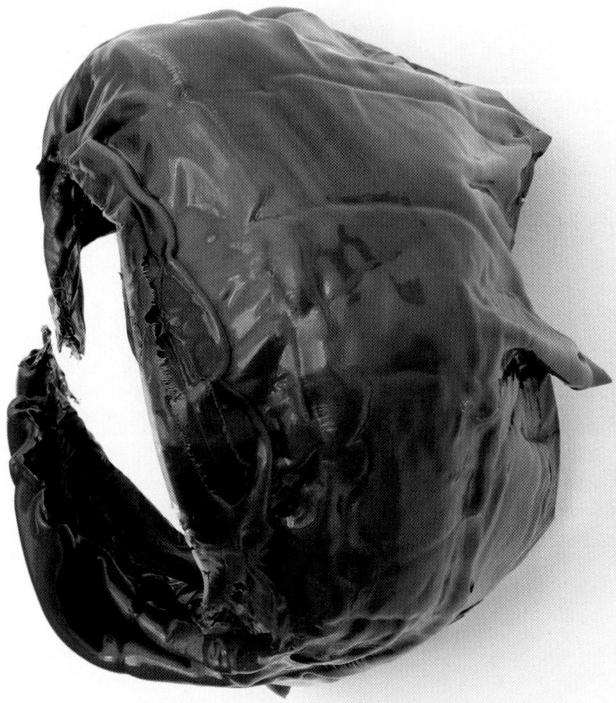

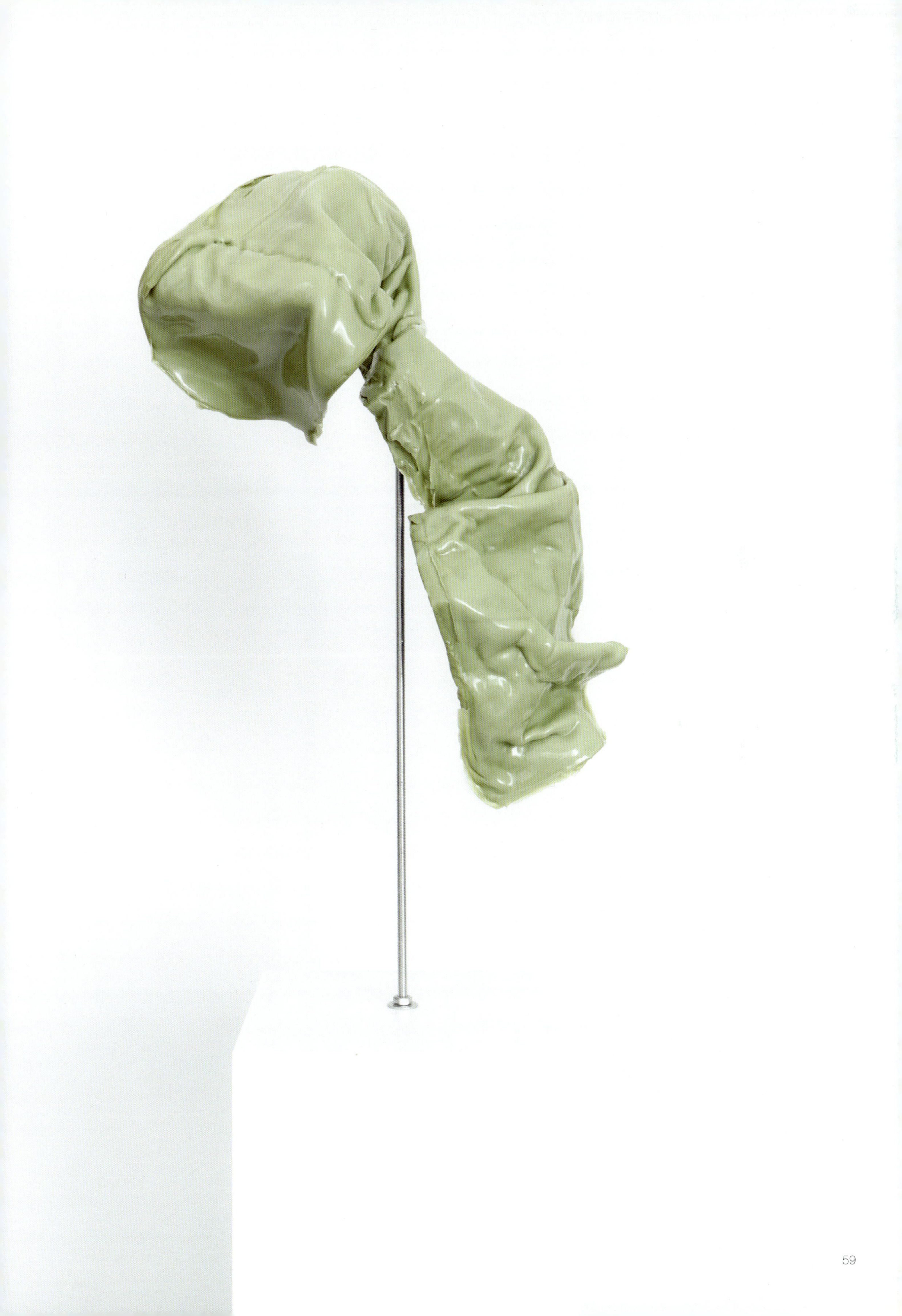

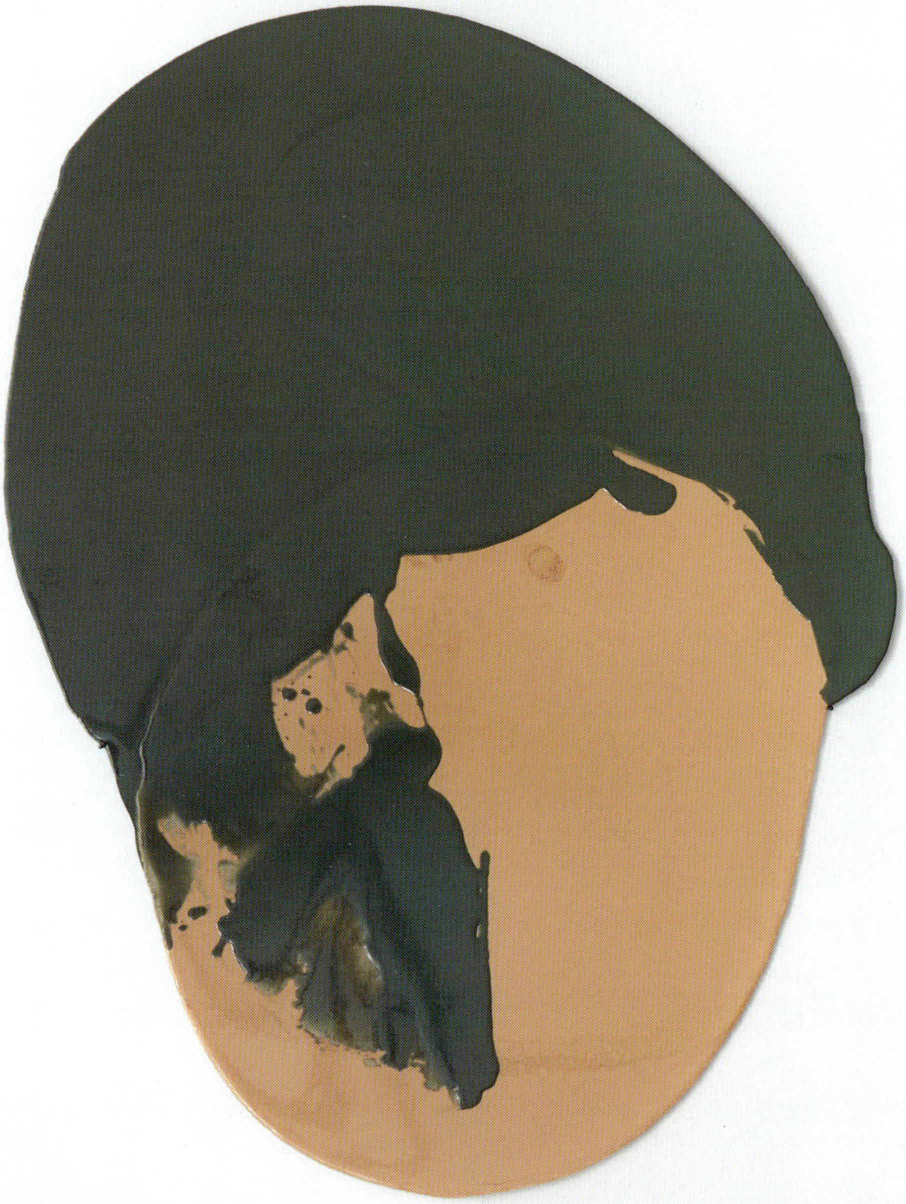

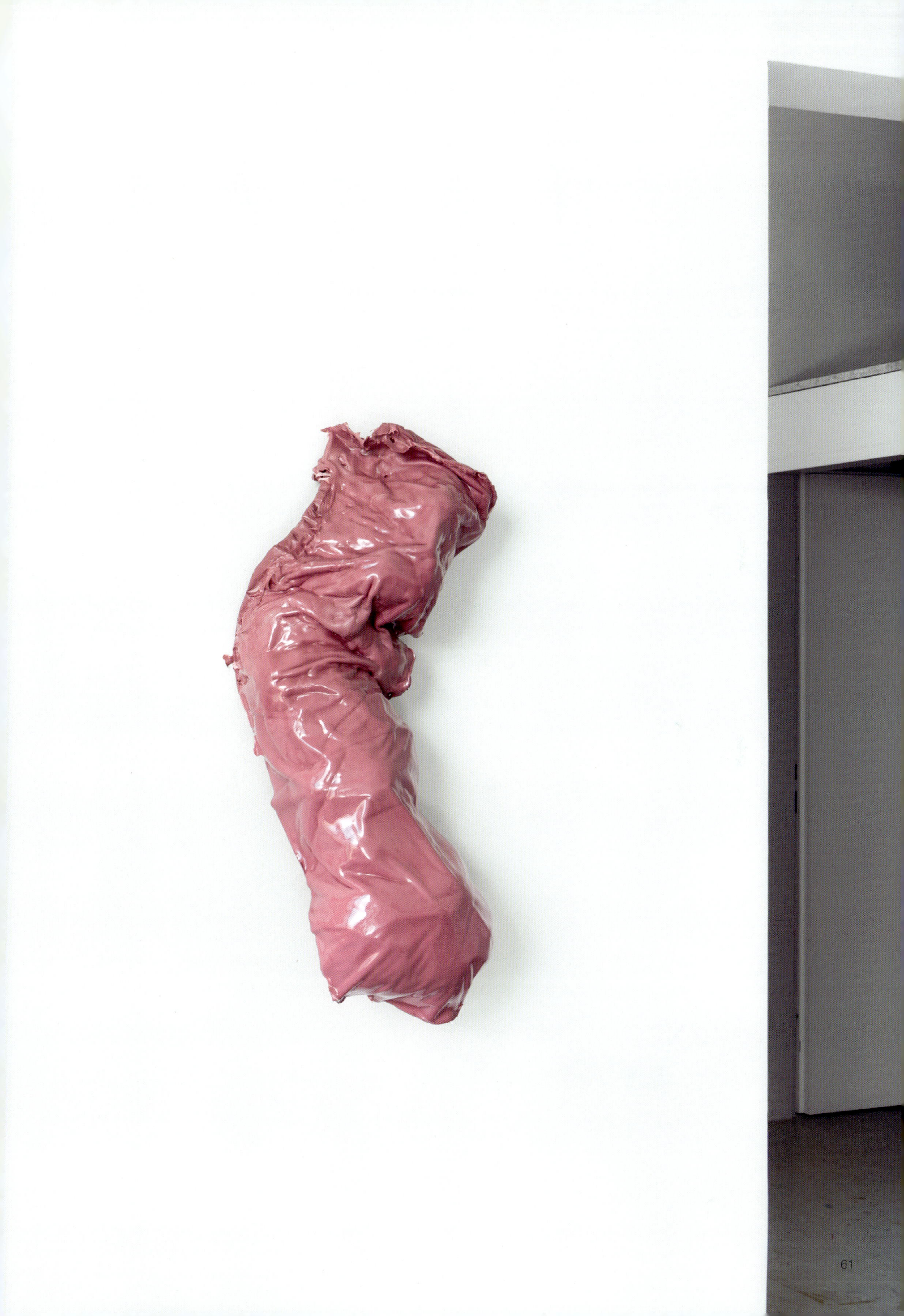

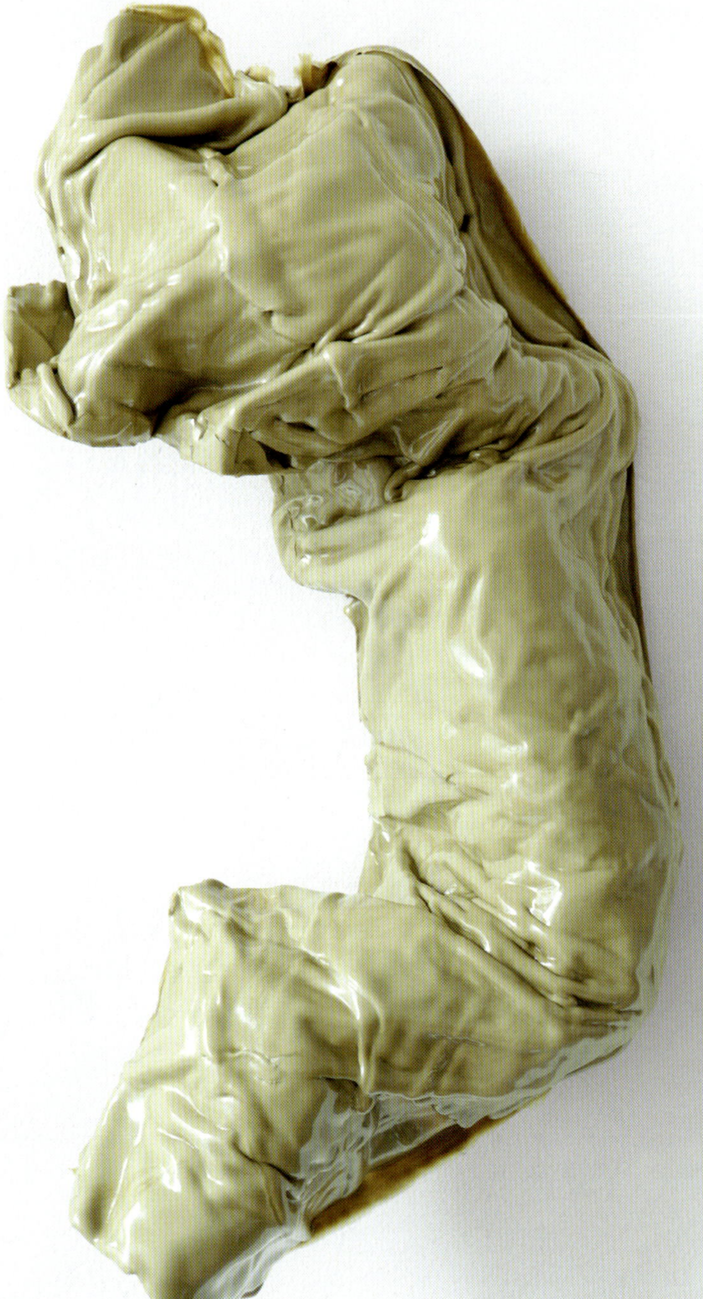

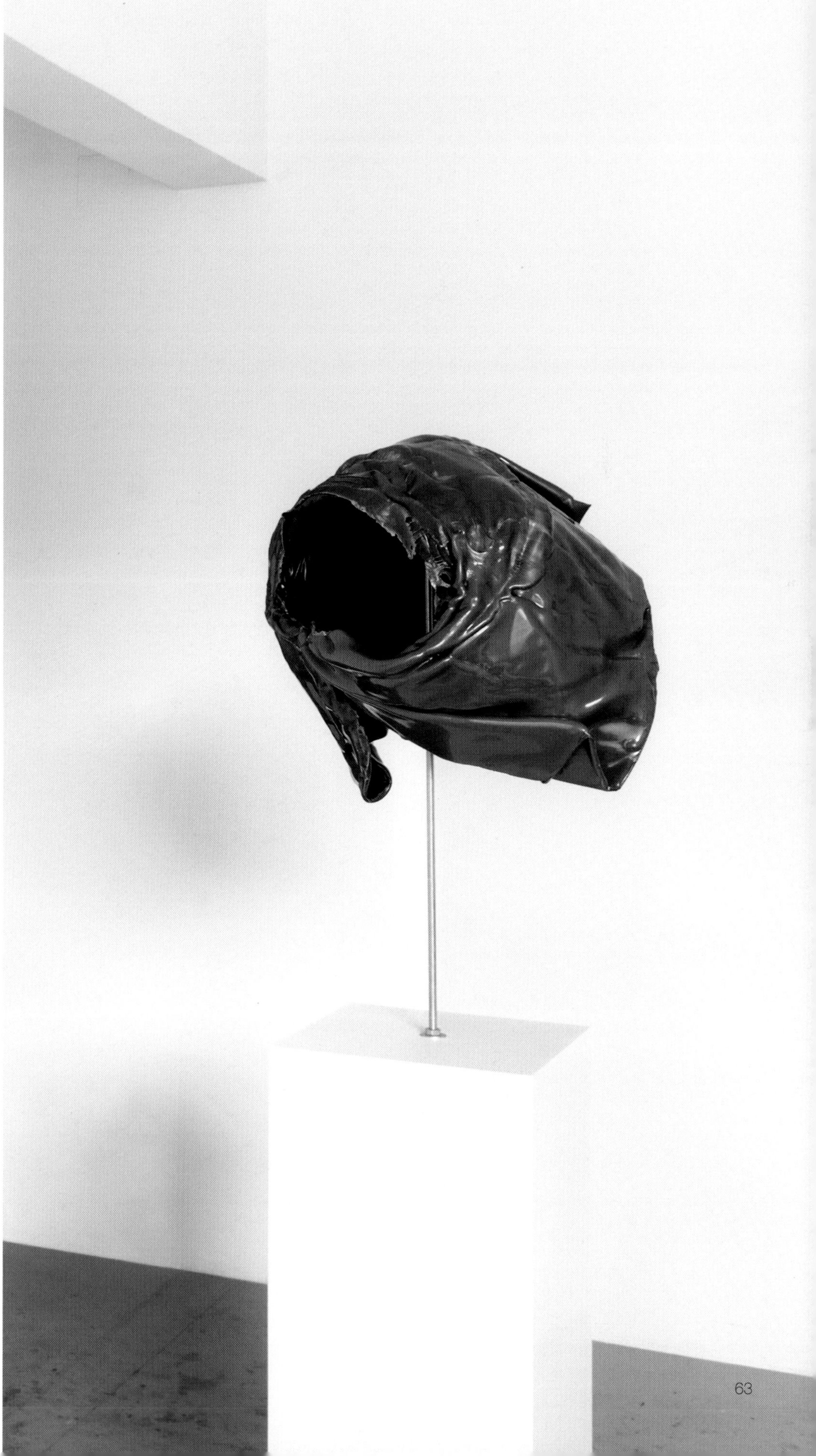

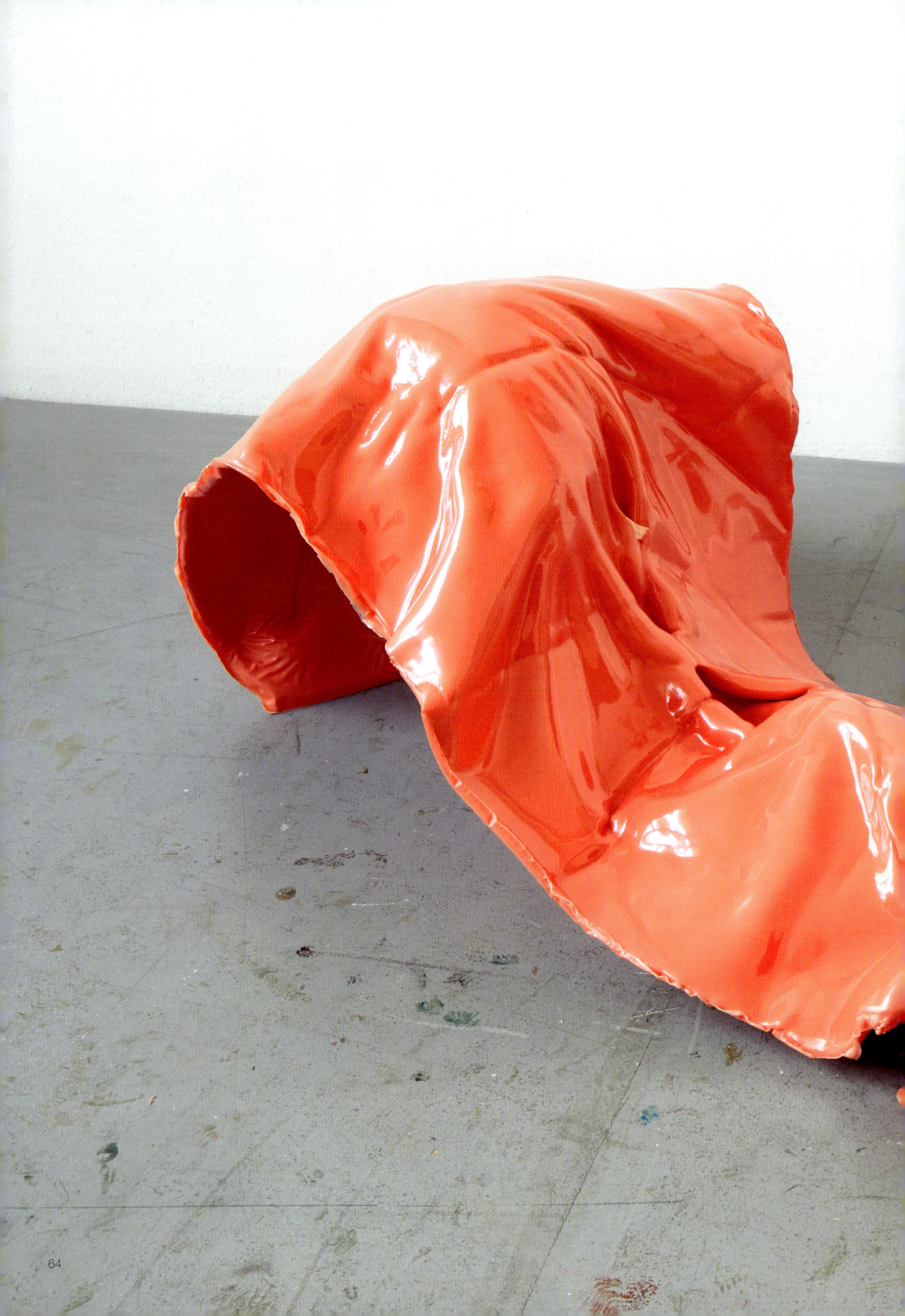

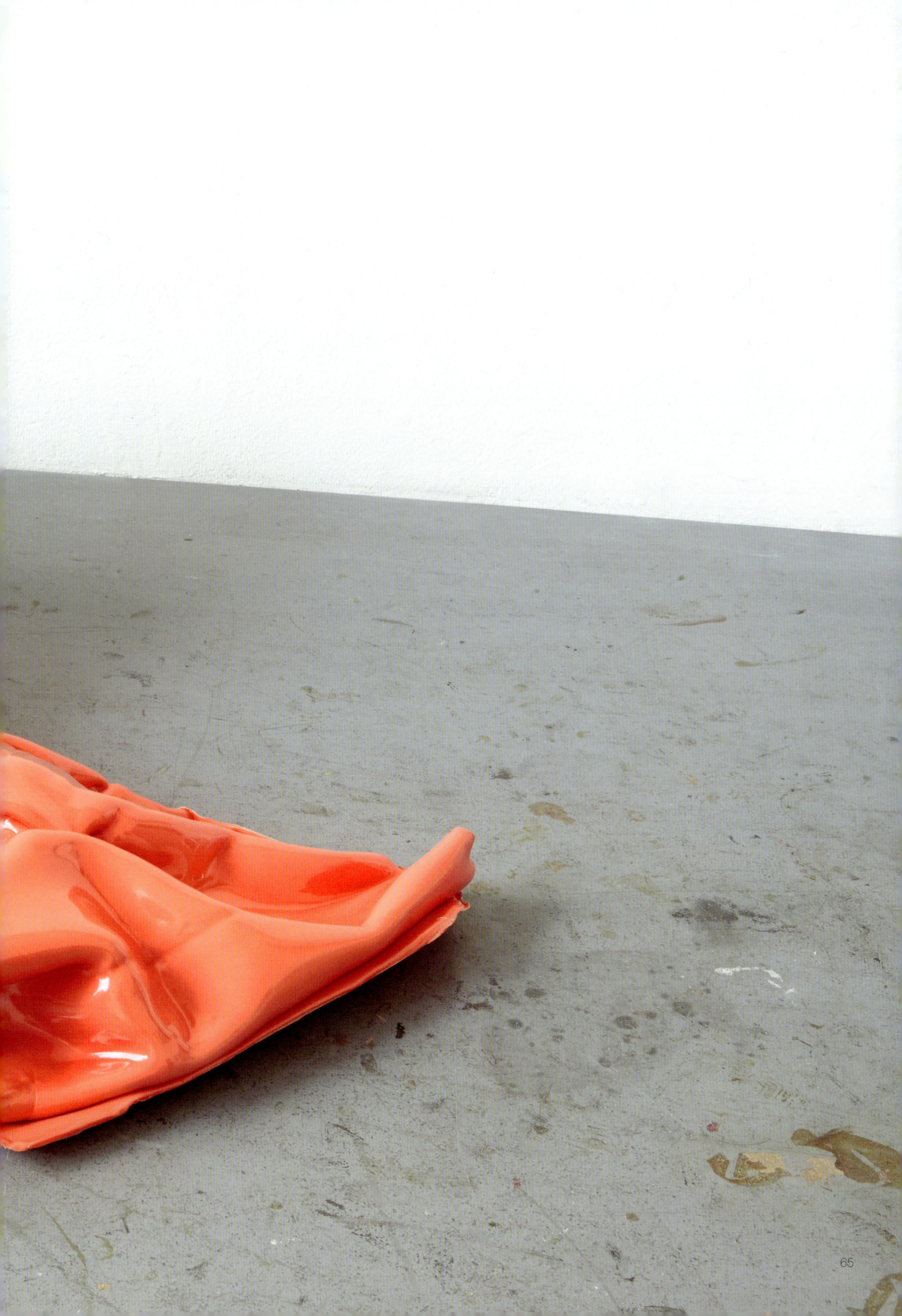

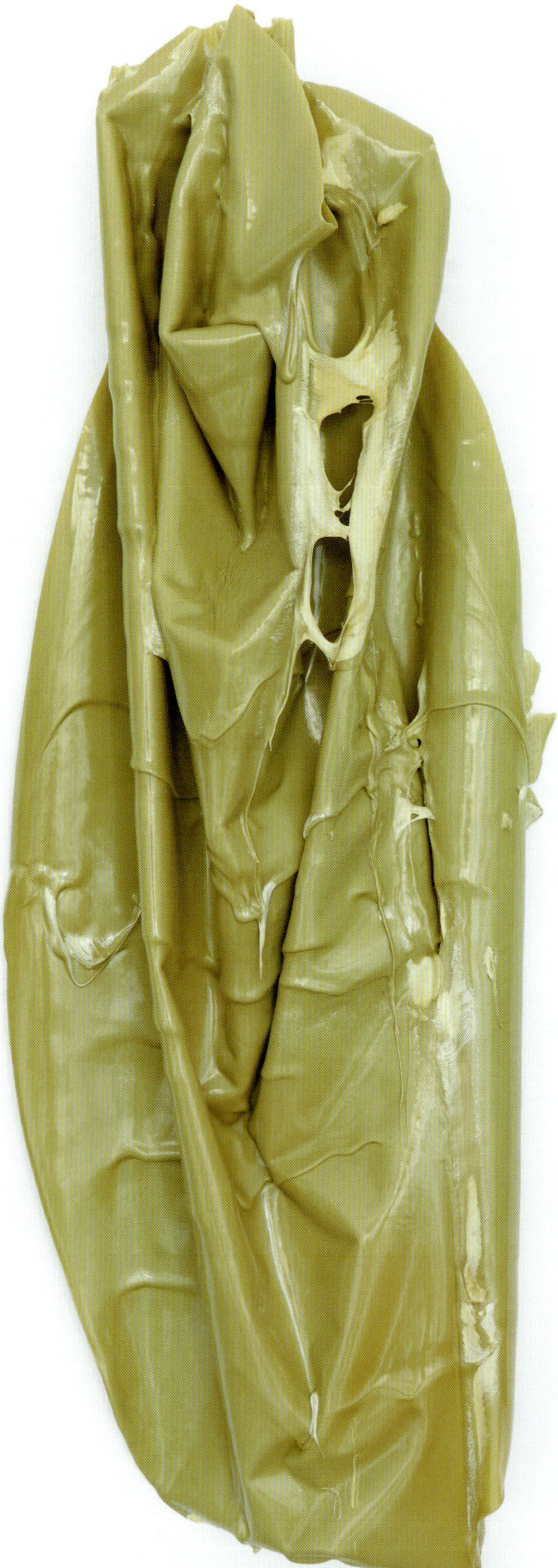

Embodying Colour

Michael Post, Heiner Thiel – Künstler | *Artists*

Zu den Farbkörpern von Eduard Tauss

On the Colour Bodies by Eduard Tauss

Im Rohzustand nehmen wir Farben als Körper wahr, seien es Anhäufungen reiner Pigmente oder deren Einbindungen in diverse flüssige bis zähflüssige Medien. Dies ist deswegen so bemerkenswert, weil sie in einem Zustand der Weiterverarbeitung nicht nur ihr Volumen zu Gunsten einer eher flächigen Erscheinungsform ausdehnen sollen, sondern auch fast ausschließlich für den Zweck einer solchen Weiterverarbeitung hergestellt werden.

Mit den Graden ihrer Verflüssigung wird ihre funktionale Bestimmung festgelegt und es ergibt sich eine erhebliche Bandbreite von Ausdehnungsmöglichkeiten, um Oberflächen einzufärben und deren Körper in einem anderen Lichte erscheinen zu lassen. Die grenzenlose Vielfalt von Farben, die in unterschiedlichen Konsistenzen zum Einsatz gebracht werden können, lässt sich allerdings in ihrer visuellen Wirkung am besten anhand der Malerei und der farbigen Skulptur in allen Epochen der Kunstgeschichte ablesen. Unsere Wahrnehmung von Bildinhalten, im Kontext der verschiedenen künstlerischen Absichten, wird maßgeblich durch deren farbmalerische Komponenten bestimmt. Diese verändern reale Körper, unterstützen die Vortäuschung dreidimensionaler Gegebenheiten im Tafelbild, definieren aber auch den konkreten Farbraum unserer Tage im

In their raw state, we perceive colours as bodies, in the form of mere pigment accumulations or of pigments bound in a range of liquid to viscous media. This is quite remarkable because colours are actually meant to expand their volume when processed to acquire a more planar appearance and – moreover – are also produced almost exclusively for the purpose of that type of processing.

The extent of their liquefaction defines the future function of colours, and a considerable range of expansion options are available for colouring surfaces to let their bodies appear in a new light. The visual effects of the unlimited variety of colours which can be applied in differing consistencies can best be appreciated in the paintings and coloured sculptures of all epochs in the history of art. Our perception of pictorial contents in their context of differing artistic intentions is shaped decisively by their colour-painted components. Colour changes real bodies, supports the feint of three-dimensional facts in panel paintings – and it also defines the real colour spaces of our time in their decidedly planar manifestations. In all the different types of these phenomena, the respective consistencies of the colour substances is what permits using them flexibly in the most diverse painterly genres, be they representational, abstract or concrete. The physical

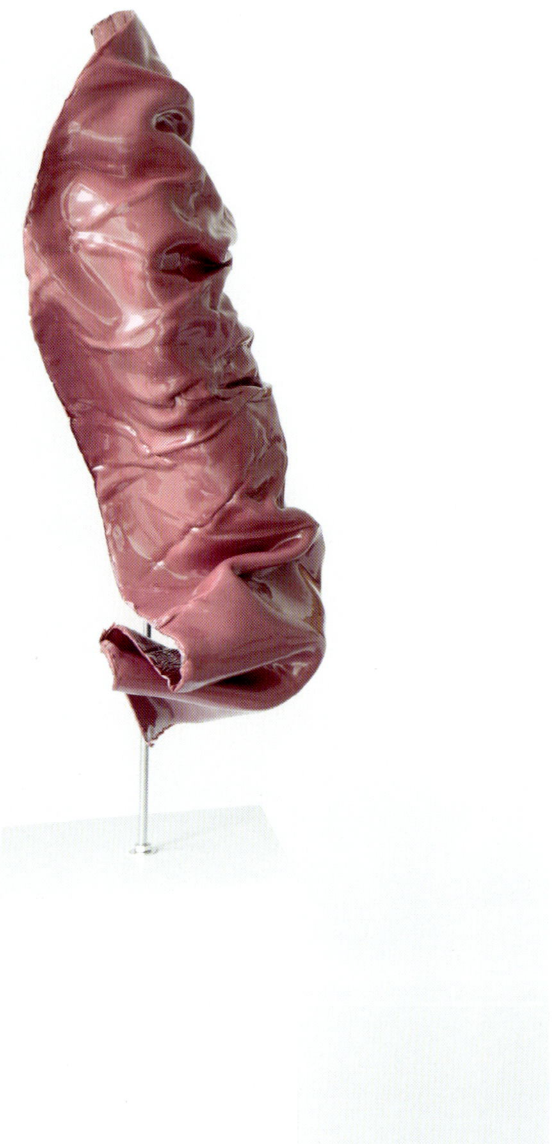

Ausdruck einer dezidierten Flächigkeit. In allen Ausprägungen dieser Phänomene ist es den jeweiligen Konsistenzen von Farbsubstanzen zu verdanken, in den unterschiedlichsten Bezügen von Malerei flexibel eingesetzt werden zu können, seien diese gegenständlicher, abstrakter oder konkreter Natur. Die materielle Existenz der Farbe ist an der Wirkung eines Gemäldes genauso beteiligt, wie umgekehrt der Farbe das Bildhafte immanent zu sein scheint. Hier knüpft Eduard Tauss mit seinen skulpturalen Farbsubstanzen an:
„Die Arbeiten von Eduard Tauss relativieren die tradierten Vorstellungen von Malerei, besonders die Erwartungen des Betrachters von einem Bild. Ihm geht es allerdings weniger um die höchst komplexe Realität der Farbe, sondern um den Prozess der Herstellung, um die Substanz des Materials, um die Beziehung zwischen Farbe und Stoff. Damit thematisiert er auf innovative Weise ein bisher kaum beachtetes, ontologisch aber elementares Problem. Der Unterschied zwischen der vom Licht bedingten Präsenz der Farbe und der kompakten Masse des Kunstharzes ist für Tauss Quelle der Inspiration.“[1]

Die Autonomie der Farbe, ein Begriff, der im Kontext der gegenstandsfreien Malerei entstanden ist, erfährt hier seinen Fortgang: Die Farbe hat sich sogar von ihrem Bildträger befreit und macht sich mittels ihrer eigenen plastischen Substanz zum Ausdruck ihrer selbst und zum Gegenstand ihrer Betrachtung im Raum.

Während des Herstellungsprozesses seiner Arbeiten kommen die für Tauss idealen Materialeigenschaften der in Kunstharz gebundenen Farben entgegen, um die geeigneten skulpturalen Formen zu finden: „Die Farbe wird

---

1 Heinz Gappmayr: Eduard Tauss, Katalog, edition ps, Wien, 2003, S. 14.

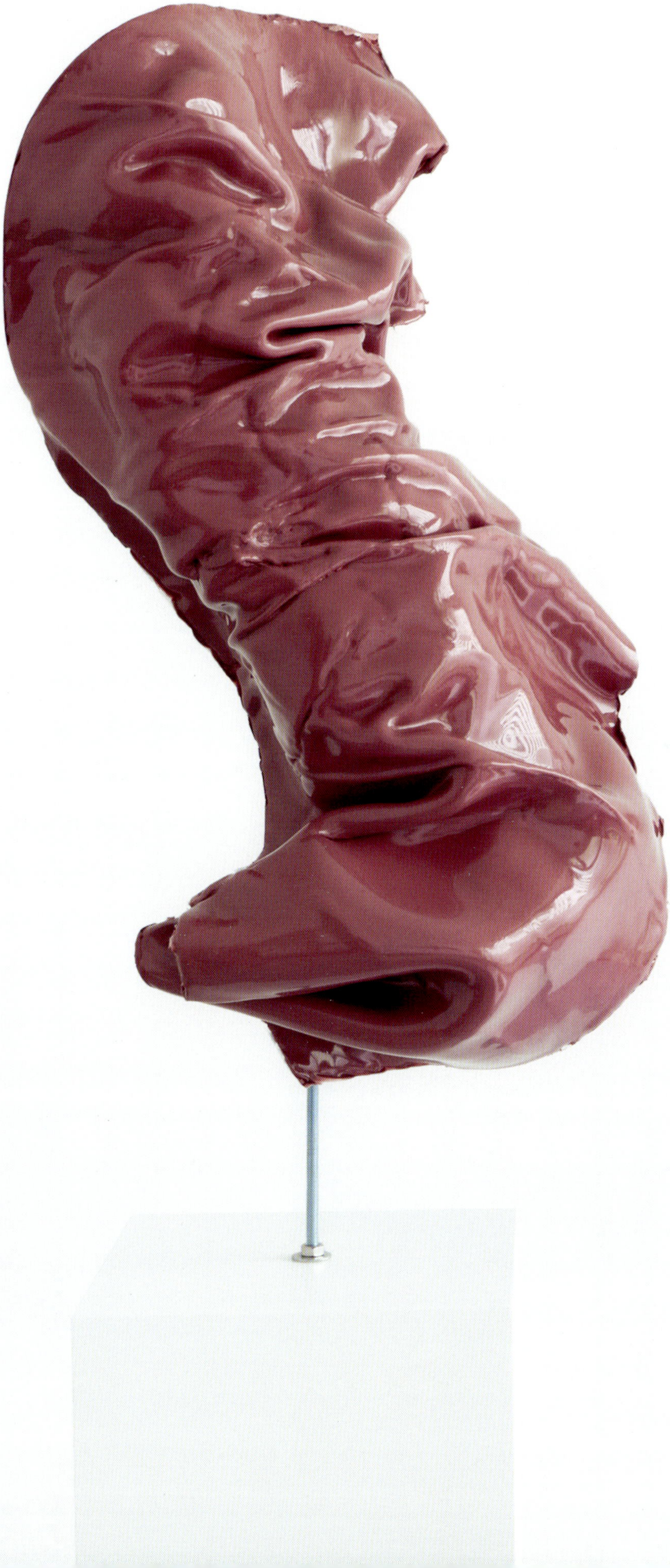

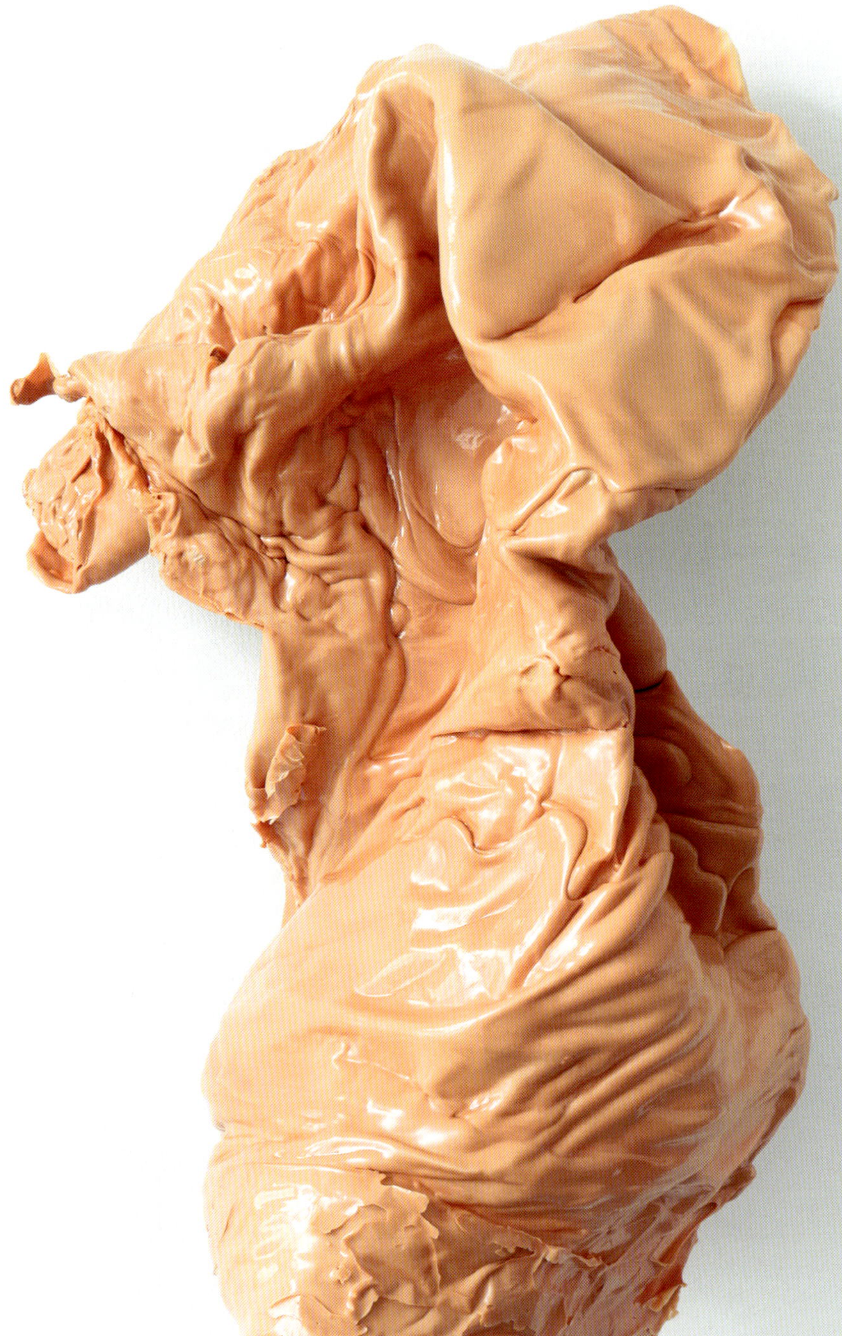

presence of colour participates in the effect of a painting just as, in turn, the pictorial appears to be immanent in colour. This is the starting point of Eduard Tauss's sculptural colour substances:

"The works by Eduard Tauss relativise traditional conceptions of painting and, in particular, viewers' expectations as to what constitutes a picture. But he is less concerned with the highly complex reality of colour than with the process of its production, the substance of its material and the relationship between colour and materials. In an innovative form, Tauss addresses a problem that has so far found little attention, but in fact presents an elementary ontological problem. The difference between the presence of a colour conditioned by light and the compact mass of the synthetic resin is a source of inspiration for Tauss."[1]

The autonomy of colour, a concept that emerged in the context of nonrepresentational painting, is taken one step further here: Colour has even emancipated itself from its picture substrate, turning itself into an expression of itself and an object for perception in space through its own plastic substance. In creating his works, Tauss is supported in finding the appropriate sculptural forms by what he regards as the ideal physical properties of colours bound in synthetic resin: "The colour is not painted, but cast. It is at first a dynamic mass, which ultimately solidifies. Casting is itself part of the act of forming. The transformation of the initially flat cast form into the plastic form takes place in direct dialogue with the material."[2] *During the phase of hardening, there are stages which permit forming*

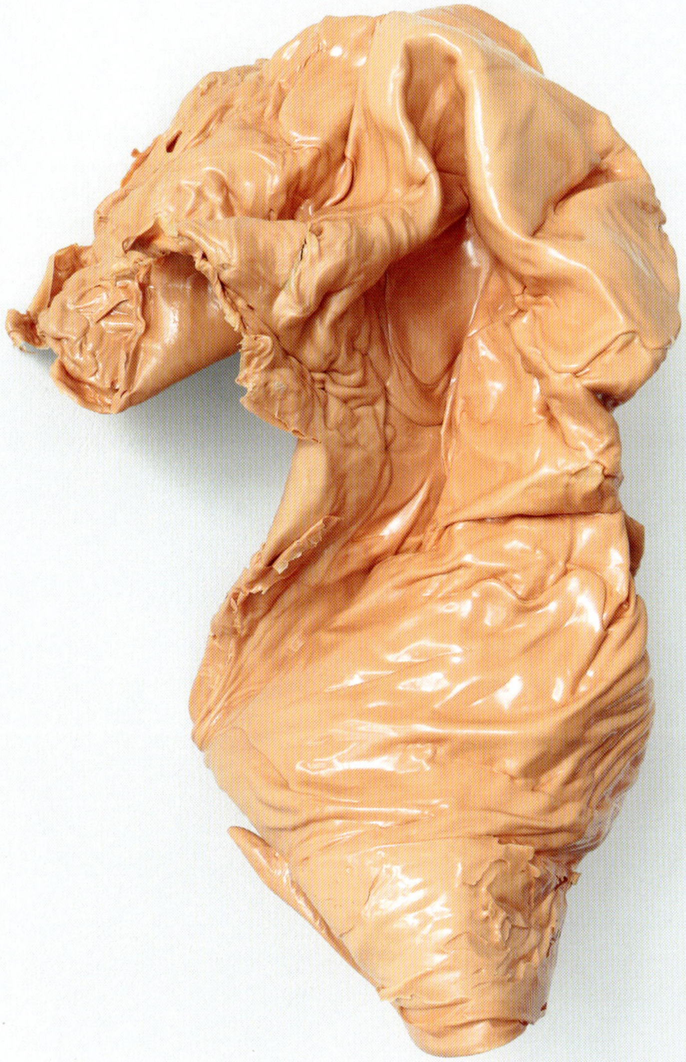

1 *Heinz Gappmayr: Eduard Tauss, exh. cat., edition ps, Vienna, 2003, p. 14.*

2 *Michael Post and Heiner Thiel in conversation with Eduard Tauss in the artist's studio, 2013, Vienna.*

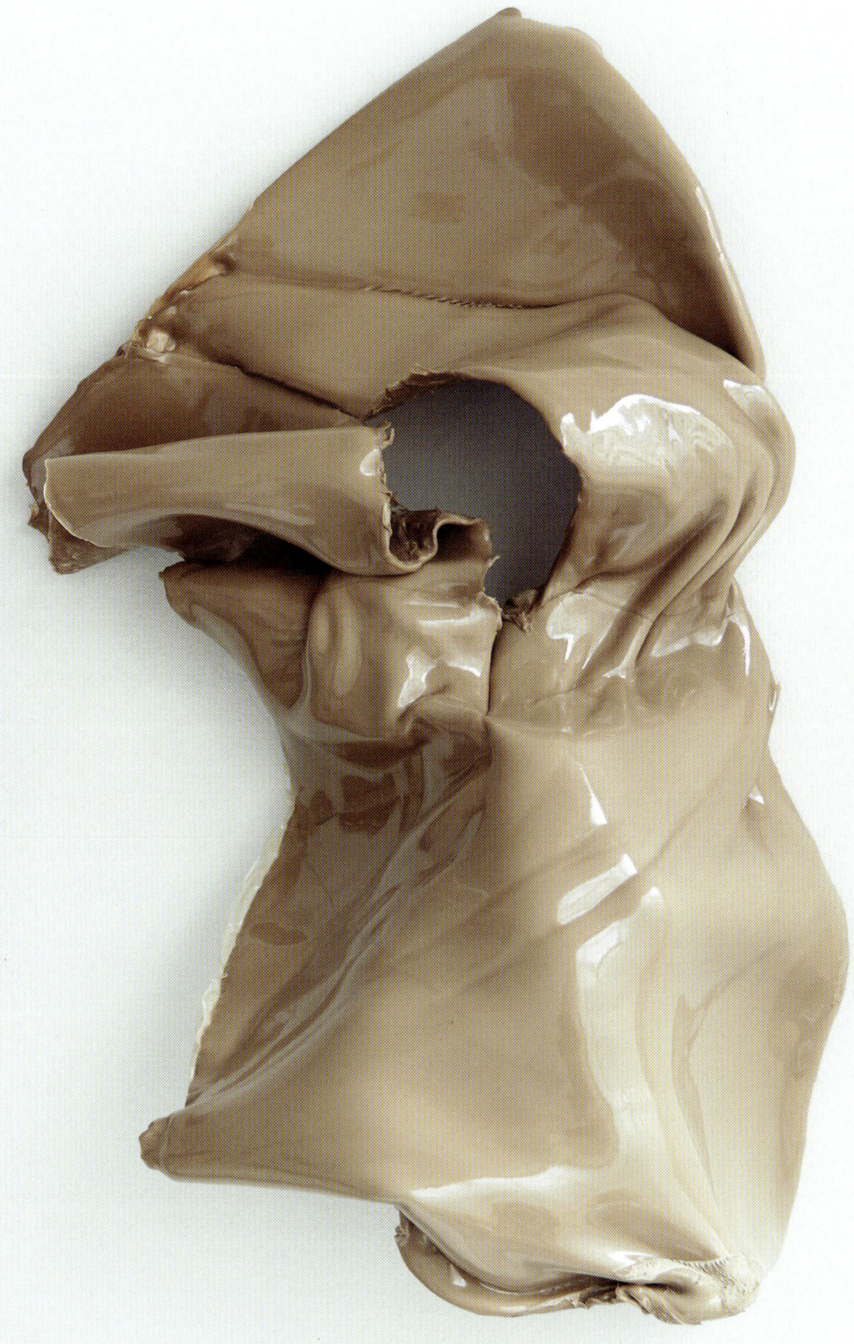

nicht gemalt, sondern gegossen, sie ist zunächst eine dynamische Masse, die schließlich erstarrt. Das Gießen selbst ist ein Teil des Formalaktes. Die Transformation der anfänglich flachen Gussform in die plastische Form erfolgt im unmittelbaren Dialog mit dem Material."[2] In der Phase der Aushärtung ergeben sich Stadien, welche die Formgebung mittels Biegen, Falten, Drücken, Pressen oder Zwängen ermöglichen. Die Gestaltung muss materialbedingt zügig verlaufen und verlangt schnelles Reagieren. Die spontane Einflussnahme auf die formbare Masse durch persönliche Kraftausübung, bezieht hierbei den

by bending, folding, pushing, pressing or forcing. The nature of the material requires fast conformation and swift reactions. The spontaneous influence on the formable mass by exertion of personal force involves the acting body in the process. Tauss ascribes a performative character to the respective psychical and physical preconditions of the creative act. In their finished state, his sculptural wall objects and fully plastic works not only render traces of the actions on the material and its specific reactions clearly apparent. They are themselves the expression of a past temporary course of action that has

2 Michael Post und Heiner Thiel im Gespräch mit Eduard Tauss im Atelier des Künstlers, 2013, Wien.

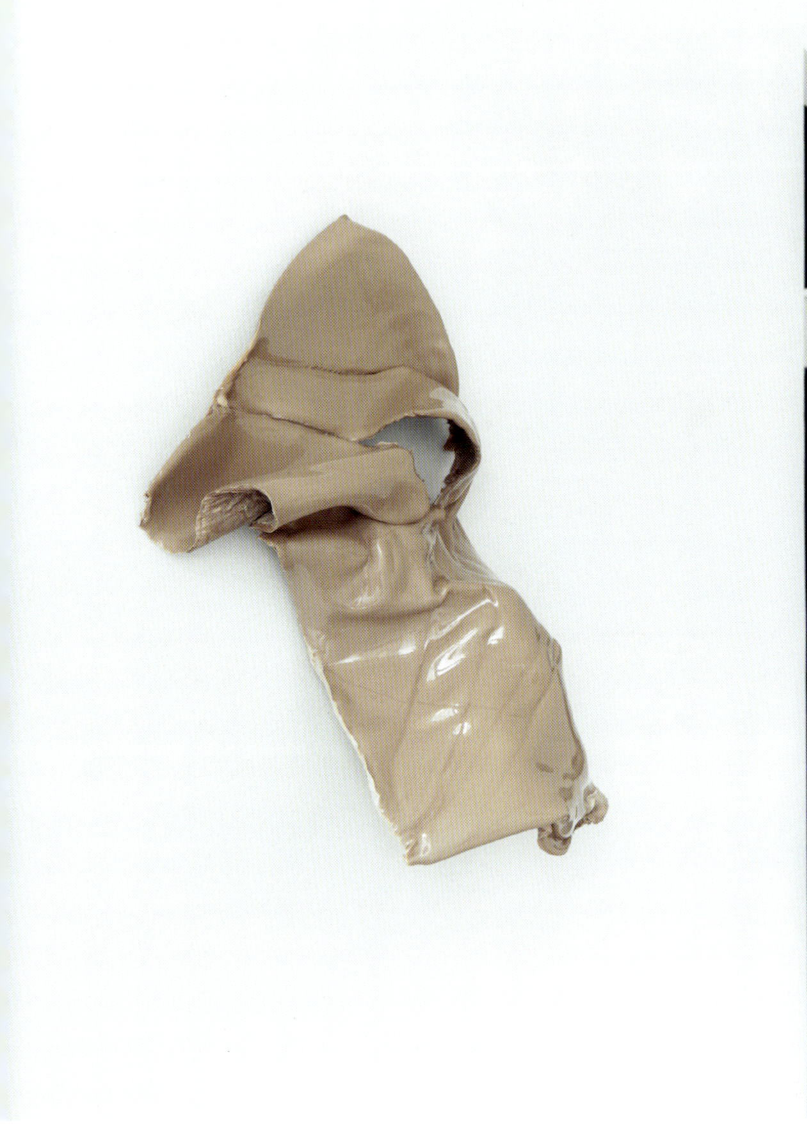

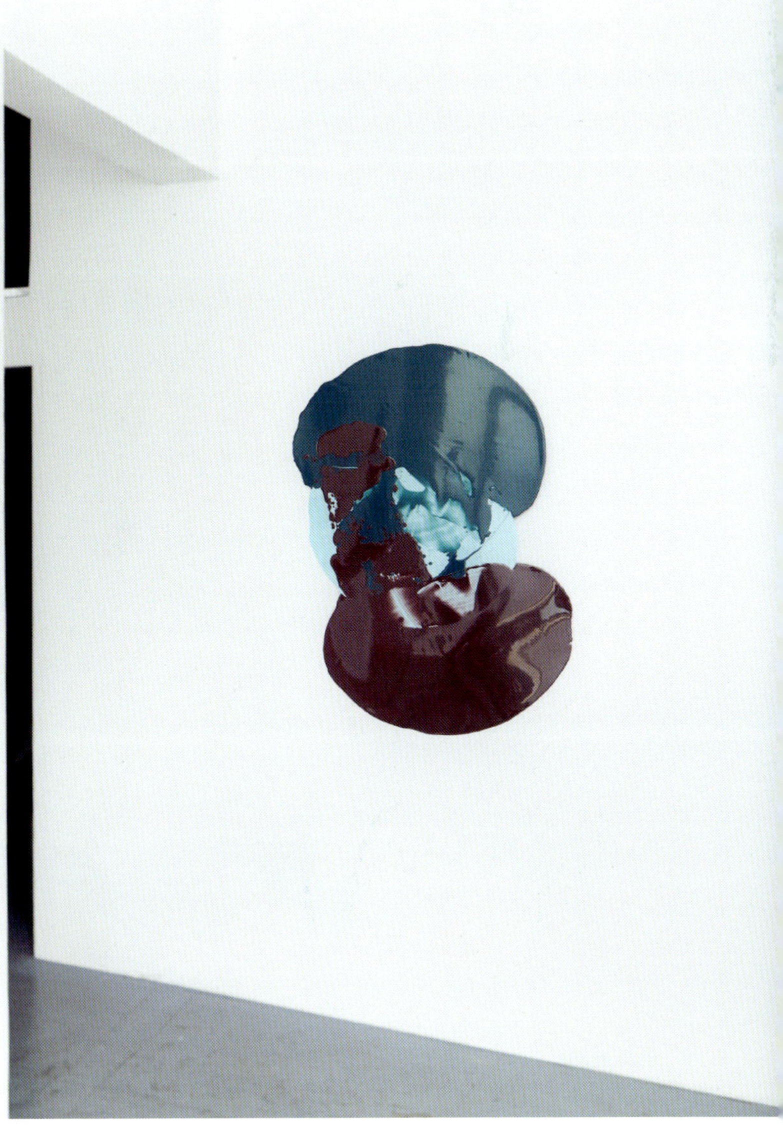

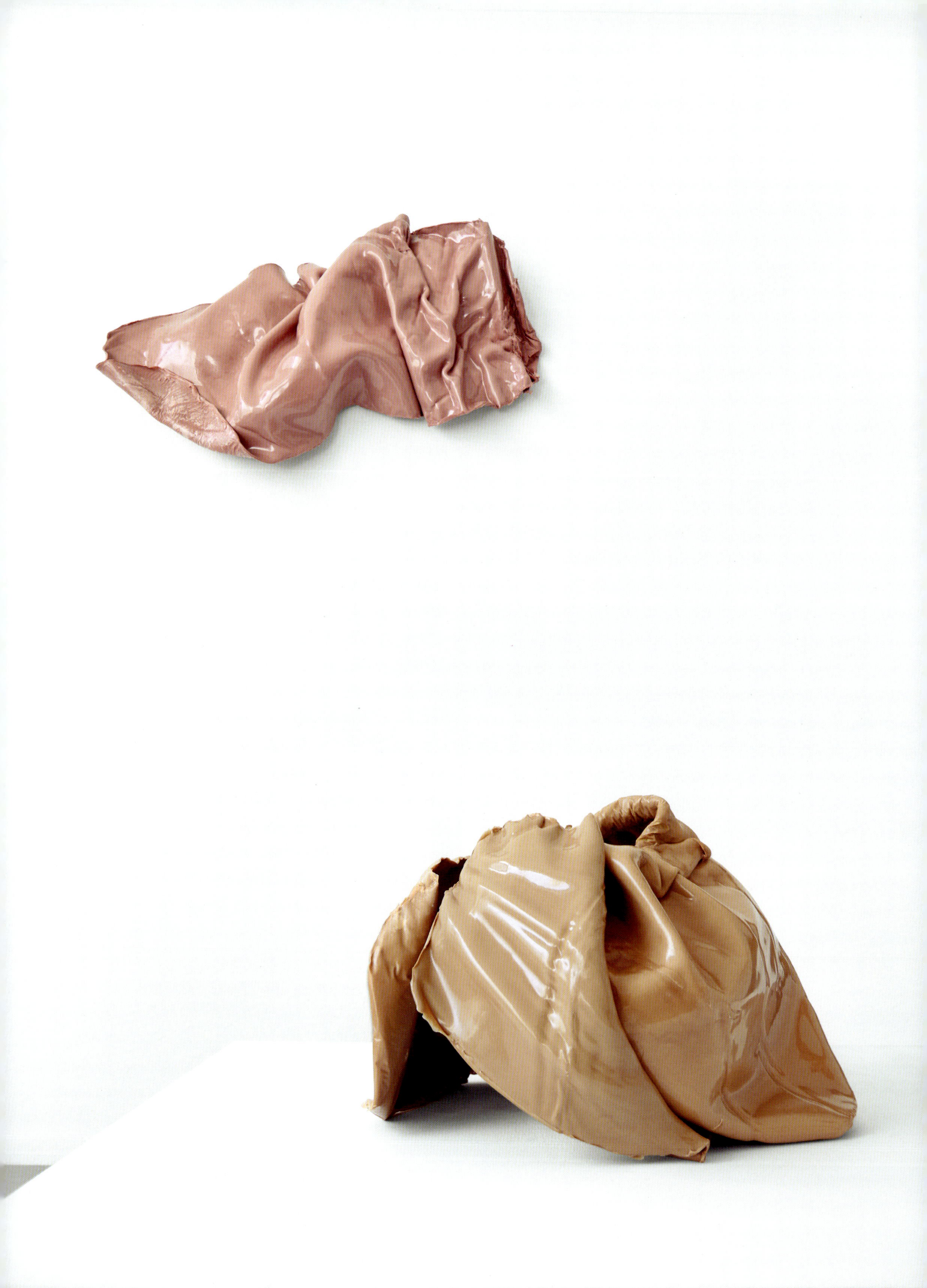

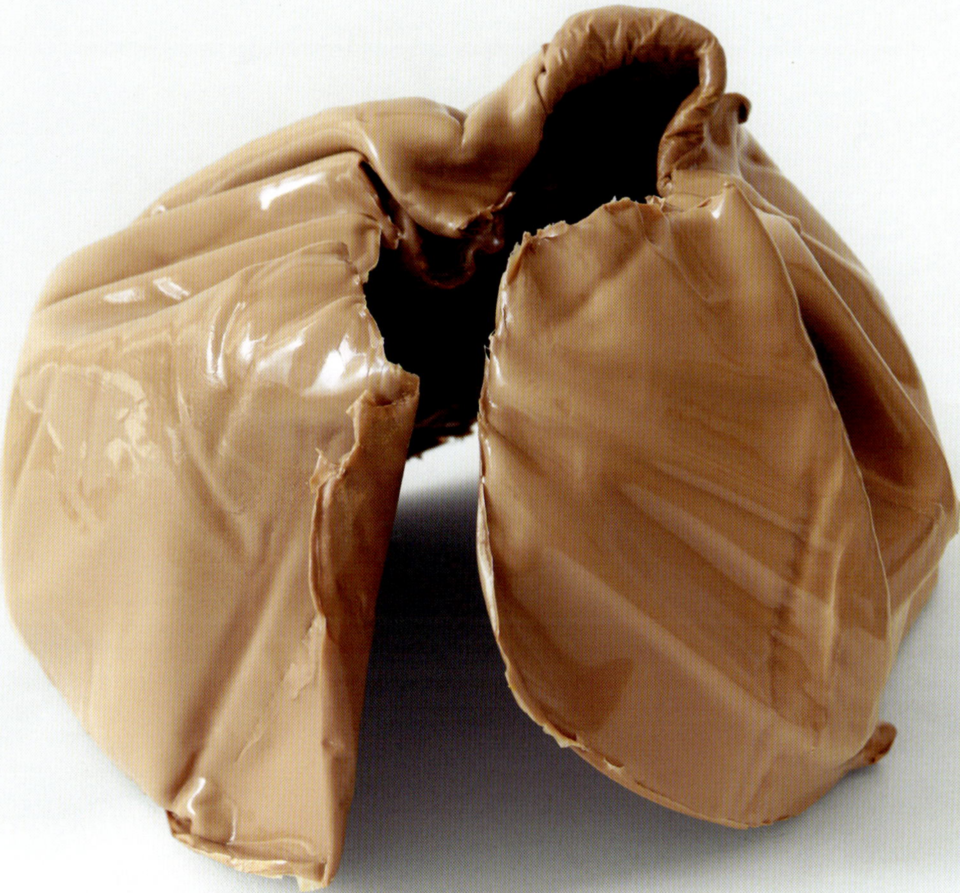

handelnden Körper mit ein. Den jeweiligen psychischen und physischen Voraussetzungen der Aktion schreibt Tauss einen performativen Charakter zu.
Im fertigen Zustand lassen sich bei seinen skulpturalen Wandstücken und vollplastischen Arbeiten Spuren der Einflussnahmen auf das spezifisch reagierende Material nicht nur deutlich nachvollziehen, sie sind vielmehr auch der Ausdruck eines in Erstarrung geratenen, ehemals zeitlich limitierten Handlungsablaufs. Den Gesetzen der Schwerkraft folgend, haben die Arbeiten, während sie noch weich sind, die Tendenz nach unten zu fließen, was bei Betrachtung der ausgehärteten Formen, vor allem wenn sie an der Wand hängen, Vorstel-

solidified. Based on the laws of gravity, the works tend to flow downward while still soft, which evokes notions of lowering or falling when viewing the hardened forms, especially if they hang on a wall.

What we really see is three-dimensional, like colour in its raw state described at the start. The transformation of this material in the described artistic context presumes the recognition that the phenomenon of painting which appears constitutive for our perception, i.e. that it usually unfolds on two-dimensional surfaces, enters into Tauss's works in a paradoxical manner and coalesces with them.

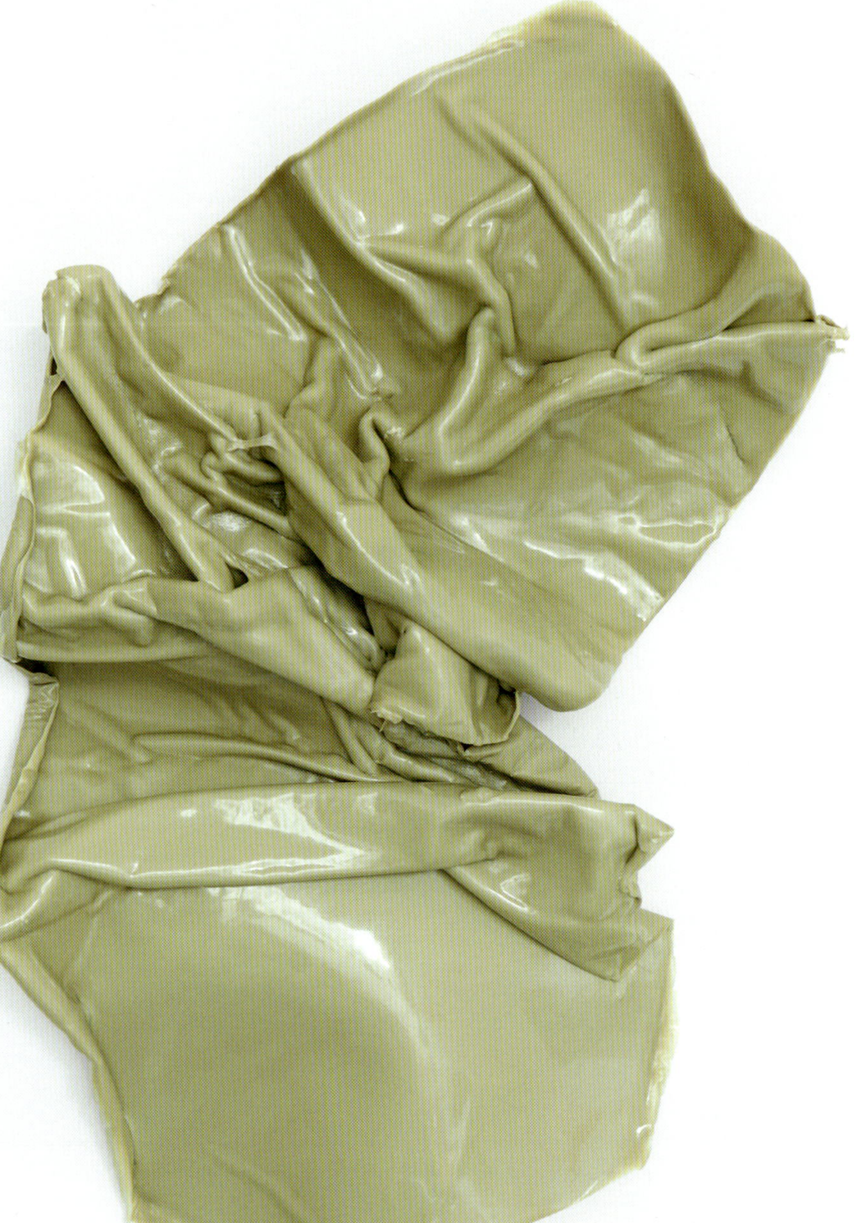

lungen des Herunterlassens oder Fallens auslösen.

Was wir wirklich sehen, ist dreidimensional, auch die eingangs beschriebene Farbe in ihrem Rohzustand. Die Transformation dieses Materials in den beschriebenen Kontext der Kunst setzt die Erkenntnis voraus, dass das für unsere Wahrnehmung prägende Phänomen der Malerei, nämlich sich gewöhnlich auf zweidimensionalen Flächen zu entfalten, auf paradoxe Weise in seine plastischen Arbeiten Einzug hält und mit ihnen verschmilzt.

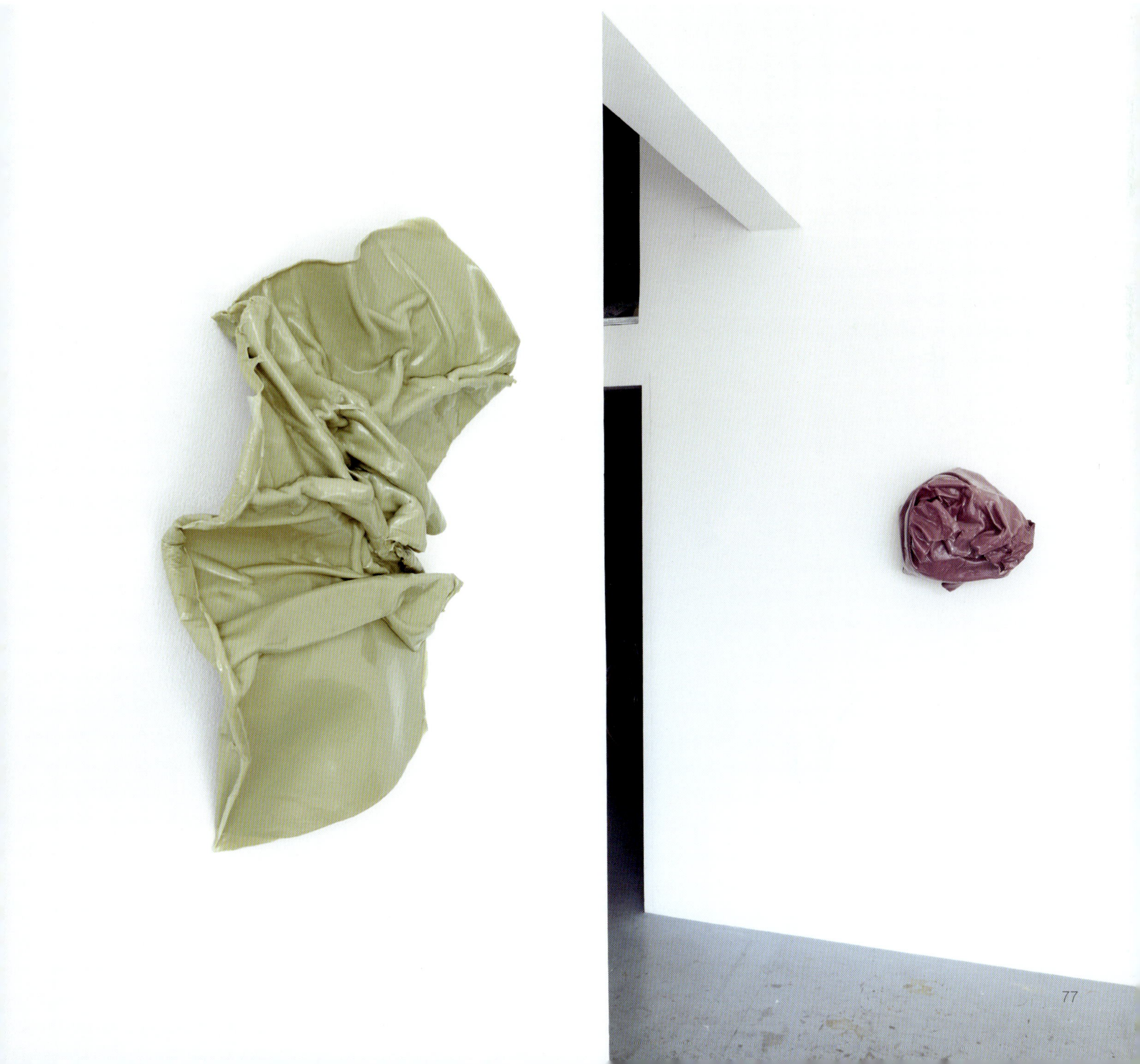

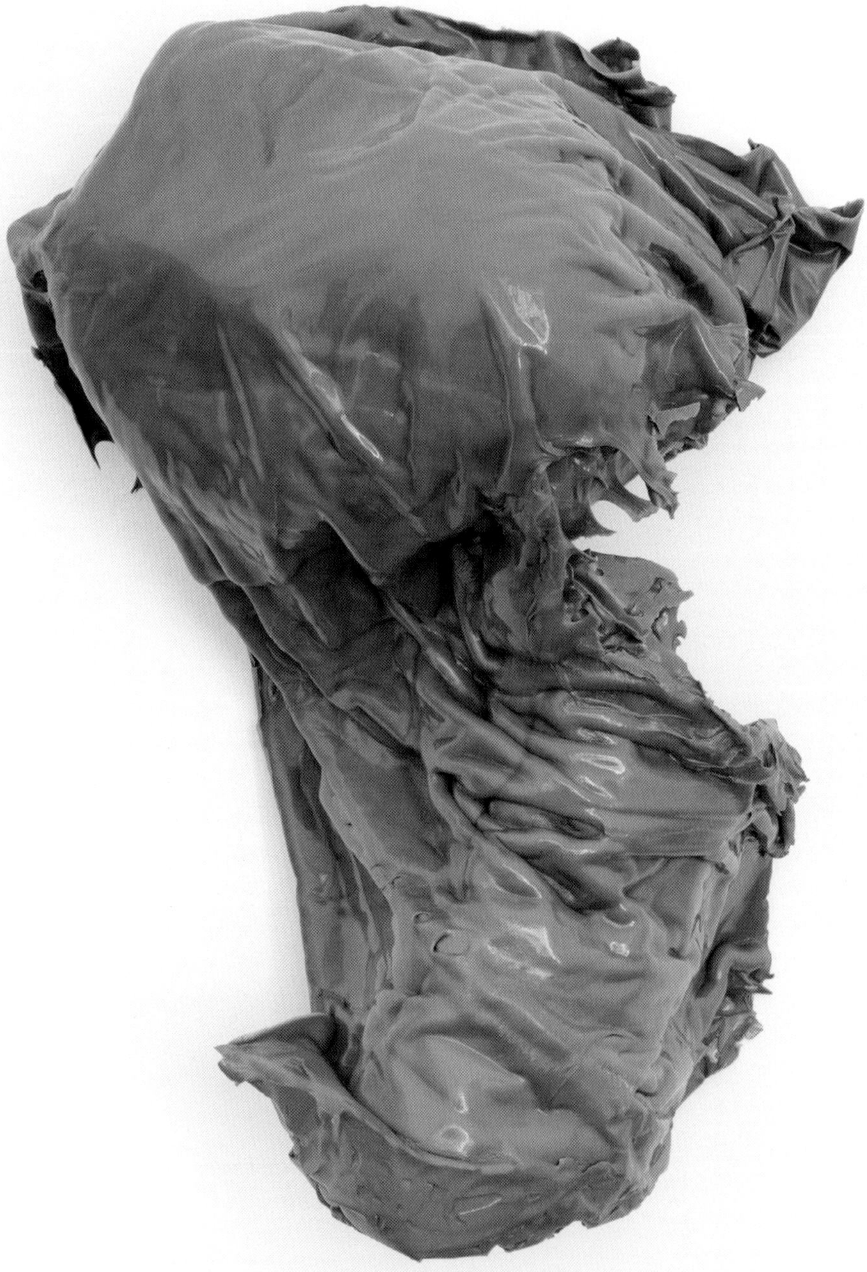

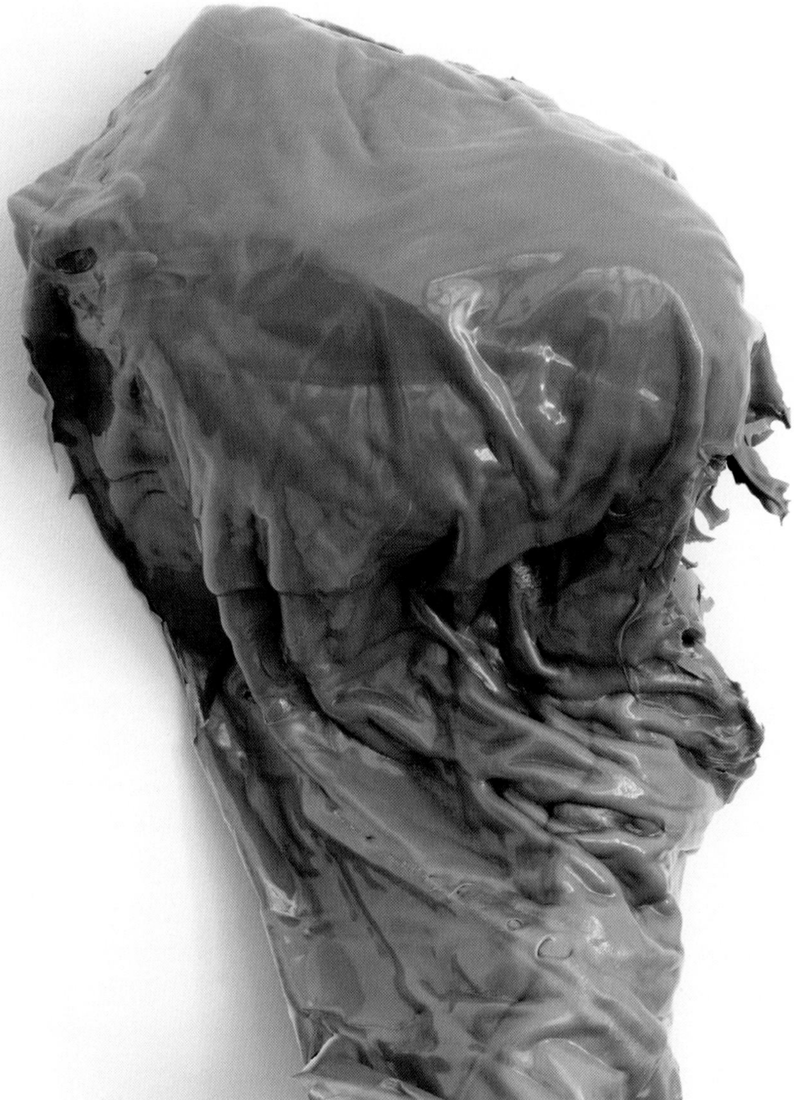

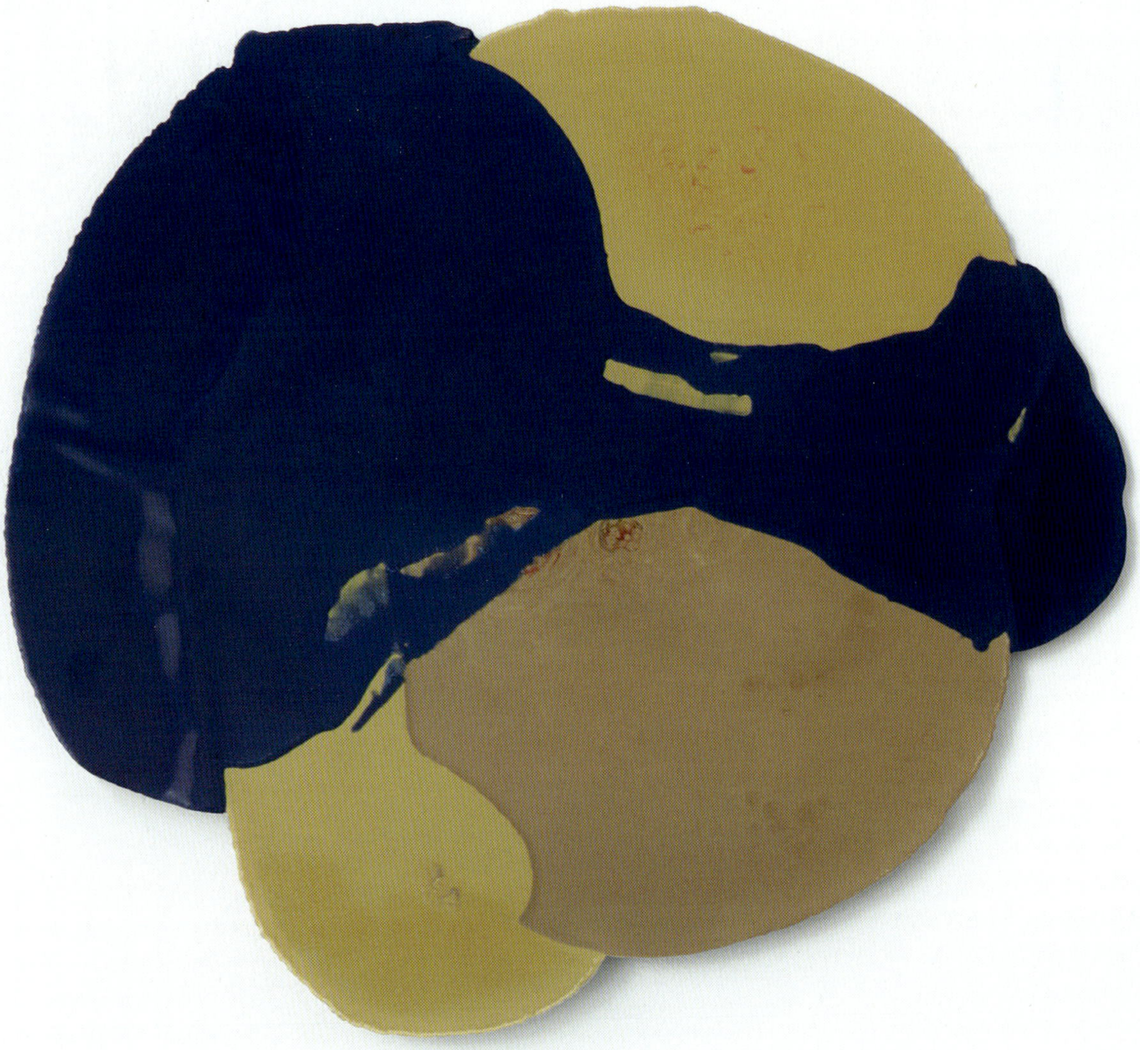

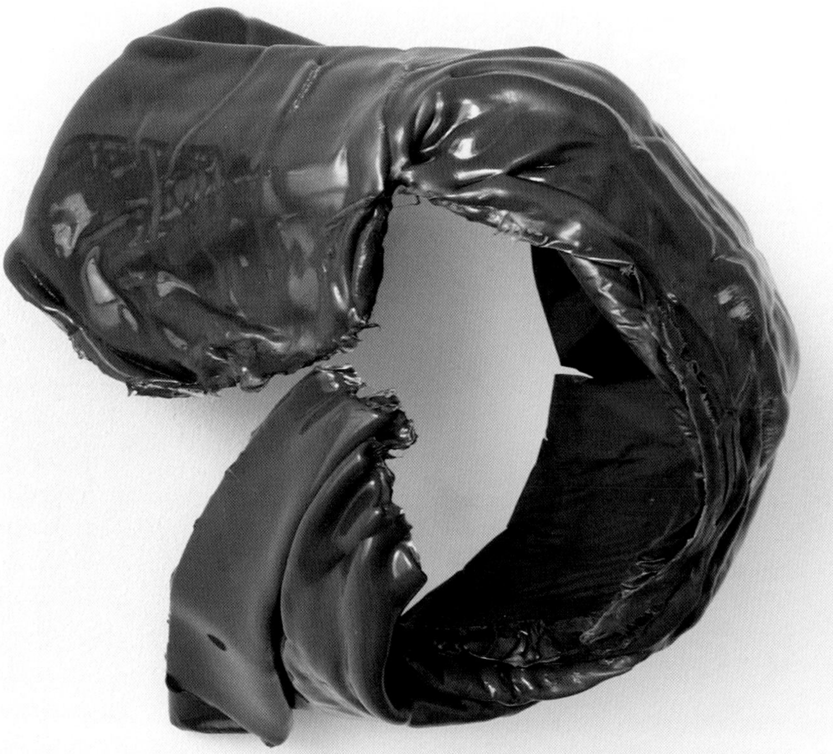

Manisha Jothady

Kunstkritikerin

Malerei als plastischer Prozess

Im Rückblick erscheint der Ausstellungstitel, mit dem Eduard Tauss eine Solopräsentation vor rund 20 Jahren in einer Wiener Galerie überschrieben hat, programmatisch: „itself" lautete dieser und bezog sich auf eine Reihe von monochromen Bildobjekten und an die Wand applizierten Farbflächen aus Kunstharz, die im Sinne der L'art pour l'art ihre Autonomie und Selbstbezüglichkeit behaupteten.[1] Seitdem hat der Künstler konsequent an einem erweiterten Malereibegriff weitergearbeitet, den „Ausstieg aus dem Bild"[2], wie es der Kunsthistoriker Laszlo Glozer 1981 mit Blick auf die zunehmende Hybridisierung der Gattungen formulierte, vollzogen. Die Verweigerung eines Narrativs, das sich auf ein Außerhalb der Arbeiten und deren Entstehungsprozess richten könnte, bildet dabei nach wie vor eine Konstante in seinem Werk, ebenso die materielle Substanz, auf der seine Arbeiten basieren – pigmentiertes Polyurethan.

---

1 Eduard Tauss: itself, Galerie Lindner, Wien, 2002.

2 Laszlo Glozer: Westkunst. Zeitgenössische Kunst seit 1939, Museen der Stadt Köln, Köln, 1981.

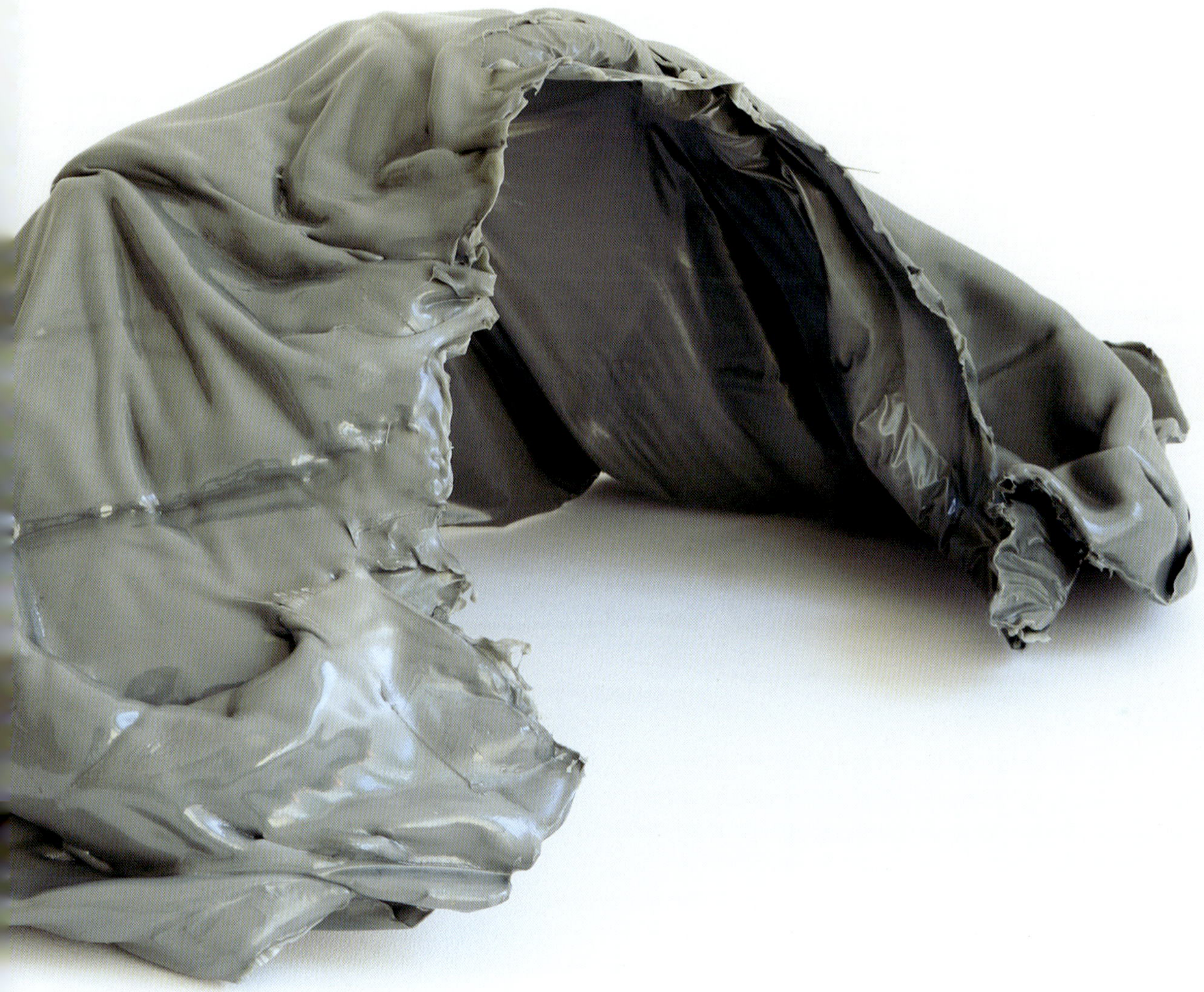

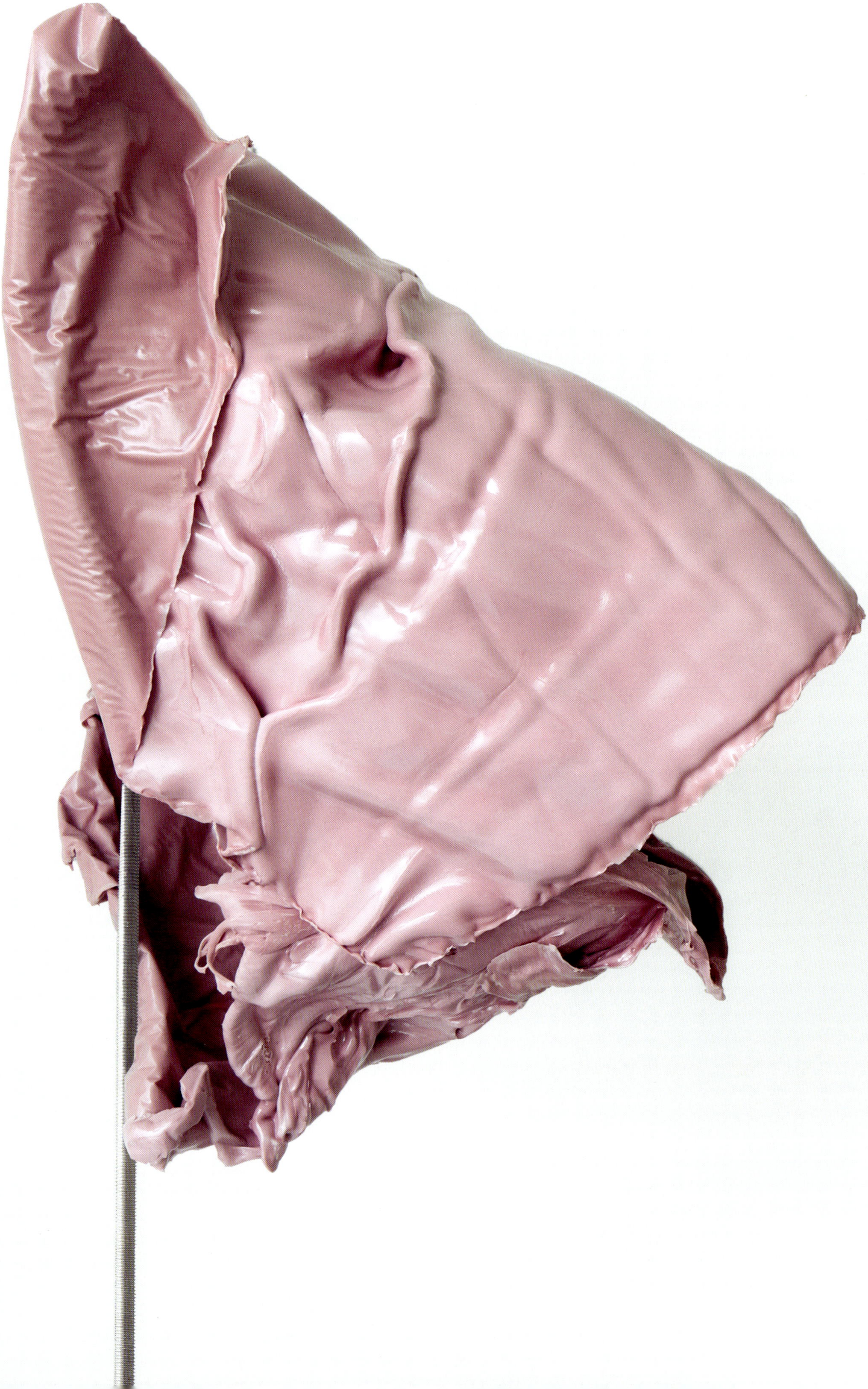

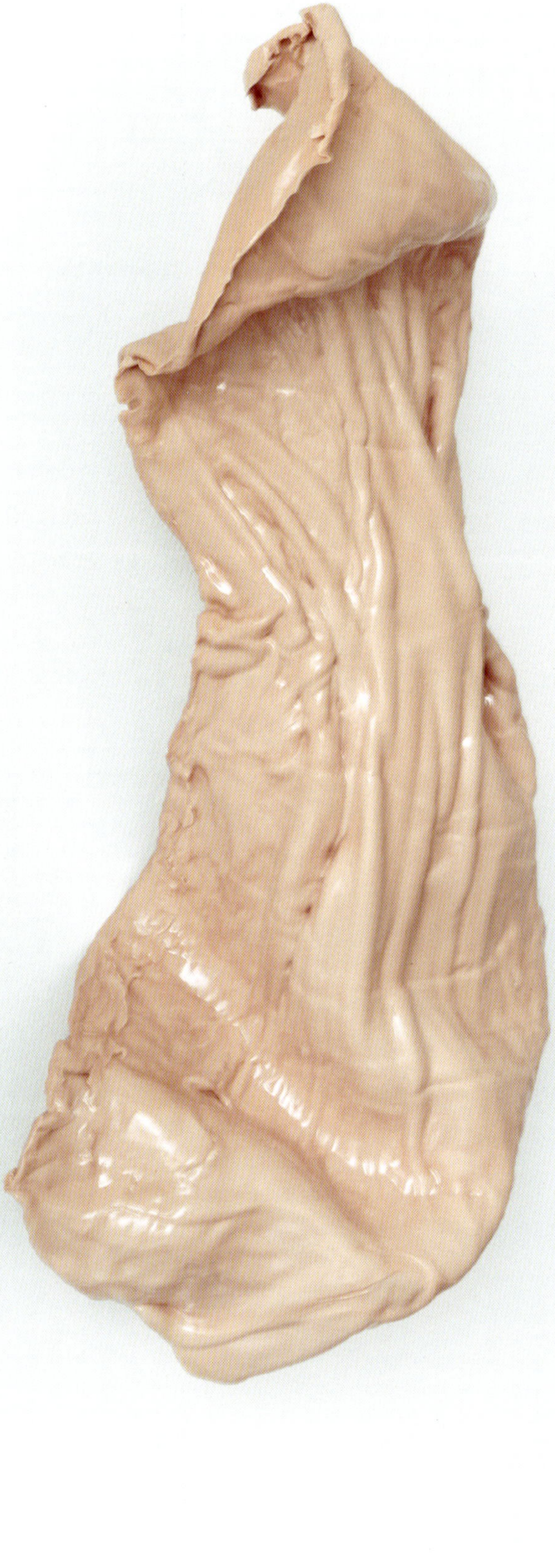

„Meine Ideen kommen aus der Malerei, selbst wenn ich nicht male“[3], sagte Donald Judd einst und verdeutlichte damit, wie sehr Aspekte der Malerei in das Konzept einer interdisziplinären Kunstpraxis einfließen können. Auch Eduard Tauss' Kunst basiert auf diesem Ansatz. In seinen Arbeiten treten Farbe, Textur und Licht als wesentliche Parameter hervor, wenngleich der Herstellungsprozess ein bildhauerischer ist. Der Künstler gießt den flüssigen und meist monochrom eingefärbten Kunststoff in eigens angefertigte Becken und lässt das Material nur bis zu jenem Grad aushärten, an dem es noch formbar ist. Er dekliniert die Bandbreite von offenen zu geschlossenen Formen durch, von sich mehr in der Fläche entfaltenden zu dreidimensionalen Arbeiten. Werkgruppen wie „Farbplatten“ und „Offene Formen“ lassen sich unmittelbar mit Malerei assoziieren, während andere, darunter Tauss' „Farbkörper“, durch Ausbuchtungen und Eindellungen, Drehungen und Faltungen, Ein- und Umstülpungen deutlich objekthaft ausformuliert sind. Der Formbildungsprozess lässt sich dabei nur bedingt steuern. Denn bei der Übertragung von der flachen Farbmasse aus der Gussvorrichtung in ein dreidimensionales Farbobjekt im Raum entfalten Bewegung und Schwerkraft ihre Wirkung. Sie setzen eine Materialdynamik frei, die sich als Farb- beziehungsweise Materialspuren in den ausgehärteten Zustand der Objekte einschreibt. Der plastischen Formwerdung wohnt bei Eduard Tauss somit immer eine vorangegangene Aktion, ein performatives Moment inne. Die abstrakten Gebilde erscheinen dabei wie inmitten ihrer Metamorphose erstarrt. Ein Vorgang, der an den fotografischen Schnappschuss erinnert, an das Einfrieren eines Handlungsablaufs im entscheidenden Augenblick.

3 Das Zitat ist dem Katalog zur Ausstellung „Malerei ohne Malerei“ vorangestellt, hg. v. Dirk Luckow, Hans-Werner Schmidt, Museum der bildenden Künste Leipzig, Leipzig, 2002.

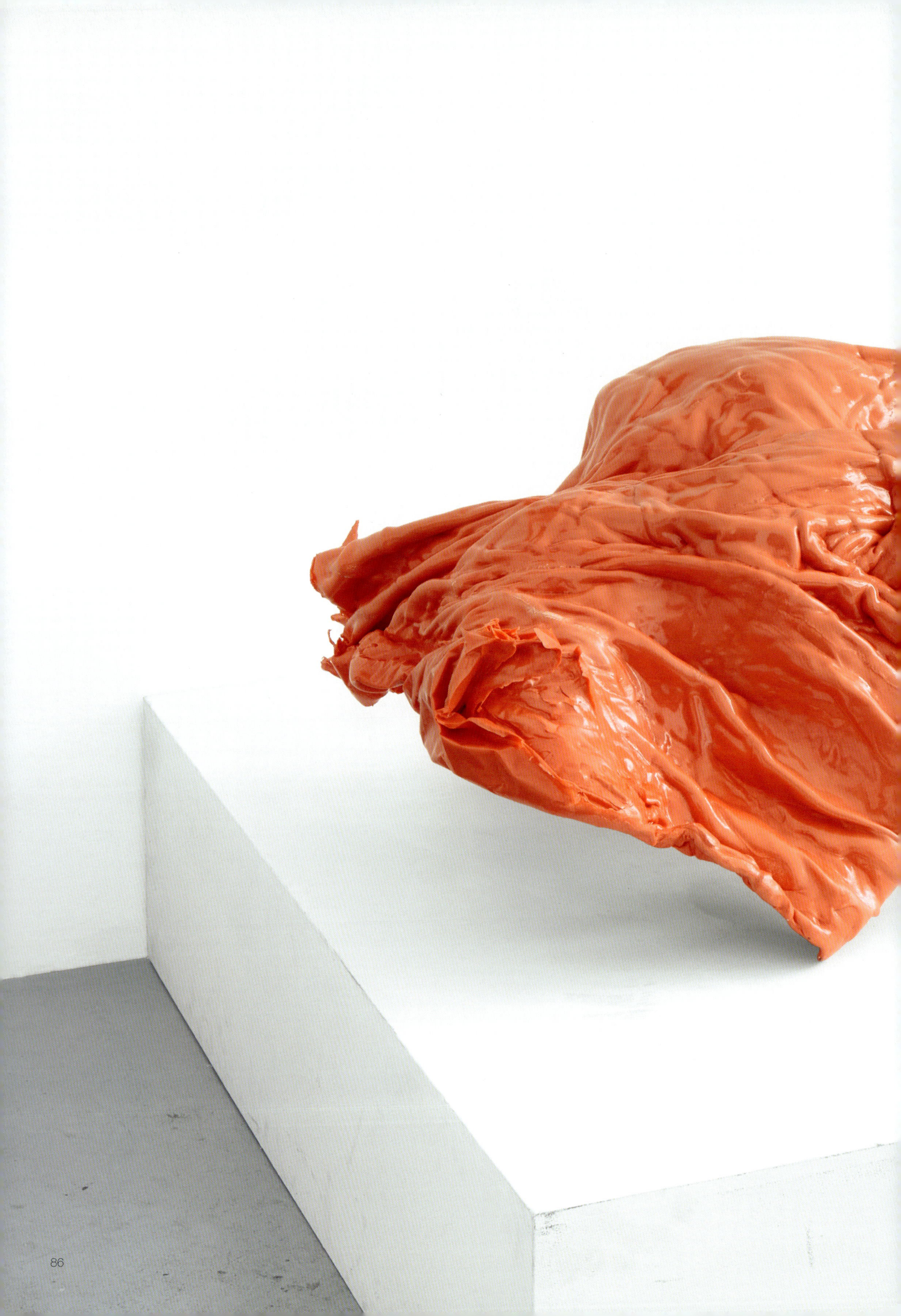

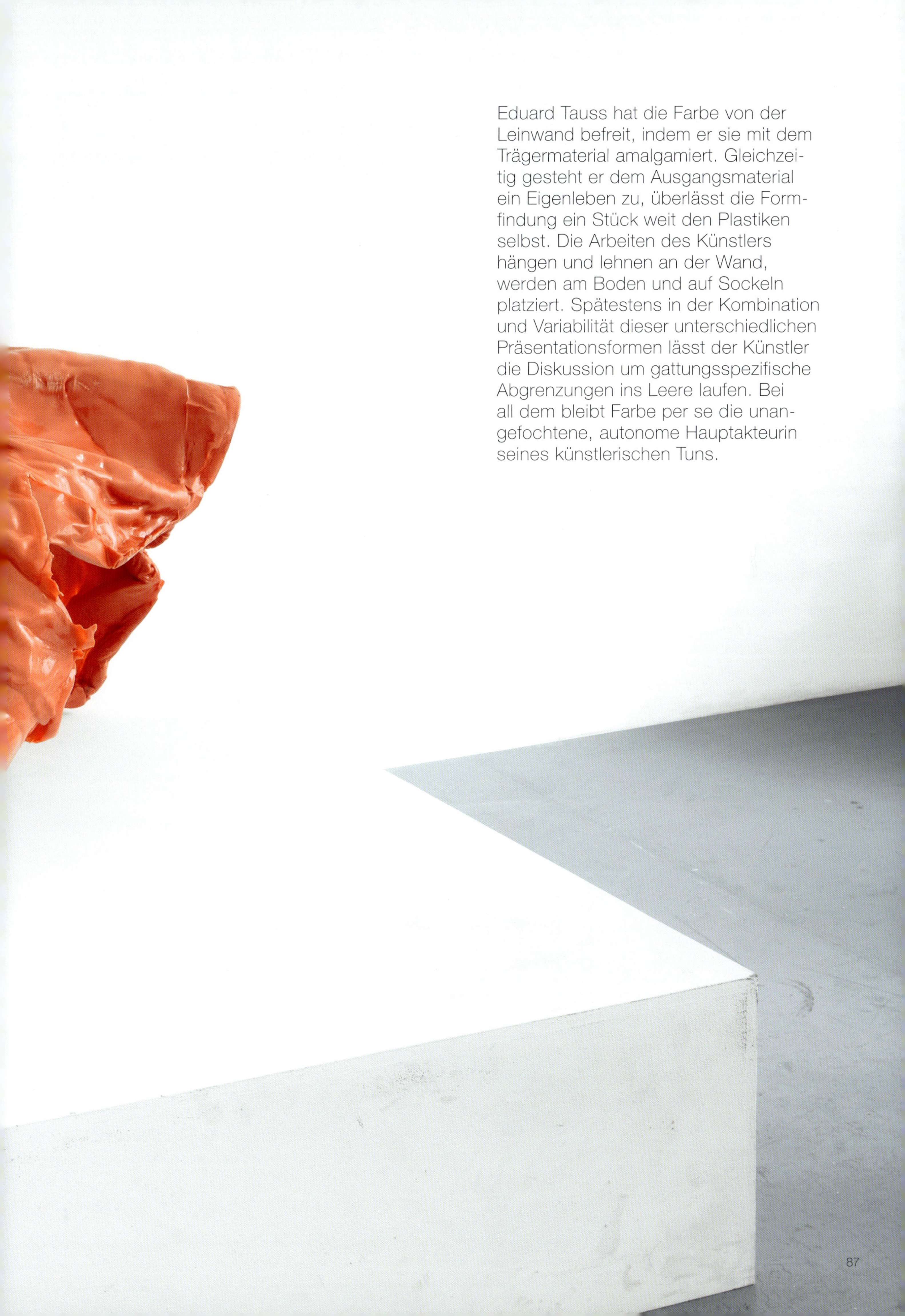

Eduard Tauss hat die Farbe von der Leinwand befreit, indem er sie mit dem Trägermaterial amalgamiert. Gleichzeitig gesteht er dem Ausgangsmaterial ein Eigenleben zu, überlässt die Formfindung ein Stück weit den Plastiken selbst. Die Arbeiten des Künstlers hängen und lehnen an der Wand, werden am Boden und auf Sockeln platziert. Spätestens in der Kombination und Variabilität dieser unterschiedlichen Präsentationsformen lässt der Künstler die Diskussion um gattungsspezifische Abgrenzungen ins Leere laufen. Bei all dem bleibt Farbe per se die unangefochtene, autonome Hauptakteurin seines künstlerischen Tuns.

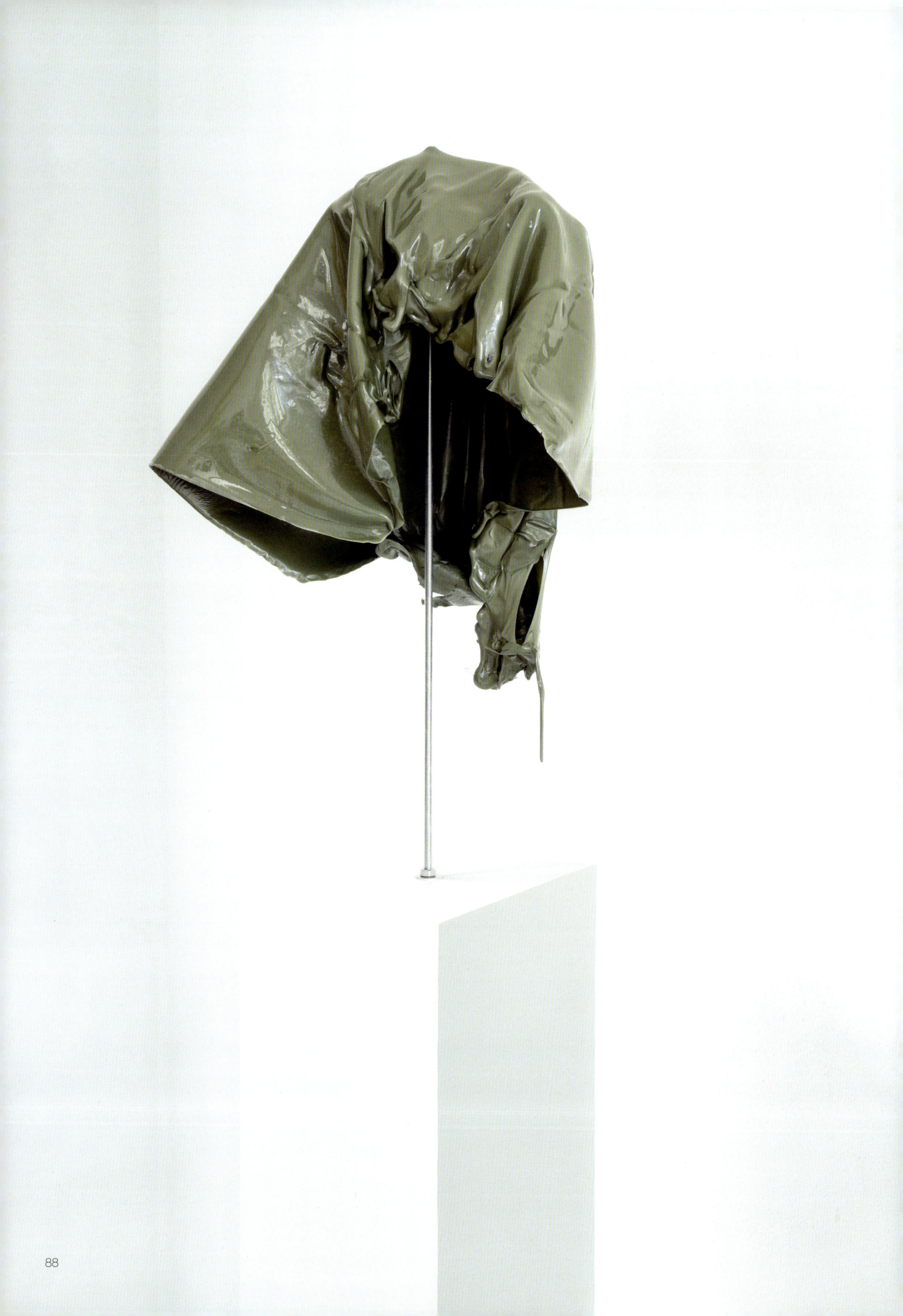

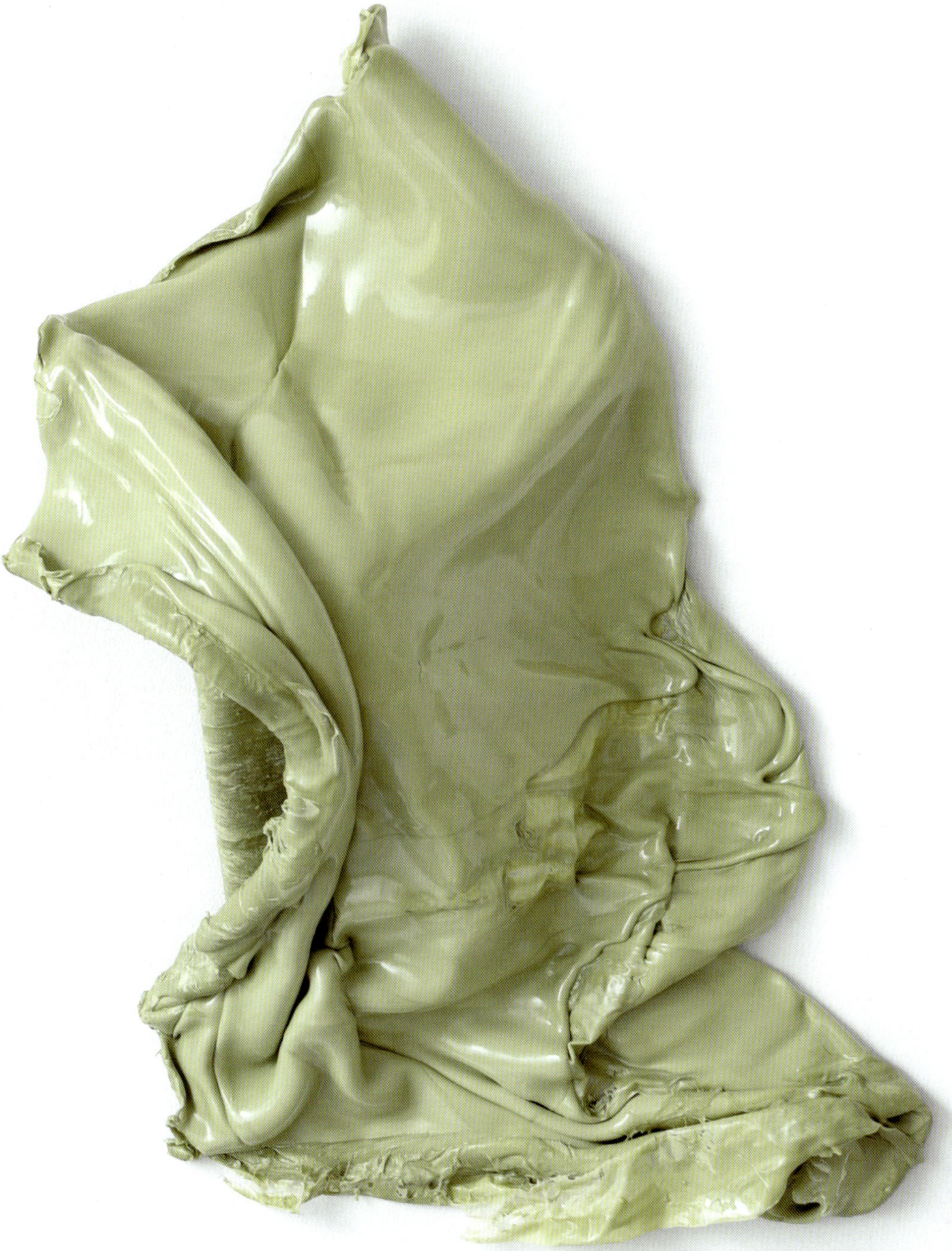

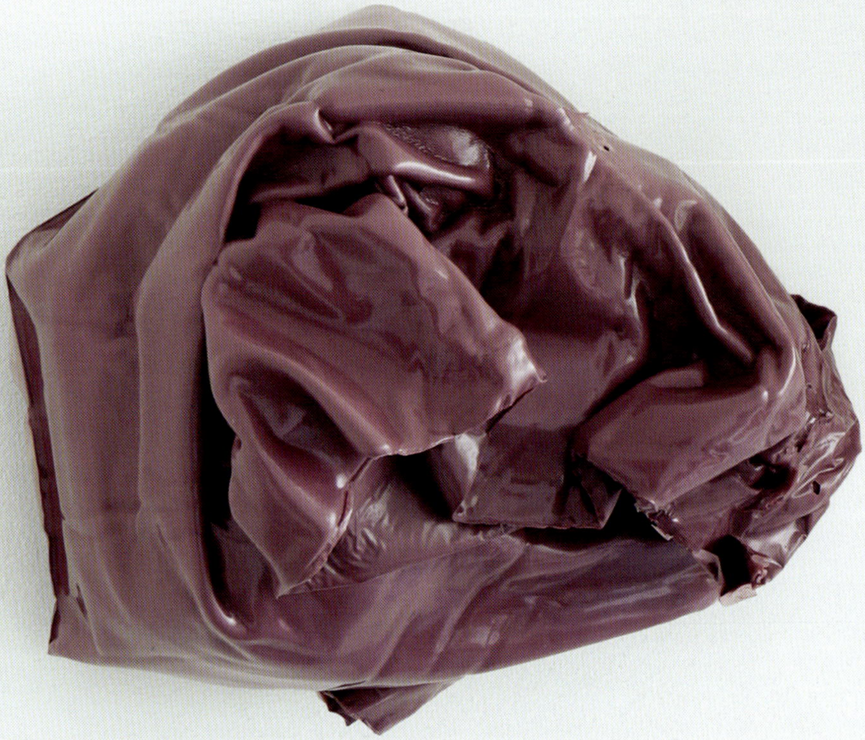

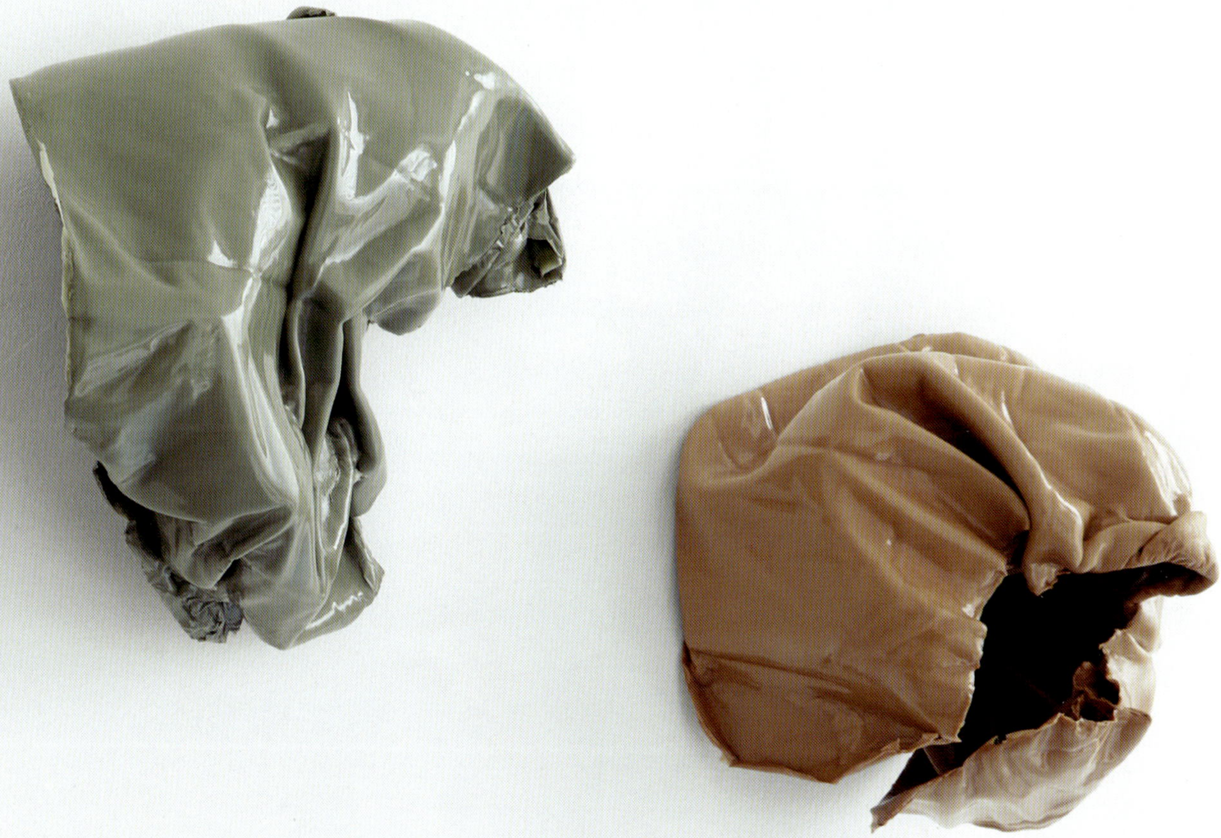

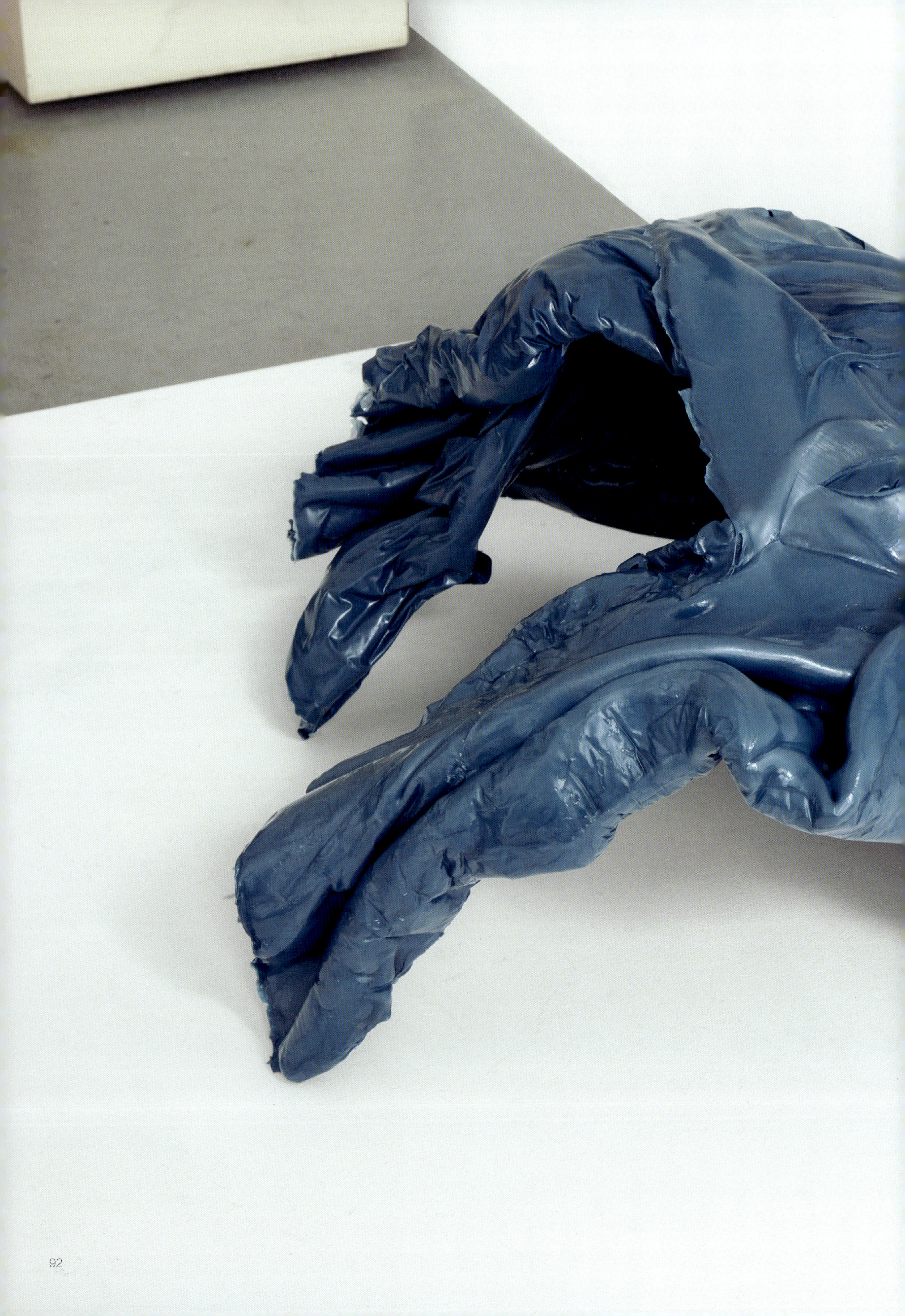

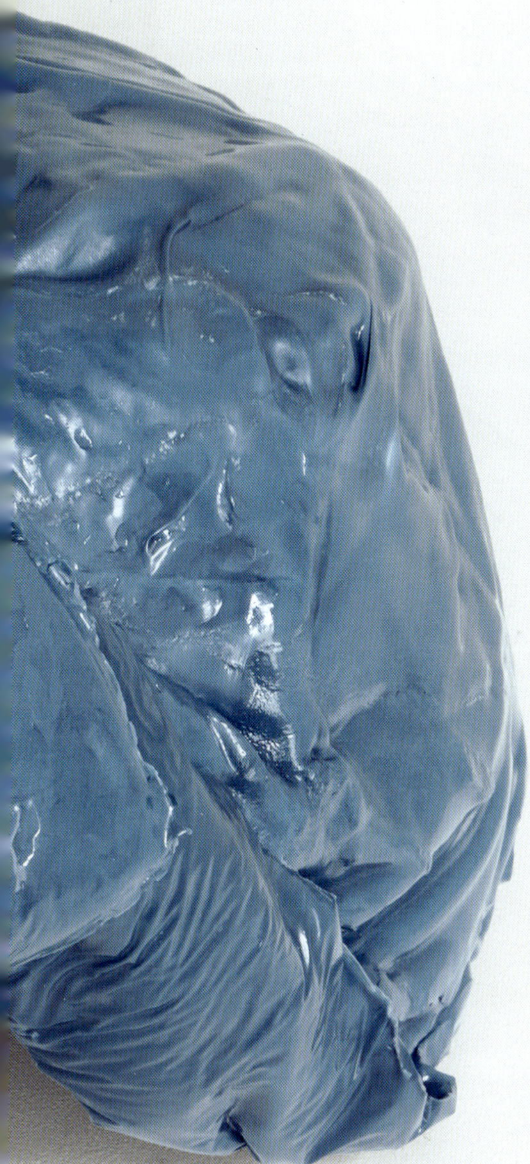

Manisha Jothady

Art critic

Painting as Sculptural Process

In retrospect, the exhibition title that was chosen by Eduard Tauss to headline a solo presentation in a Vienna gallery around twenty years ago seems programmatic: called "itself", it referred to a series of monochrome pictorial objects and synthetic resin colour fields applied to the wall, which proclaimed their autonomy and self-reference in the spirit of l'art pour l'art.[1] *Since then, Tauss has been working consistently on an extended concept of painting; he has taken the ultimate step by "Stepping Out Of the Picture"*[2] *as formulated by the art historian Laszlo Glozer in 1981 when viewing the increasing hybridisation of the genres. The rejection of a narrative that could be oriented on one that exists outside the works and their creational process still forms a constant in his work, likewise the material substance upon which his works are based – pigmented polyurethane.*

"My ideas come from painting even when I'm not painting"[3]*, Donald Judd once said, thus stressing how intensively aspects of painting can flow into the concept of an interdisciplinary artistic praxis. Eduard Tauss's art is also*

1 Eduard Tauss: itself, Galerie Lindner, Vienna, 2002.

2 Laszlo Glozer: Westkunst. Zeitgenössische Kunst seit 1939, Museen der Stadt Köln, Cologne, 1981.

3 The quote precedes the catalogue for the exhibition "Malerei ohne Malerei", ed. Dirk Luckow, Hans-Werner Schmidt, Museum der bildenden Künste Leipzig, Leipzig, 2002.

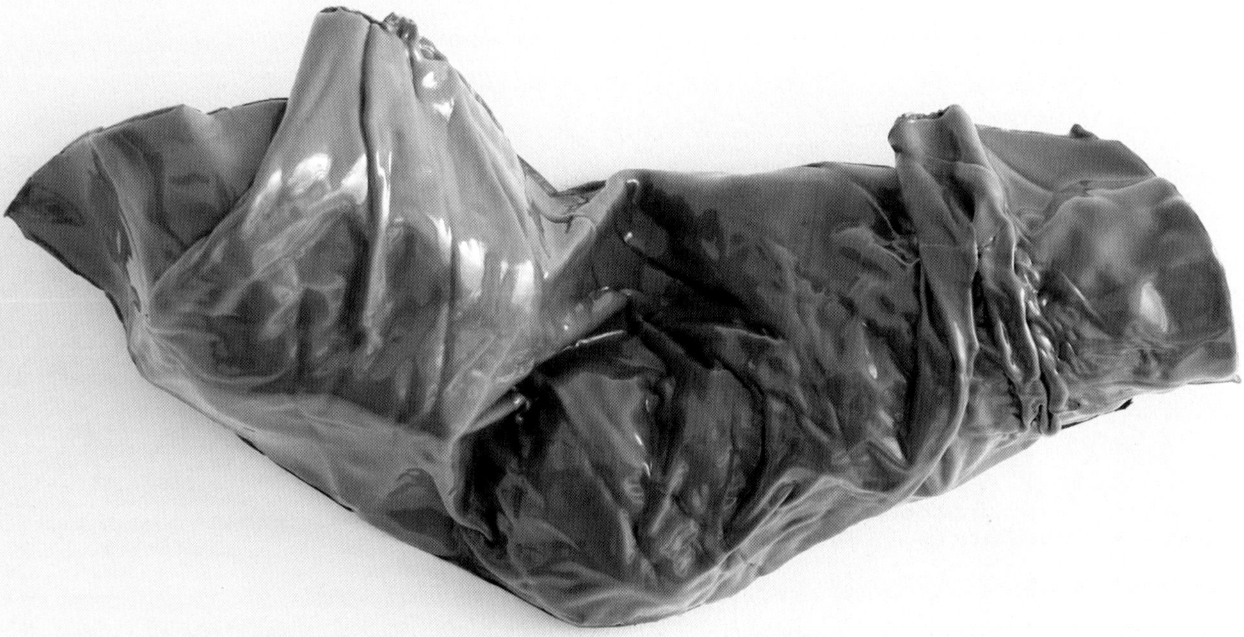

based on this approach. Colour, texture and light predominate in his works as essential parameters, even though the production process is sculptural. He casts the liquid and usually monochrome coloured plastic into a specially made basin and lets the material harden only to the degree that it is still mouldable. He runs the gamut from open to closed forms, from forms that unfold more on the flat surface to three-dimensional works. Work groups like "Colour Plate" and "Open Shape" can be directly associated with painting, while others, such as Tauss's "Colour Bodies", with their protuberances, indentations, twisting, invaginations and inversions, are shaped as distinctly object-like. This configuration process can be controlled only partially. Namely, transferring the flat mass of paint out of the casting device into a three-dimensional coloured object in space enables movement and gravitational force to unfold their effects. They release a material dynamic that inscribes itself as traces of colour and material in the objects' hardened state. Thus in Tauss's work the sculptural genesis of the objects always involves a previous action, a performative moment. It is as though the abstract shapes seem petrified in the middle of their metamorphosis – a process reminiscent of the snapshot in photography, freeze-framing an ongoing action at the decisive moment.

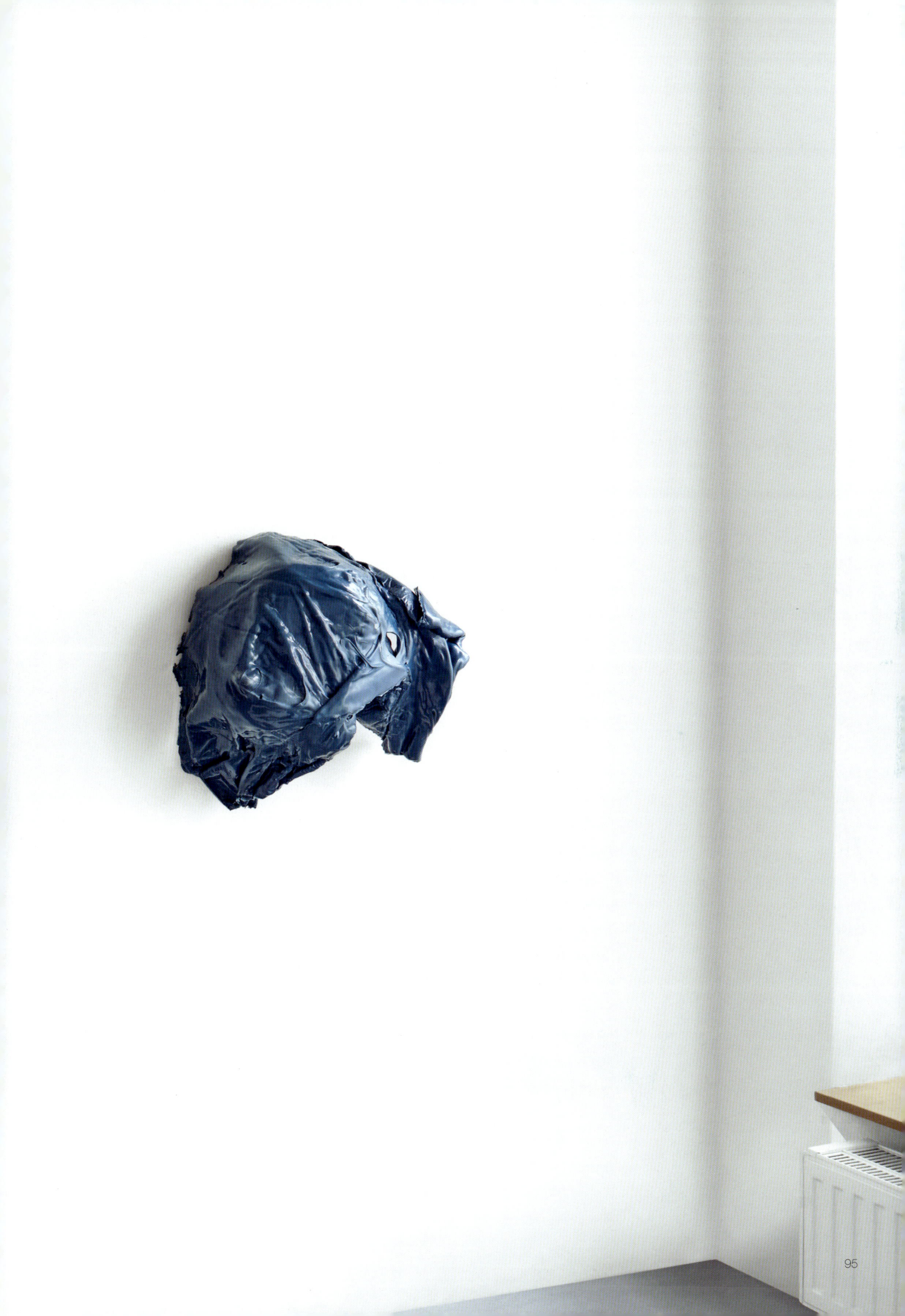

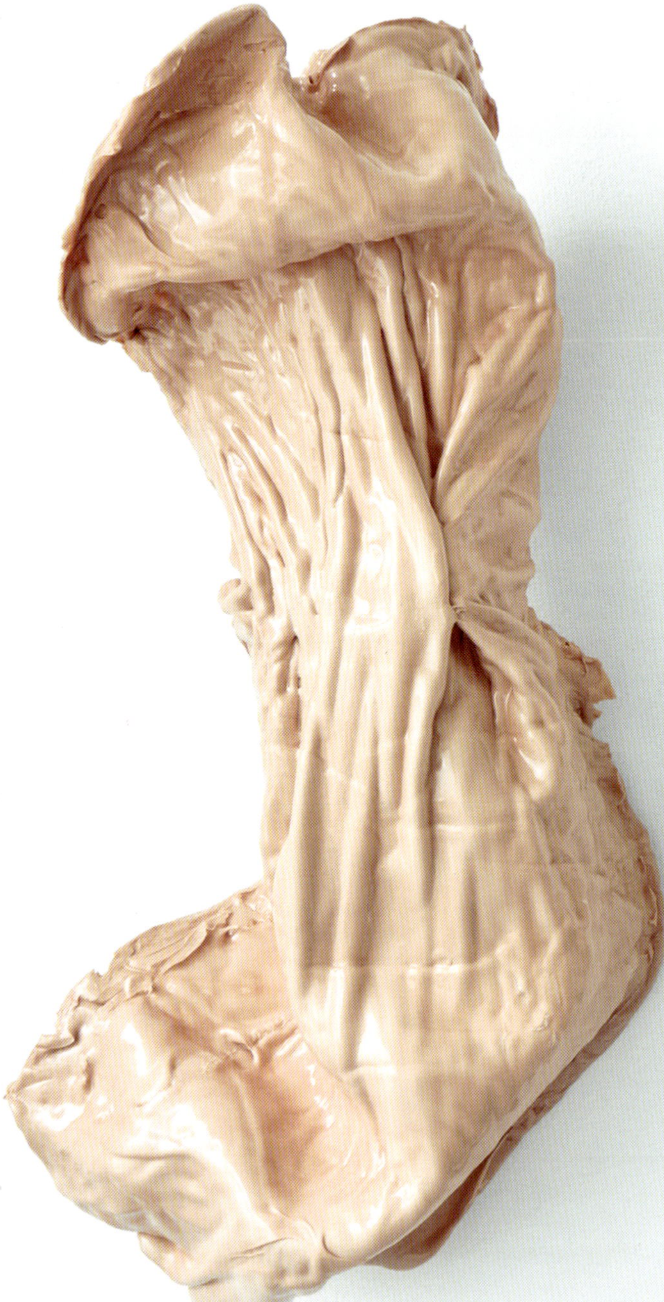

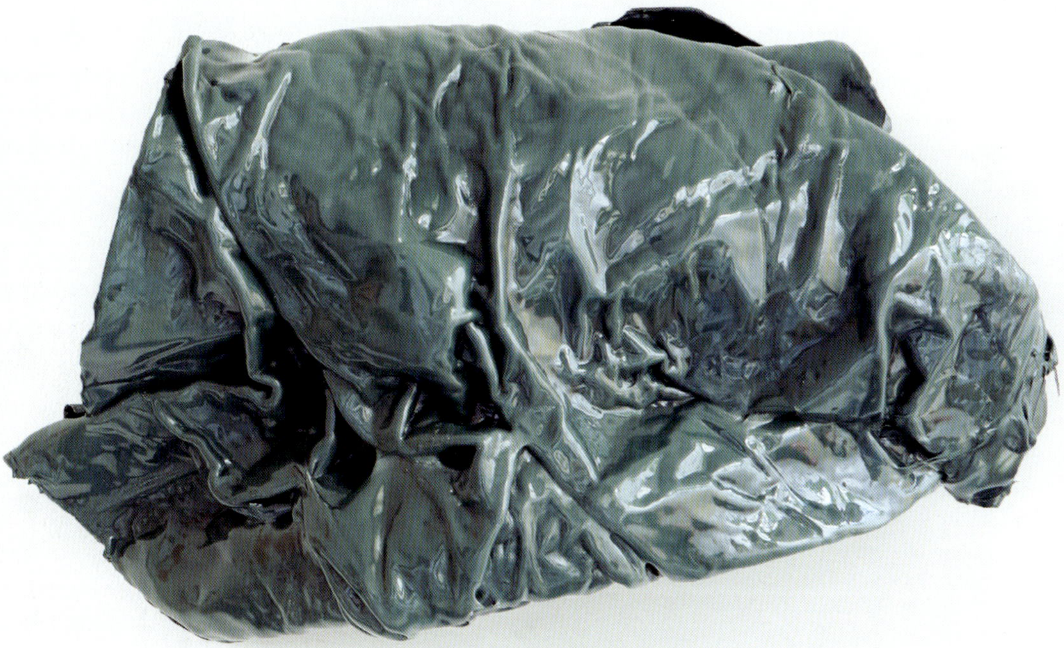

Eduard Tauss has liberated the paint from the canvas by amalgamating it with the substrate material itself. At the same time, he grants the starting material a life of its own, leaves the genesis of form to some extent to the sculptures themselves. His works hang, lean against the wall, are placed on the floor and on pedestals. At the latest in the combination and variability of these different forms of presentation, the artist takes the wind out of the sails of the discussion about genre-specific boundaries. Meanwhile, paint per se remains the incontrovertible and autonomous main protagonist in his artistic activity.

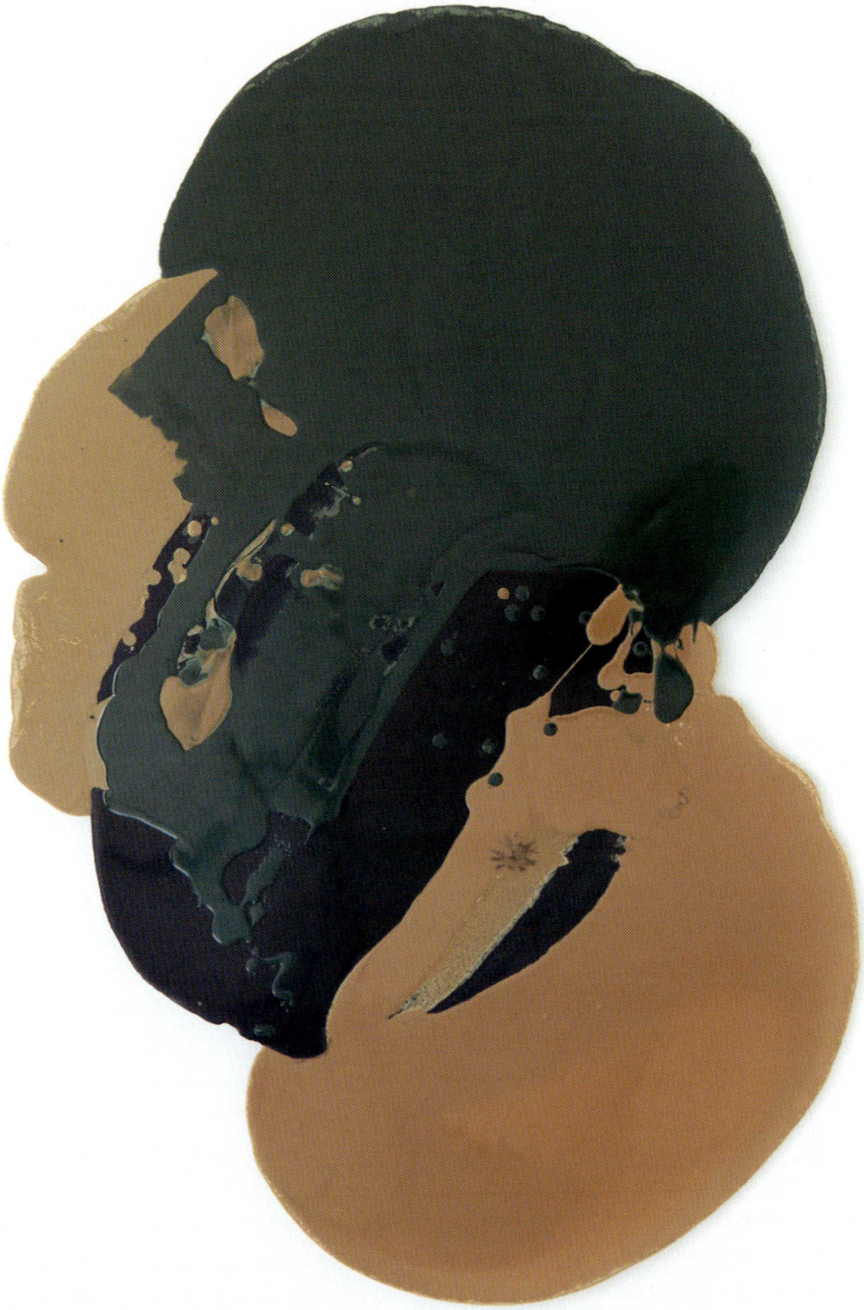

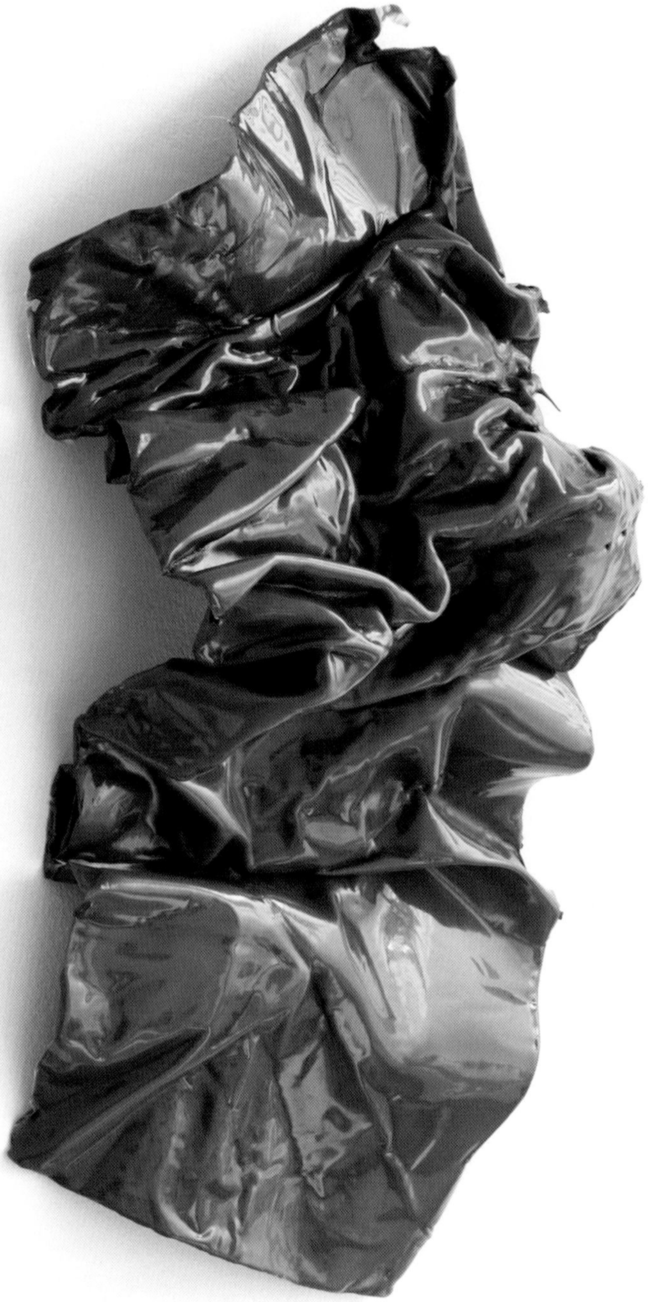

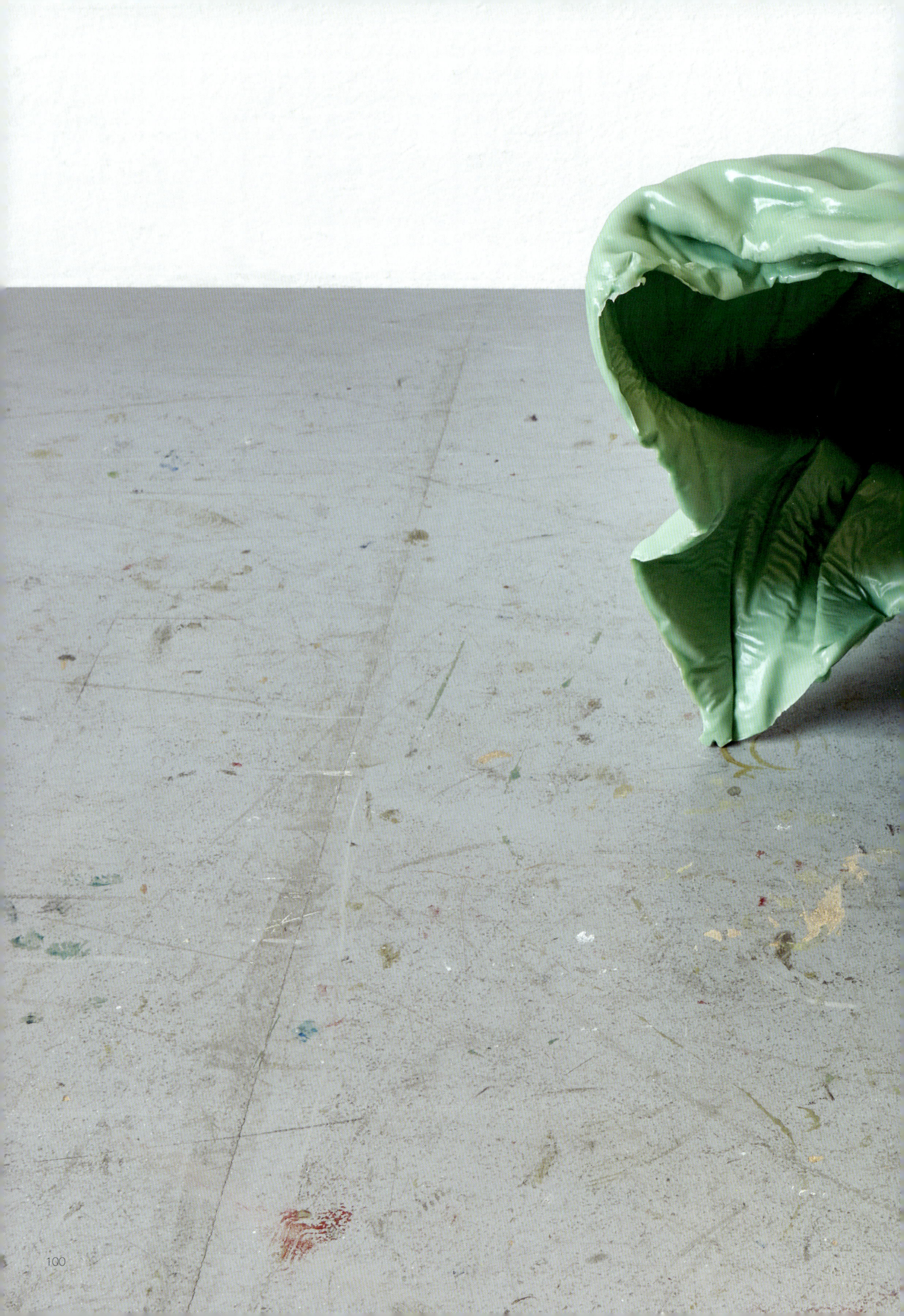

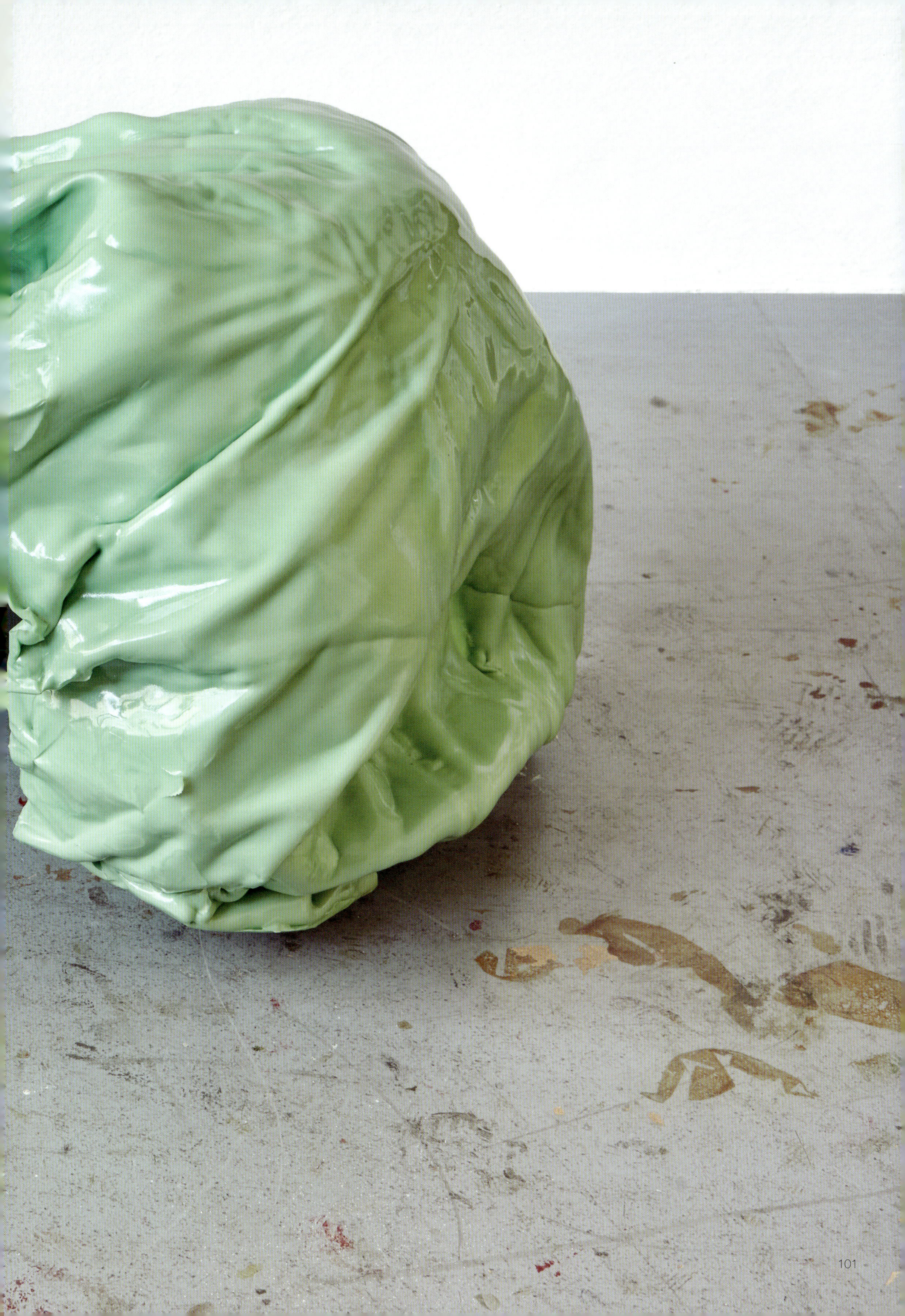

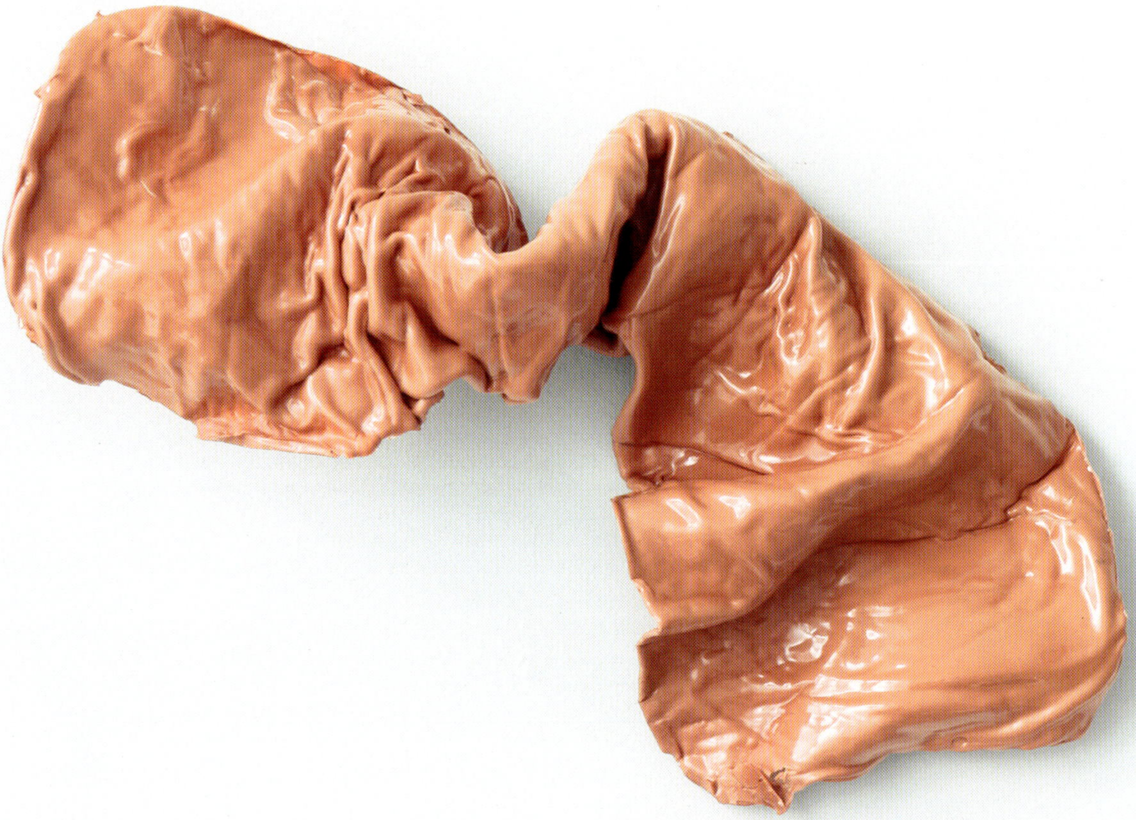

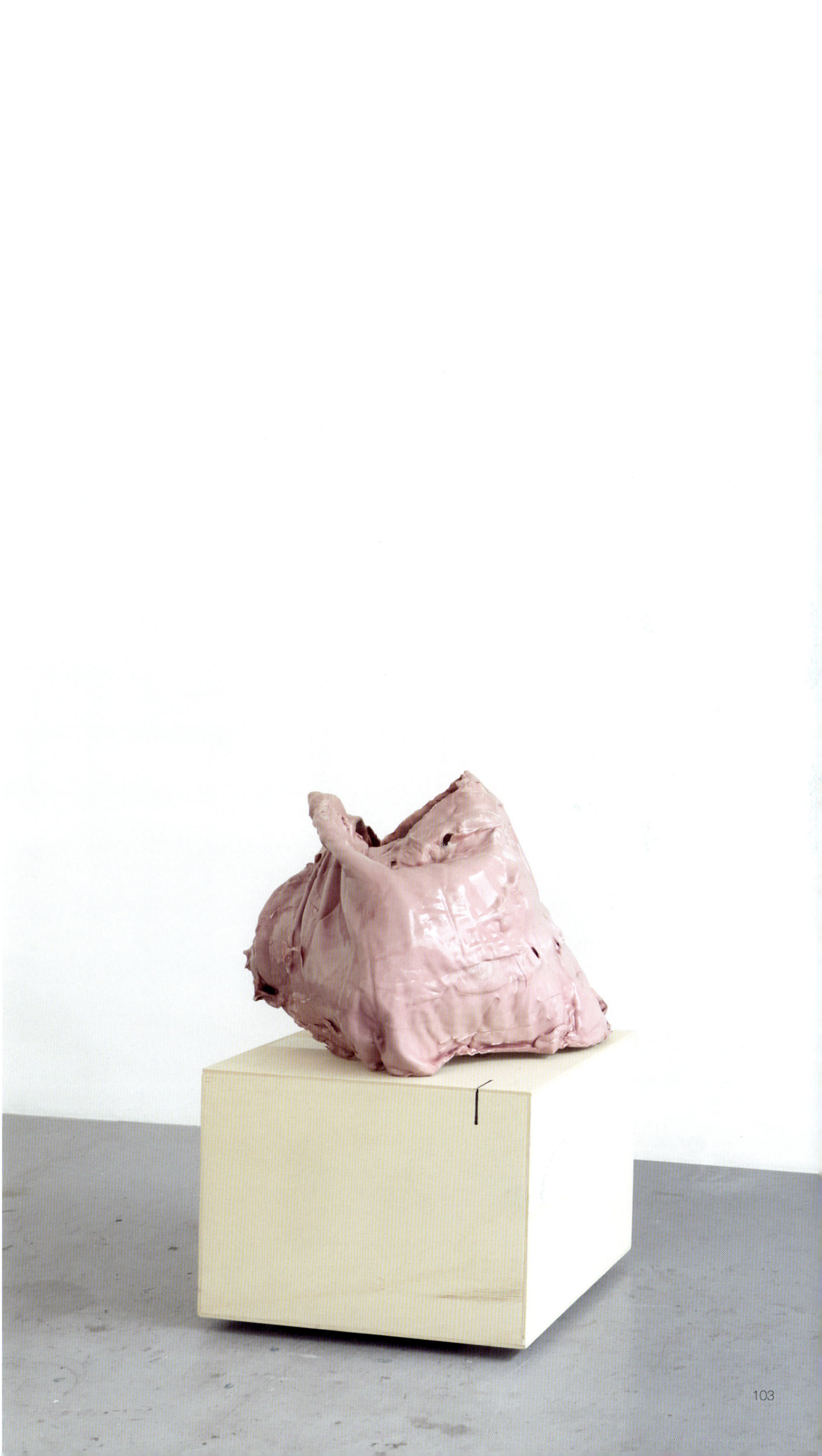

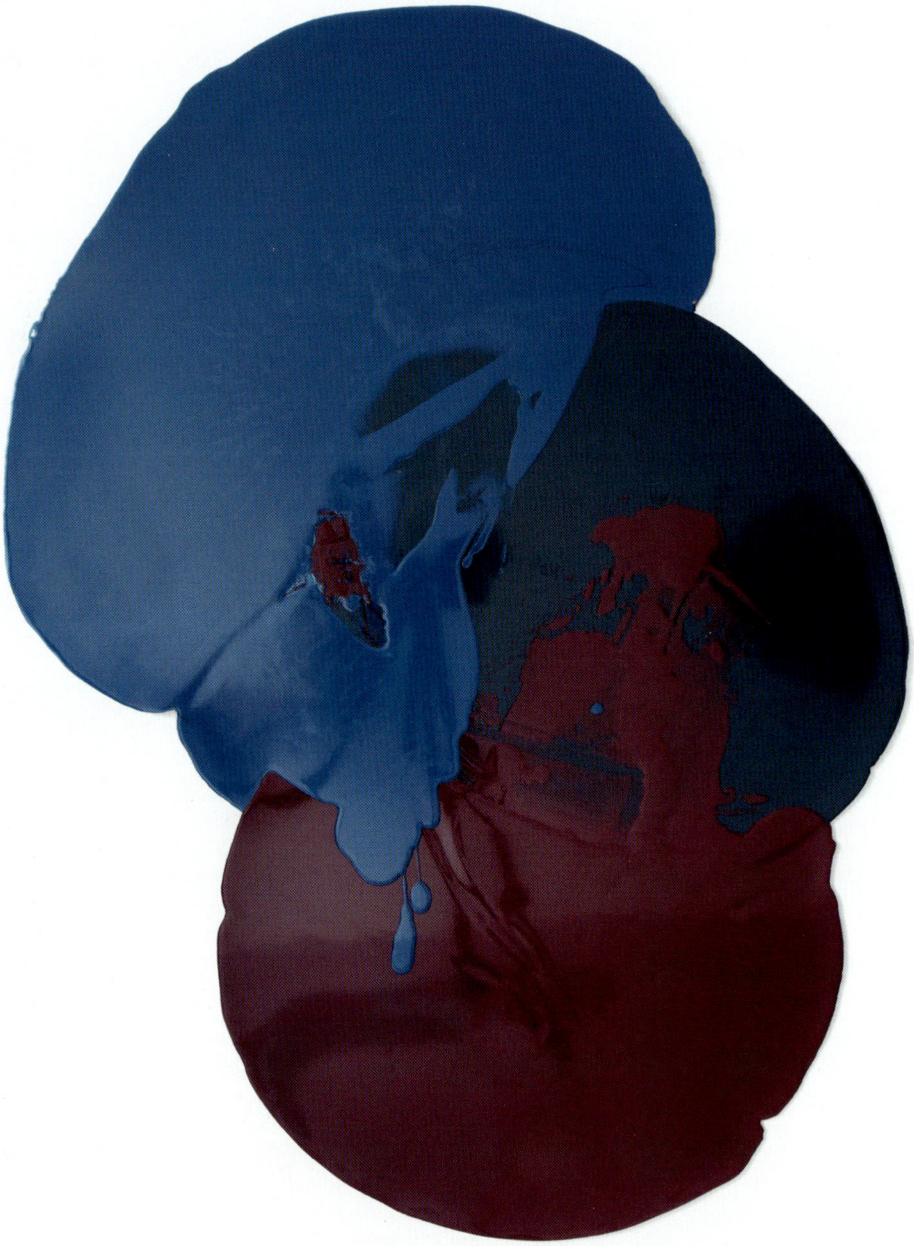

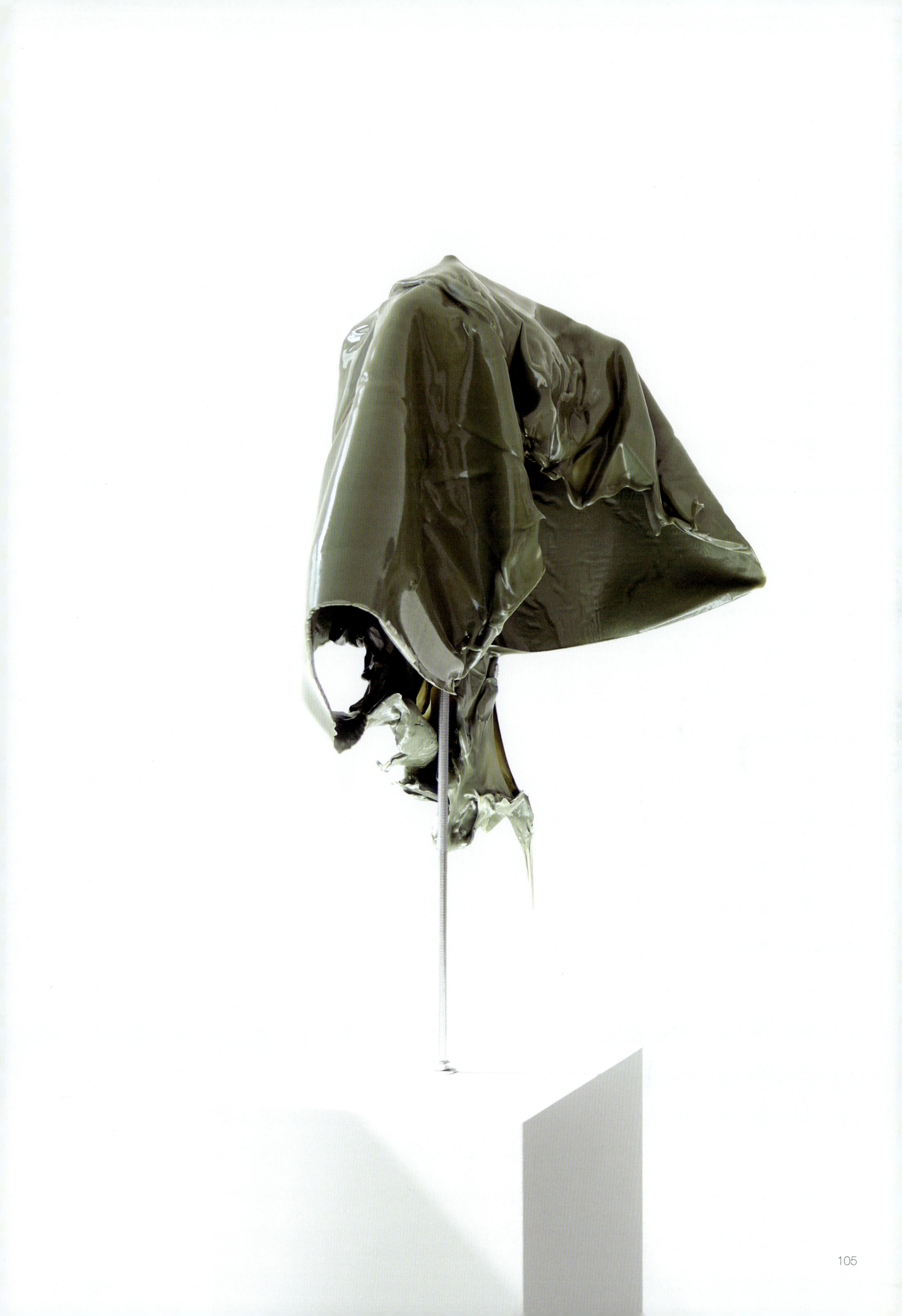

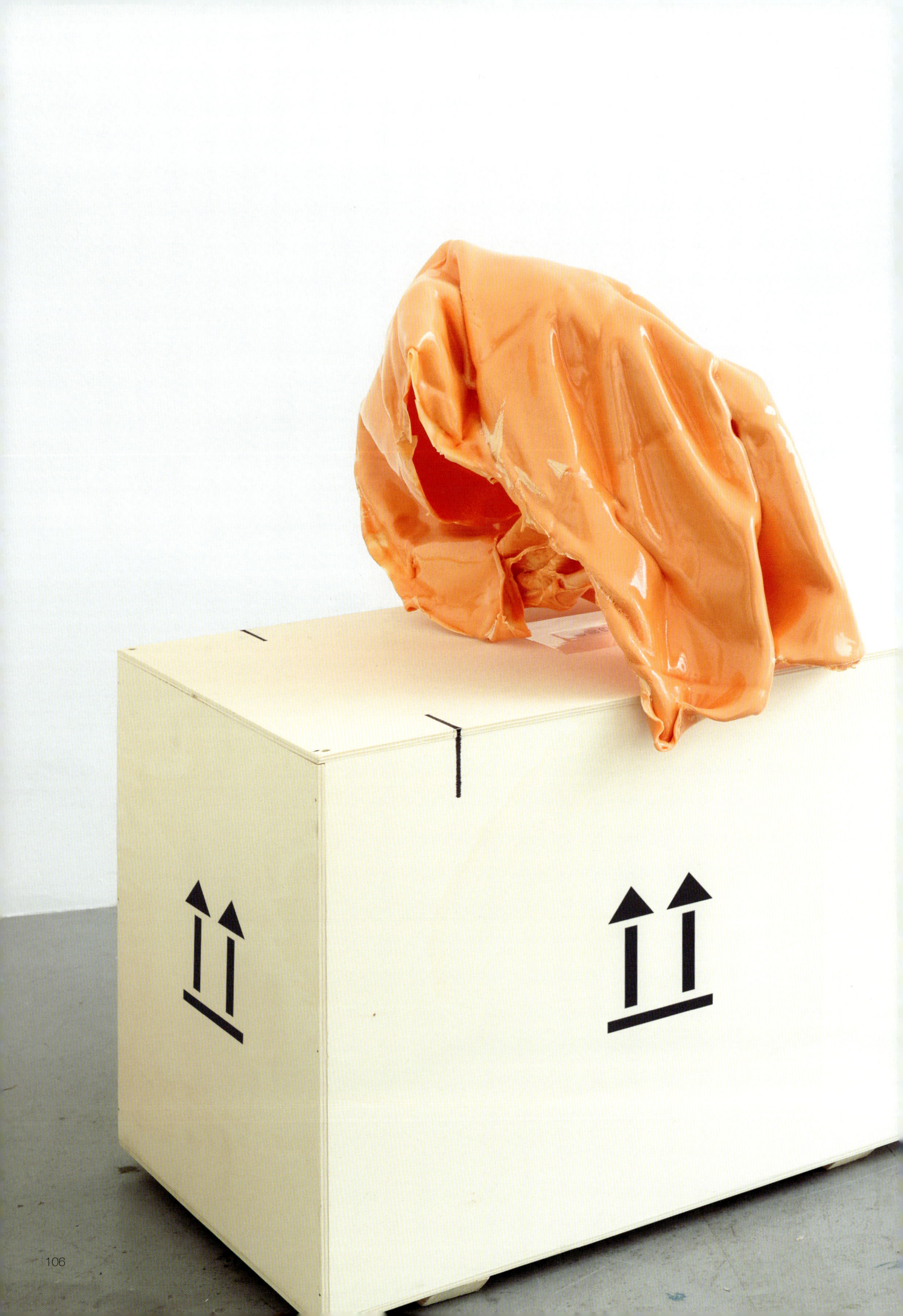

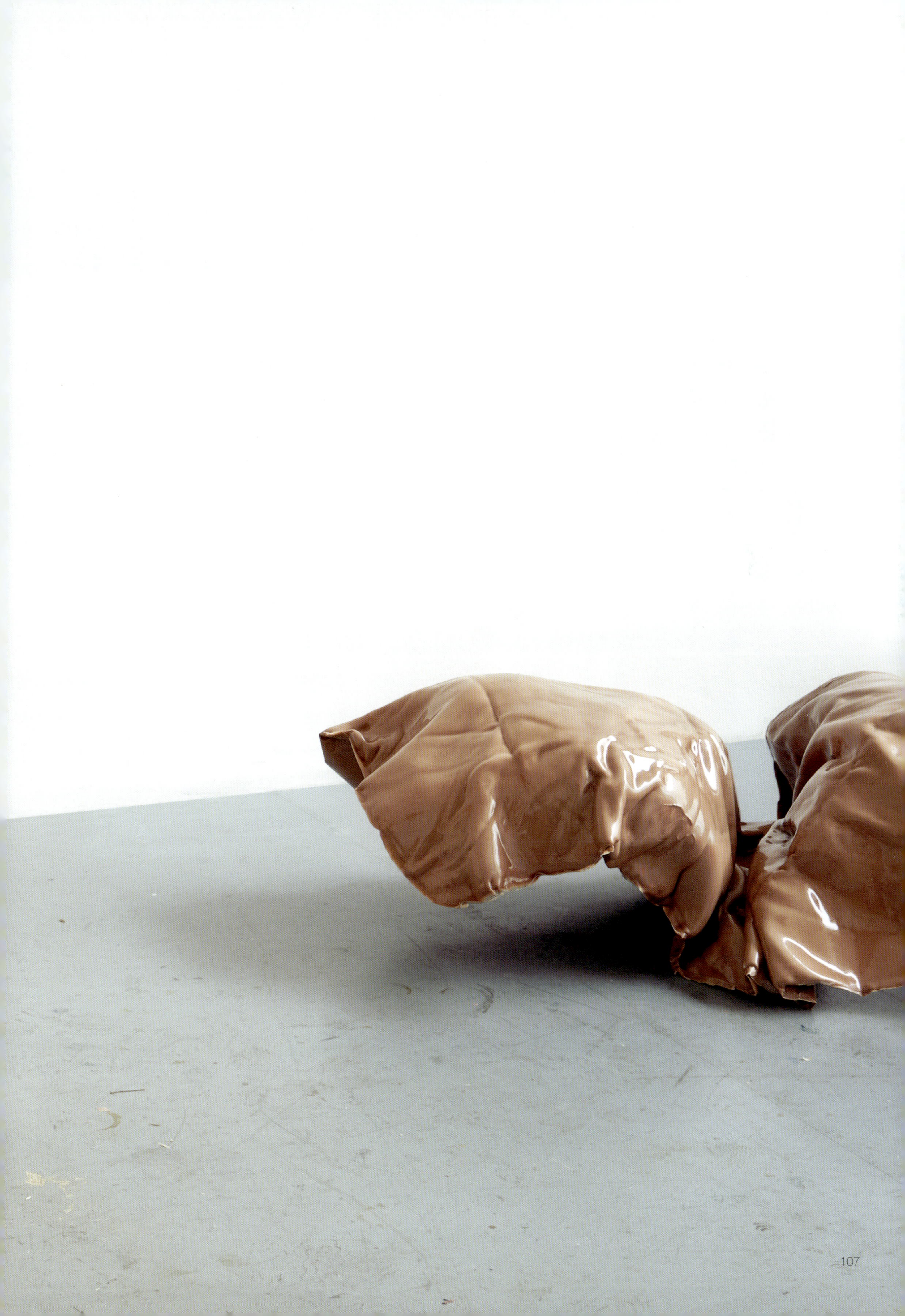

Objektinformationen | *Object information*

Seite | *Page*

4
5 Farbkörper | *Colour Bodies*, 2020
Polyurethan, Pigment | *polyurethane, pigment*

7 Detailansicht | Detail view
Polyurethan, Pigment | *polyurethane, pigment*

8 Farbobjekt | Colour Object, 2007
Polyurethan, Pigment | *polyurethane, pigment*
ca. | *approx.* 130 x 130 x 65 cm

10
11 Farbkörper | *Colour Body*, 2020
Polyurethan, Pigment | *polyurethane, pigment*
ca. | *approx.* 75 x 37 x 26 cm

12
13 Farbkörper | *Colour Body*, 2020
Polyurethan, Pigment | *polyurethane, pigment*
ca. | *approx.* 72 x 43 x 28 cm

14
15 Farbkörper | *Colour Body*, 2022
Polyurethan, Pigment | *polyurethane, pigment*
ca. | *approx.* 98 x 48 x 37 cm

16
17 Farbkörper | *Colour Body*, 2021
Polyurethan, Pigment | *polyurethane, pigment*
ca. | *approx.* 56 x 45 x 36 cm

19 Farbkörper | *Colour Body*, 2022
Polyurethan, Pigment | *polyurethane, pigment*
ca. | *approx.* 79 x 47 x 40 cm

20 Farbkörper | *Colour Body*, 2022
Polyurethan, Pigment | *polyurethane, pigment*
ca. | *approx.* 50 x 106 x 24 cm

22
23 Farbkörper | *Colour Body*, 2018
Polyurethan, Pigment | *polyurethane, pigment*
ca. | *approx.* 65 x 73 x 20 cm

24
25 Farbkörper | *Colour Body*, 2014
Polyurethan, Pigment | *polyurethane, pigment*
ca. | *approx.* 93 x 74 x 15 cm

26
27 Farbkörper | *Colour Body*, 2018
Polyurethan, Pigment | *polyurethane, pigment*
ca. | *approx.* 130 x 48 x 19 cm

28
29 Farbkörper | *Colour Body*, 2021
Polyurethan, Pigment | *polyurethane, pigment*
ca. | *approx.* 82 x 38 x 30 cm

30 Farbkörper | *Colour Body*, 2021
Polyurethan, Pigment | *polyurethane, pigment*
ca. | *approx.* 79 x 43 x 31 cm

31 Farbkörper | *Colour Body*, 2018
Polyurethan, Pigment | *polyurethane, pigment*
ca. | *approx.* 107 x 58 x 26 cm

32
33 Farbkörper | *Colour Body*, 2022
Polyurethan, Pigment | *polyurethane, pigment*
ca. | *approx.* 96 x 43 x 28 cm

34
35 Farbkörper | *Colour Body*, 2022
Polyurethan, Pigment | *polyurethane, pigment*
ca. | *approx.* 83 x 57 x 24 cm

36
37 Farbkörper | *Colour Body*, 2021
Polyurethan, Pigment | *polyurethane, pigment*
ca. | *approx.* 58 x 42 x 31 cm

38 Farbkörper | *Colour Body*, 2021
Polyurethan, Pigment | *polyurethane, pigment*
ca. | *approx.* 96 x 38 x 23 cm

39 Offene Form | *Open Shape*, 2021
Polyurethan, Pigment | *polyurethane, pigment*
ca. | *approx.* 101 x 68 x 0,3 cm

40
41 Farbplatten | *Colour Plates*, 2019
Polyurethan, Pigment | *polyurethane, pigment*

42
43 Farbkörper | *Colour Body*, 2021
Polyurethan, Pigment | *polyurethane, pigment*
ca. | *approx.* 84 x 49 x 28 cm

44 Farbkörper | *Colour Body*, 2021
Polyurethan, Pigment | *polyurethane, pigment*
ca. | *approx.* 84 x 49 x 28 cm

45 Farbkörper | *Colour Body*, 2020
Polyurethan, Pigment | *polyurethane, pigment*
ca. | *approx.* 64 x 48 x 17 cm

46 Farbkörper | *Colour Body*, 2021
Polyurethan, Pigment | *polyurethane, pigment*
ca. | *approx.* 44 x 37 x 38 cm

47 Offene Form | *Open Shape*, 2019
Polyurethan, Pigment | *polyurethane, pigment*
ca. | *approx.* 105 x 80 x 0,3 cm

48 Offene Form | *Open Shape*, 2019
Polyurethan, Pigment | *polyurethane, pigment*
ca. | *approx.* 84 x 65 x 0,3 cm

49 Farbkörper | *Colour Body*, 2019
Polyurethan, Pigment | *polyurethane, pigment*
ca. | *approx.* 43 x 56 x 36 cm

50 Farbkörper | *Colour Body*, 2021
Polyurethan, Pigment | *polyurethane, pigment*
ca. | *approx.* 44 x 109 x 25 cm

51 Offene Form | *Open Shape*, 2019
Polyurethan, Pigment | *polyurethane, pigment*
ca. | *approx.* 60 x 58 x 0,3 cm

52 Farbkörper | *Colour Bodies*, 2022
Polyurethan, Pigment | *polyurethane, pigment*
ca. | *approx.* 96 x 43 x 28 cm / 72 x 50 x 32 cm

53 Offene Form | *Open Shape*, 2019
Polyurethan, Pigment | *polyurethane, pigment*
ca. | *approx.* 89 x 92 x 0,3 cm

54 Farbkörper | *Colour Body*, 2021
Polyurethan, Pigment | *polyurethane, pigment*
ca. | *approx.* 68 x 47 x 20 cm

55 Offene Form | *Open Shape*, 2020
Polyurethan, Pigment | *polyurethane, pigment*
ca. | *approx.* 120 x 70 x 0,3 cm

56 Farbkörper | *Colour Body*, 2021
Polyurethan, Pigment | *polyurethane, pigment*
ca. | *approx.* 56 x 39 x 41 cm

57 Offene Form | *Open Shape*, 2019
Polyurethan, Pigment | *polyurethane, pigment*
ca. | *approx.* 130 x 77 x 0,3 cm

58 Farbkörper | *Colour Body*, 2021
Polyurethan, Pigment | *polyurethane, pigment*
ca. | *approx.* 50 x 47 x 38 cm

59 Farbkörper | *Colour Body*, 2021
Polyurethan, Pigment | *polyurethane, pigment*
ca. | *approx.* 68 x 47 x 20 cm

60 Offene Form | *Open Shape*, 2019
Polyurethan, Pigment | *polyurethane, pigment*
ca. | *approx.* 102 x 73 x 0,3 cm

61 Farbkörper | *Colour Body*, 2021
Polyurethan, Pigment | *polyurethane, pigment*
ca. | *approx.* 102 x 40 x 30 cm

62 Farbkörper | *Colour Body*, 2021
Polyurethan, Pigment | *polyurethane, pigment*
ca. | *approx.* 85 x 43 x 26 cm

63 Farbkörper | *Colour Body*, 2021
Polyurethan, Pigment | *polyurethane, pigment*
ca. | *approx.* 50 x 47 x 38 cm

64 Farbkörper | *Colour Body*, 2021
65 Polyurethan, Pigment | *polyurethane, pigment*
ca. | *approx.* 80 x 42 x 32 cm

66 Farbkörper | *Colour Body*, 2018
Polyurethan, Pigment | *polyurethane, pigment*
ca. | *approx.* 130 x 46 x 14 cm

68 Farbkörper | *Colour Body*, 2020
69 Polyurethan, Pigment | *polyurethane, pigment*
ca. | *approx.* 81 x 48 x 22 cm

70 Farbkörper | *Colour Body*, 2022
71 Polyurethan, Pigment | *polyurethane, pigment*
ca. | *approx.* 91 x 55 x 38 cm

72 Farbkörper | *Colour Body*, 2018
Polyurethan, Pigment | *polyurethane, pigment*
ca. | *approx.* 91 x 55 x 31 cm

73 Offene Form | *Open Shape*, 2019
Polyurethan, Pigment | *polyurethane, pigment*
ca. | *approx.* 108 x 68 x 0,3 cm

74 Farbkörper | *Colour Body*, 2020
Polyurethan, Pigment | *polyurethane, pigment*
ca. | *approx.* 44 x 89 x 16 cm

75 Farbkörper | *Colour Body*, 2020
Polyurethan, Pigment | *polyurethane, pigment*
ca. | *approx.* 42 x 46 x 30 cm

76 Farbkörper | *Colour Body*, 2020
Polyurethan, Pigment | *polyurethane, pigment*
ca. | *approx.* 75 x 46 x 14 cm

77 Farbkörper | *Colour Body*, 2020
Polyurethan, Pigment | *polyurethane, pigment*
ca. | *approx.* 42 x 45 x 29 cm

78 Farbkörper | *Colour Body*, 2022
79 Polyurethan, Pigment | *polyurethane, pigment*
ca. | *approx.* 72 x 50 x 32 cm

80 Offene Form | *Open Shape*, 2019
Polyurethan, Pigment | *polyurethane, pigment*
ca. | *approx.* 71 x 65 x 0,3 cm

81 Farbkörper | *Colour Body*, 2021
Polyurethan, Pigment | *polyurethane, pigment*
ca. | *approx.* 50 x 47 x 38 cm

82 Farbkörper | *Colour Body*, 2021
83 Polyurethan, Pigment | *polyurethane, pigment*
ca. | *approx.* 79 x 43 x 31 cm

84 Farbkörper | *Colour Body*, 2021
Polyurethan, Pigment | *polyurethane, pigment*
ca. | *approx.* 56 x 39 x 41 cm

85 Farbkörper | *Colour Body*, 2022
Polyurethan, Pigment | *polyurethane, pigment*
ca. | *approx.* 109 x 47 x 36 cm

86 Farbkörper | *Colour Body*, 2022
87 Polyurethan, Pigment | *polyurethane, pigment*
ca. | *approx.* 80 x 58 x 43 cm

88 Farbkörper | *Colour Body*, 2019
Polyurethan, Pigment | *polyurethane, pigment*
ca. | *approx.* 66 x 47 x 46 cm

89 Farbkörper | *Colour Body*, 2018
Polyurethan, Pigment | *polyurethane, pigment*
ca. | *approx.* 98 x 58 x 26

90 Farbkörper | *Colour Body*, 2020
Polyurethan, Pigment | *polyurethane, pigment*
ca. | *approx.* 42 x 45 x 29 cm

91 Farbkörper | *Colour Bodies*, 2020
Polyurethan, Pigment | *polyurethane, pigment*
ca. | *approx.* 47 x 53 x 25 cm / 42 x 46 x 30 cm

92 Farbkörper | *Colour Body*, 2022
93 Polyurethan, Pigment | *polyurethane, pigment*
ca. | *approx.* 54 x 52 x 29 cm

94 Farbkörper | *Colour Body*, 2022
Polyurethan, Pigment | *polyurethane, pigment*
ca. | *approx.* 108 x 52 x 34 cm

95 Farbkörper | *Colour Body*, 2022
Polyurethan, Pigment | *polyurethane, pigment*
ca. | *approx.* 54 x 52 x 29 cm

96 Farbkörper | *Colour Body*, 2022
Polyurethan, Pigment | *polyurethane, pigment*
ca. | *approx.* 109 x 47 x 36 cm

97 Farbkörper | *Colour Body*, 2022
Polyurethan, Pigment | *polyurethane, pigment*
ca. | *approx.* 50 x 87 x 26 cm

98 Offene Form | *Open Shape*, 2020
Polyurethan, Pigment | *polyurethane, pigment*
ca. | *approx.* 110 x 74 x 0,3 cm

99 Farbkörper | *Colour Body*, 2020
Polyurethan, Pigment | *polyurethane, pigment*
ca. | *approx.* 88 x 44 x 15 cm

100 Farbkörper | *Colour Body*, 2022
101 Polyurethan, Pigment | *polyurethane, pigment*
ca. | *approx.* 50 x 49 x 38 cm

102 Farbkörper | *Colour Body*, 2021
Polyurethan, Pigment | *polyurethane, pigment*
ca. | *approx.* 49 x 97 x 26 cm

103 Farbkörper | *Colour Body*, 2021
Polyurethan, Pigment | *polyurethane, pigment*
ca. | *approx.* 56 x 39 x 41 cm

104 Offene Form | *Open Shape*, 2019
Polyurethan, Pigment | *polyurethane, pigment*
ca. | *approx.* 108 x 76 x 0,3 cm

105 Farbkörper | *Colour Body*, 2019
Polyurethan, Pigment | *polyurethane, pigment*
ca. | *approx.* 66 x 47 x 46 cm

106 Farbkörper | *Colour Bodies*, 2020 / 2022
107 Polyurethan, Pigment | *polyurethane, pigment*

6 „Matter Matters, oder: Nichts als Farbe", erschienen im Katalog Eduard Tauss, Farbplastiken, 2017 | *„Matter Matters, or: Nothing but Paint", published in the catalogue Eduard Tauss, Colour Sculptures, 2017*

67 "Zu den Farbkörpern von Eduard Tauss", erschienen anlässlich der Ausstellung Embodying Colour in der Kunsthalle Wiesbaden, 2013 | *„On the Colour Bodies by Eduard Tauss", published to accompany the exhibition Embodying Colour at the Kunsthalle Wiesbaden, 2013*

Eduard Tauss

1968 geboren in Vorau, Steiermark, AT | *born in Vorau, Styria, AT*
1987-92 Akademie der bildenden Künste, Wien | *Academy of Fine Arts, Vienna*

Lebt und arbeitet in Wien |
Lives and works in Vienna

Arbeiten wurden international in Einzel- und Gruppenausstellungen gezeigt: Deutschland, Frankreich, Italien, Mexiko, Schweiz, Slovakei, Tschechien, Ungarn, USA |
Works were shown internationally in solo and group exhibitions: Germany, France, Italy, Mexico, Switzerland, Slovakia, Czech Republic, Hungary, USA

Impressum | *Colophon*

Danke schön!
I Couldn´t Have Done It Without You!
Arnold Berger, Elisabeth Mauerhofer

Erschienen im | *Published by:*
VfmK Verlag für moderne Kunst GmbH
Schwedenplatz 2/24
A-1010 Wien | *Vienna*
hello@vfmk.org
www.vfmk.org

ISBN-Nr. 978-3-903439-87-0

Vertrieb | *Distribution*
Europa | *Europe*: LKG, www.lkg-va.de
UK: Cornerhouse Publications,
www.cornerhousepublications.org
USA: D.A.P., www.artbook.com

Bibliografische Information der Deutschen Nationalbibliothek
Die Deutsche Nationalbibliothek verzeichnet diese Publikation in der Deutschen Nationalbibliografie; detaillierte bibliografische Daten sind im Internet über dnb.de abrufbar

Bibliographic information published by the Deutsche Nationalbibliothek
The Deutsche Nationalbibliothek lists this publication in the Deutsche Nationalbibliografie; detailed bibliographic data is available in the Internet at dnb.de

Herausgeber | *Editor*
Eduard Tauss
www.eduard-tauss.com

Textbeiträge | *Contributions*
Manisha Jothady, Michael Post/
Heiner Thiel, Florian Steininger,
Angela Stief

Übersetzung | *Translation*
Douglas Deitemyer, Abigail Prohaska,
Sabine Reul

Lektorat, Korrektorat | *Editing, Proofreading*
Theodor Maier, Elisabeth Mauerhofer

Fotos, Grafik | *Photos, Layout*
Eduard Tauss

Druck | *Printing*
Gerin Druck GmbH

Auflage | *Print Run*
500

Mit freundlicher Unterstützung von |
With the kind support of

Bundesministerium
Kunst, Kultur,
öffentlicher Dienst und Sport

Das Land
Steiermark
→ Kultur, Europa,
Außenbeziehungen

Bildrecht

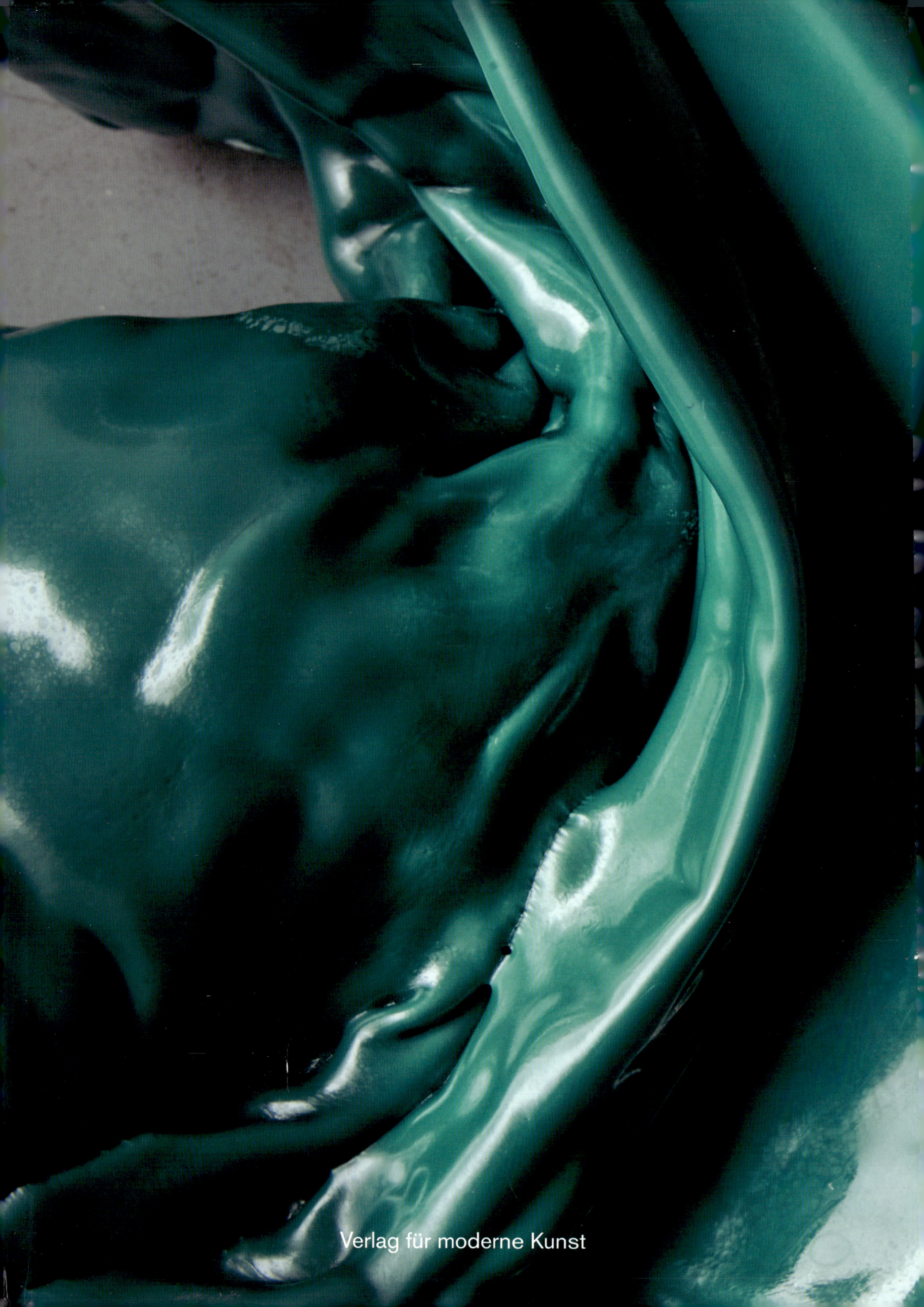

Verlag für moderne Kunst